Moral Error Theory

Jonas Olson presents an original account of the historical background of moral error theory, and examines in particular J. L. Mackie's influential contributions to the debate. In Part I (History), Olson provides the historical context of the debate, and discusses the moral error theories of David Hume and of some more or less influential twentieth century philosophers, including Axel Hägerström, Bertrand Russell, Ludwig Wittgenstein, and Richard Robinson. He argues that the early cases for moral error theory are suggestive but that they would have been stronger had they included something like Mackie's arguments that moral properties and facts are metaphysically queer. Part II (Critique) focuses on these arguments. Olson identifies four queerness arguments, concerning supervenience, knowledge, motivation, and irreducible normativity, and goes on to establish that while the first three are not compelling, the fourth has considerable force, especially when combined with debunking explanations of why we tend to believe that there are moral properties and facts when in fact there are none. One conclusion of Part II is that a plausible error theory takes the form of an error theory about irreducible normativity. In Part III (Defence), Olson considers challenges according to which that kind of error theory has problematic ramifications regarding hypothetical reasons, epistemic reasons, and deliberation. He ends his discussion with a consideration of the upshots of moral error theory for ordinary moral thought and talk, and for normative theorizing.

Moral Error Theory

History, Critique, Defence

Jonas Olson

OXFORD
UNIVERSITY PRESS

OXFORD
UNIVERSITY PRESS

Great Clarendon Street, Oxford, OX2 6DP,
United Kingdom

Oxford University Press is a department of the University of Oxford.
It furthers the University's objective of excellence in research, scholarship,
and education by publishing worldwide. Oxford is a registered trade mark of
Oxford University Press in the UK and in certain other countries

First published 2014
First published in paperback 2017

Published in the United States of America by Oxford University Press
198 Madison Avenue, New York, NY 10016, United States of America

British Library Cataloguing in Publication Data
Data available

Library of Congress Cataloging in Publication Data
Data available

ISBN 978–0–19–870193–4 (Hbk.)
ISBN 978–0–19–876997–2 (Pbk.)

Acknowledgements

In the process of writing this book I have been helped by many people. In the autumn of 2012, Jens Johansson organized a reading group at Uppsala University on the entire manuscript. I am deeply grateful to Jens and the other participants, Per Algander, Erik Carlson, Karl Ekendahl, Johan Gustafsson, Magnus Jedenheim, Victor Moberger, Henrik Rydéhn, Frans Svensson, and Folke Tersman, for their generous feedback. Having such insightful and constructive critics is the closest a secular philosopher can get to being blessed. Russ Shafer-Landau and his students read drafts of Parts II and III in a graduate seminar on metaethics at the University of Wisconsin, Madison. I am very grateful to Russ and his students for extremely helpful comments.

Most of the book was written at the department of philosophy at Stockholm University, which is an excellent workplace. I have benefitted from sustained discussions with my Stockholm colleagues Henrik Ahlenius, Gustaf Arrhenius, Björn Eriksson, Sofia Jeppsson, Hasse Mathlein, Niklas Olsson-Yaouzis, and Torbjörn Tännsjö. Parts of the book were written while I was a visiting fellow at CEPPA (Centre for Ethics, Philosophy, and Public Affairs) at the University of St Andrews in the spring of 2012. This was a productive period and I am very grateful to John Haldane and the other members of the department of moral philosophy at St Andrews for making the stay so pleasant and stimulating.

Drafts of the material in this book have been presented at seminars at the universities of Reading, Oxford, Nottingham, Glasgow, Edinburgh, and St Andrews; at the 2012 Ratio Conference on Irrealism in Ethics at the University of Reading, at the 2012 SPAWN Conference on Normative Realism at Syracuse University, and at two workshops at Insel Reichenau, organized by Attila Tanyi in 2011 and 2012. I am grateful to the many people who gave helpful comments on these occasions.

I have benefitted from conversations with, and/or written comments from, the following people: Krister Bykvist, Ruth Chang, Terence Cuneo,

Sven Danielsson, David Enoch, Kent Hurtig, Wouter Floris Kalf, Uri Leibowitz, Susanne Mantel, Thomas Mautner, Brian McElwee, Tristram McPherson, Graham Oddie, Ragnar Francén Olinder, Andrew Reisner, Mike Ridge, Richard Rowland, John Skorupski, Shanna Slank, Michael Smith, Philip Stratton-Lake, Bart Streumer, and Jussi Suikkanen. Two anonymous readers for OUP, one of whom turned out to be Matt Bedke, provided extremely useful and detailed comments on the content as well as the organization of the material. Peter Momtchiloff at OUP has been very helpful in the editorial process. All of these people contributed to making the book much better than it otherwise would have been. Needless to say, they bear no responsibility for the faults that remain.

I wish to acknowledge a special debt of gratitude to the late Jordan Howard Sobel, from whom I learnt a lot about metaethics and about Hume's philosophy. My deepest and most heartfelt thanks go to LMH and LEOH. This book is dedicated to them.

***

Parts of this book are based on the following previously published material:

Olson, J. 2011. 'In Defence of Moral Error Theory'. In *New Waves in Metaethics*, edited by M. Brady. Basingstoke: Palgrave, Macmillan, 62–84.

Olson, J. 2011. 'Error Theory and Reasons for Belief'. In *Reasons for Belief*, edited by A. Reisner and A. Steglich-Petersen. Cambridge: Cambridge University Press, 75–93.

Olson, J. 2011. 'Getting Real about Moral Fictionalism'. In *Oxford Studies in Metaethics* vol. 6, edited by R. Shafer-Landau. Oxford: Oxford University Press, 181–204.

Olson, J. 2011. 'Projectivism and Error in Hume's Ethics'. *Hume Studies* 37 (2011): 19–42.

Olson, J. 'Mackie's Motivational Argument from Queerness Reconsidered'. Forthcoming in *International Journal for the Study of Skepticism*.

I thank the publishers, Palgrave Macmillan, Cambridge University Press, Oxford University Press, and Brill, for permissions to reuse the material.

Contents

Part III: Defence

1
Introduction

1.1. Rationale and Brief Overview of the Book

Virtually any area of philosophy is haunted by a sceptical spectre. In moral philosophy its foremost incarnation has for some time been the moral error theorist, who insists that that ordinary moral thought and discourse involve untenable ontological commitments and that, as a consequence, ordinary moral beliefs and claims are uniformly untrue. This book investigates the case for moral error theory from historical as well as contemporary perspectives.

The main aims of the book are reflected in the themes of its three parts. One aim is to give a historical background to the debate about moral error theory, which often begins and ends with discussions and rejections of arguments put forward in the first chapter of J. L. Mackie's seminal *Ethics: Inventing Right and Wrong* (1977). In Part I (*History*) I discuss the moral error theories of David Hume, and of some more or less influential twentieth-century philosophers, including Axel Hägerström, Bertrand Russell, Ludwig Wittgenstein, and Richard Robinson.

My aim in Part I is not to give a complete historical inventory of moral error theory and its advocates. In a historical survey like the one I intend to give one is naturally forced to be selective in at least two ways. One first needs to settle on a starting point. My story begins with Hume, but arguments and ideas that have spurred the development of moral error theory can certainly be traced farther back in the history of philosophy. Mackie mentions, among others, Thomas Hobbes as one historical source of inspiration.[1] According to Hobbes, moral rules are human inventions. More particularly, they are the outcomes of bargaining between rational

[1] Mackie 1977: 108–14. Mackie also mentions Hume, Protagoras, and G. J. Warnock in this context. As noted, Hume's metaethics is the topic of the next chapter. According to

and self-interested individuals who want to negotiate their way out of a war of all against all. Hobbes was thus interested in metaethics, broadly speaking, but it is difficult to determine whether he or any other philosophers who wrote in eras much earlier than the present were moral error theorists.[2] The focus on the semantics of moral judgements and the ontology of moral properties, which make it possible and meaningful to distinguish moral error theory from subjectivism, relativism, non-cognitivism and other theories on which morality is not primarily to be discovered but somehow invented, is fairly recent in the history of philosophical theorizing about morality. As we shall see in Chapter 2, it is difficult enough to attribute a position to Hume that is both coherent and faithful to Hume's texts.

The second way in which one needs to be selective concerns which philosophers from the more recent history to focus on. The selection, like the choice of a sensible starting point, will of course depend to a large extent on what one means by 'moral error theory'. We shall discuss this latter question in Section 1.3.

The philosophers to whom I give particular attention have been chosen thematically, because their arguments and theories connect in interesting ways to the contemporary debate about moral error theory, and in particular to the idea that moral thought and discourse are about moral properties and facts that are in some sense queer. I hope that these discussions bring the double benefit of contributing to the understanding and interpretation of these philosophers' works and of enabling us to understand better the forms and contents moral error theories may take, and how they might combine with other metaethical theories. In these ways I hope that Part I, as indeed the book in its entirety, will be read as a contribution to the history of metaethics as well as to contemporary metaethical theorizing.

We shall see that moral projectivism and moral error theory are closely associated views. The former is congenial to the latter, but does not entail it. We shall see in Part I that precursors of moral error theory tended to

Protagoras's allegory, moral rules are god-given and their point is to facilitate human coordination and social harmony (Plato, *Protagoras and Meno*). It is this latter idea that is congenial to moral error theorists like Mackie. Warnock's account of the human predicament and the coordinating functions of morality is in Warnock 1971: Ch. 2.

[2] For a discussion of projectivism in Hobbes, see Darwall (2000).

focus more on arguments for moral projectivism, which suggested moral error theory, than on arguments for the ontological and semantic claims that are needed to give unequivocal support to moral error theory. In this respect, Mackie's defence of moral error theory in his *Ethics: Inventing Right and Wrong* is an important advance in the debate since it involves an explicit defence of the relevant semantic claim and even more importantly, it involves an elaboration of the argument from queerness, which is intended to establish the relevant ontological claim.

Prior to Mackie, the argument from queerness had only been hinted at, but it has now become central to the debate about moral error theory and about metaethics at large. It is also the linchpin of this book and is at the centre of focus in Part II (*Critique*). In my view, the argument from queerness is complex, not always adequately understood, and often dismissed too quickly. This is probably due in part to Mackie's own presentation of the argument, which is highly compressed and sometimes opaque. Part II scrutinizes the argument even-handedly. I have the double aim of interpreting Mackie—which requires some exegesis—and of providing the clearest and strongest presentation of the argument from queerness, which requires going beyond and sometimes deviating from Mackie's discussions. For example, I shall distinguish between the argument *from* queerness and the queerness arguments. Mackie did not make this distinction explicitly, but in my view it helps clarify his case for moral error theory. I shall argue that there are four distinct queerness arguments and thus four distinct versions of the argument from queerness. Three of them do not stand up to scrutiny, whereas the fourth queerness argument, the one that targets irreducible normativity, has considerable force. As Mackie was well aware, moral error theorists need to explain why the alleged error in moral thought and discourse persists. Part II closes with a discussion of such explanations.

One of two main aims of Part III (*Defence*) is to deal with contemporary challenges to moral error theory. One conclusion reached in Part II is that the argument against irreducible normativity cannot plausibly be restricted to morality. A plausible version of error theory must take the form of an error theory not only about morality, but about irreducible normativity more generally. These ramifications of moral error theory are fatal, according to many philosophers. Chapter 8 argues that they are in fact not. The second main aim of Part III is to discuss implications of moral error theory for actual moral thought and discourse. Here I challenge moral abolitionism and moral fictionalism, and defend an alternative view, which I call moral conservationism.

The remainder of this chapter explores what moral error theory amounts to, which alternative forms it may take, and how it relates to moral projectivism. We begin with the latter question.

1.2. Moral Error Theory and Moral Projectivism

To say that we project moral properties onto the world is, of course, to speak metaphorically. Moreover, there seems to be no agreement as to what such talk amounts to. This is reflected in the fact that 'projectivism' has been used as a label for, or identified as a component of, both non-cognitivism and error theory, which can be puzzling since non-cognitivism and standard versions of error theory are very different metaethical theories. Non-cognitivism holds that moral judgements are primarily expressions of non-cognitive attitudes, whereas standard versions of error theory hold that moral judgements are assertions that attribute mind-independent (but non-instantiated) moral properties to objects and that, as a consequence, moral judgements are systematically mistaken. So 'projectivism' can evidently be used as a label for a variety of different theories. Richard Joyce has recently formulated and distinguished the following four theses often associated with projectivist views in metaethics, which I quote:

1. We experience moral wrongness, (e.g.), as an objective feature of the world.
2. This experience has its origin in some non-perceptual faculty; in particular, upon observing certain actions and characters (etc.) we have an affective attitude (e.g., the emotion of disapproval) that brings about the experience described in (1).
3. In fact, moral wrongness does not exist in the world.
4. When we utter sentences of the form 'X is morally wrong' we are misdescribing the world; we are in error (Joyce 2009: 56).

Let us comment briefly on theses (1)–(4). The first thesis concerns moral *phenomenology*. A first thing to notice is that 'experience' in (1) should be read as a non-factive verb. We may thus have experiences of moral properties as objective features of the world although there are no moral properties. To say that we experience moral properties as objective features of the world, I shall assume, is to say that we experience them as mind-independent. To say that a feature, *F*, is mind-dependent is to say that whether an object, *x*, has *F* depends constitutively on psychological responses that actual or idealized observers have or would have towards *x*. To say that whether *x* has *F* depends *constitutively* on psychological responses actual or idealized observers have or would have towards *x*, is to say that *what it is* for *x* to have *F* is for *x* to be the object of certain psychological responses of actual or hypothetical observers. For example, a view on which the property of moral wrongness just is the property of giving rise to sentiments of disapproval in impartial spectators takes moral wrongness to be mind-dependent. To say that a feature, *F*, is mind-independent is to say that whether an object, *x*, has *F* does not depend constitutively on psychological responses that actual or idealized observers have or would have towards *x*. I shall take views on which moral properties are mind-dependent to be versions of subjectivism, and views on which moral properties are mind-independent to be versions of objectivism.[3]

The second thesis is *psychological*, offering a causal explanation of this moral phenomenology. The third thesis concerns moral *ontology*, and the fourth concerns moral *semantics*, in that it tells us that in making moral judgements we perform the speech act of assertion, since in order to misdescribe the world, one has to assert something about it. A natural reading of thesis (4) is that *in* uttering sentences of the form '*x* is morally wrong' we are saying something that is false; this is the sense in which we are in error.

But there is another sense in which we might be in error *when* we utter such sentences even though we are not in error *in* uttering them. That is, it might be the case that sentences of the form '*x* is morally wrong' are sometimes true, although what we implicitly or explicitly believe about *x* when we make (sincere) utterances of that kind is false. Hence (sincere) moral judgements might involve the doxastic error of false belief in a way that does not render moral judgements uniformly false. I maintain that both views deserve the label 'error theory'. We shall return to this distinction between kinds of moral error theory in the next subsection and in

[3] Here I follow Michael Huemer's account of what it is for features to be subjective and objective (Huemer 2005: 2–3). For example, views according to which moral properties are response-dependent count as subjectivist.

the next chapter, in which it will prove to be relevant to our interpretation of Hume.

Joyce calls the conjunction of the phenomenological and the psychological theses 'minimal projectivism' and he goes on to distinguish various versions of projectivism that involve different ontological and semantic claims.[4] I shall not follow this taxonomy precisely. I shall take projectivism simply to be the conjunction of theses (1) and (2). I thus take projectivism to be a view about the phenomenology and psychology of moral judgement, according to which something 'inner', such as an emotion, or more generally an affective attitude, is experienced as a perception of something 'outer', such as a mind-independent property. Projectivism is common ground between many versions of error theory, non-cognitivism, and subjectivism.

This understanding of projectivism and the four-fold division between theses (1)–(4) is helpful because it enables us to see how and why the projection metaphor can be used to describe a variety of metaethical views. For instance, it enables us to see how all of non-cognitivism, subjectivism, and error theory can be understood as projectivist views. Non-cognitivsts can, and typically do, accept some version of theses (1)–(3), but they replace (4) with a thesis to the effect that when we utter sentences like 'Murder is wrong' we are not (primarily) describing anything.[5] Because on the non-cognitivist's view moral sentences conventionally express non-cognitive attitudes, we are not misdescribing the world in uttering them. In particular, contemporary non-cognitivists known as expressivists have emphasized that on their view, ordinary moral thinking and ordinary moral judgements do not involve systematic errors.

However, the claim that non-cognitivists can, and typically do, accept (1) may seem to commit expressivists to the view that moral phenomenology is misleading. This in turn may suggest that moral thinking after all does embody error in the form of false belief. We will see in Chapter 3 that some non-cognitivists have held that ordinary moral thinking does involve systematically false beliefs about what we are up to when we make

[4] Joyce 2009: 57. See also P. J. E. Kail's recent distinction between *feature projection* and *explanatory projection* (Kail 2007: 3–4). Kail is not concerned exclusively with projectivism in metaethics, but in this context, explanatory projection corresponds roughly to theses (1) and (2) and feature projection roughly to theses (1) through (4).

[5] For an accommodation of (1) in an expressivist theory, see Horgan and Timmons 2007.

moral judgements. As we have just mentioned, however, many expressivists do not want to maintain that it does. Does this mean that expressivists are committed to rejecting (1)?

No. First of all, that we experience something as being in a certain way does not mean that we believe it to be that way. For example, most people believe that the two lines in the Müller-Lyer illusion differ in length. But once the illusion has been pointed out to us, we no longer believe, on reflection, that they differ in length although our perceptual experiences continue to suggest that they do. Similarly, we might experience wrongness to be an objective feature of the world, but expressivists might maintain that we do not believe that it is.[6]

Second, what we said above about objectivity and mind-independence is compatible with an expressivist-friendly account of these notions, on which our experiences of wrongness as an objective feature of the world are not misleading. On this account, to experience the wrongness of kicking dogs as mind-independent is simply to experience the wrongness as independent of our attitudes, in the sense that no matter what our attitudes to kicking dogs are or would be, kicking dogs is wrong; one is against kicking dogs even in the counterfactual event that one's attitudes to kicking dogs should change and one would no longer be against it.[7] Expressivists can grant that many people have such attitudes, and that they need not involve error.

Expressivists can reject (3) if they take the claim that moral wrongness exists in the world to be true in a minimal sense. They might say, for instance, that 'Murder is wrong' is true (in a minimal sense) and from this, they can say, it follows that moral wrongness does exist in the world. For what it is for moral wrongness to exist in the world just is for some sentence like 'Murder is wrong' to be true.

Subjectivists may hold that wrongness just is projected attitudes, that the meaning of moral judgements is reducible to judgements about attitudes—either attitudes of the speaker, or of the speaker's community, or yet again of some idealized subject. They can thus accept projectivism and reject the ontological thesis.[8] They can then either reject outright the

[6] Joyce (2009: 58–9) makes a similar point.

[7] Blackburn 1984: 217–20.

[8] Since it comprises only a phenomenological and a psychological thesis, projectivism is not logically incompatible with objectivist realism. However, the marriage between projectivism and objectivist realism may not be a very happy or appealing one.

semantic thesis and maintain that moral thought and discourse involve no systematic errors, or they can maintain that we ordinary speakers are systematically mistaken about the nature of moral properties and facts but that this does not render moral judgements uniformly false. We shall see in the next chapter that Hume may have endorsed a version of this view. Another case in point is the philosopher and sociologist Edward Westermarck, who endorsed a relativistic analysis of moral judgements but maintained that ordinary speakers are typically under the illusion that moral judgements may be and sometimes are objectively true. The illusion has its source in the fact that moral judgements are based on objectification of emotions.[9]

Error theorists, by contrast, typically accept all of (1) through (4). There are complications to be added, however, and we shall discuss some of them in the next subsection. In discussing Hume's view in Chapter 2, we shall see that moral error theory may be compatible with subjectivist realism, and in discussing Hägerström's views in Chapter 3, we shall see that moral error theory may be compatible with non-cognitivism.

1.3. The Many Moral Error Theories

Projectivism and moral error theory are a natural couple, but as we have seen, projectivism may be combined with a variety of metaethical views. What, then, is definitive or error theory? Error theory about some area of thought and discourse, D, is commonly defined as the view that D involves systematically false beliefs and that, as a consequence, all D-judgements, or some significant subset thereof, are false.[10] Thus moral error theory is commonly defined as the view that moral thinking involves systematically false beliefs—typically about moral properties and facts—and that, as a consequence, all moral judgements, or some significant subset thereof,[11] are false. These seem to me satisfactory definitions of what we might call *standard error theory* and *standard moral error theory*, respectively. But we also need to accommodate some non-standard versions of error theory.

[9] Westermarck (1932). For Mackie's appraisal of Westermarck's work, see, e.g., Mackie 1977: 105, 241; 1985a.

[10] Cf., e.g., Daly and Liggins (2010).

[11] More on this presently.

According to some error theorists about some area of thought and discourse, D, the systematically false beliefs involved in D amount to a presupposition failure and, as a consequence, all D-judgements are uniformly neither true nor false. For example, some moral error theorists hold that moral thought and discourse presuppose that there are moral properties and facts, but since this presupposition is unfulfilled, moral judgements uniformly lack truth-value.[12] This complication is easily accommodated. We can make room for this non-standard version of error theory by defining an error theory about D as the view that D involves systematically false beliefs and that, as a consequence, all D-judgements are untrue, either in the sense that they are uniformly false or in the sense that they are uniformly neither true nor false.

However, as I indicated in Section 1.2, I believe that there is another important version of non-standard error theory. I shall illustrate this by focusing on moral thought and discourse. We might be systematically mistaken about the nature of moral properties and facts, but there might nevertheless be moral properties and facts. Our systematically false beliefs about the nature of moral properties and facts need not affect the meaning of our moral terms and therefore need not render our moral judgements uniformly false or untrue. Although they are not what we think they are, we might sometimes succeed in correctly attributing moral properties and reporting moral facts.[13] As I have already mentioned, I shall argue in Chapter 2 that Hume may have endorsed a view like this. According to another version of this general view, moral thinking involves systematically false beliefs about moral properties and facts, and we are mistaken about what we are up to when we make moral judgements. On this view, all moral judgements are uniformly untrue, but this is not a consequence of the systematically false beliefs about moral properties and facts, but because of the purported fact that moral judgements do not express beliefs at all. I shall argue in Chapter 3 that the early non-cognitivist Axel Hägerström at one point endorsed a view like this.

[12] This version of moral error theory is defended in Sobel (ms, ch. 13). See also Joyce (2001: 6–9).

[13] An anonymous reviewer suggested the following non-normative example to illustrate the point: physicists once believed that electrons are the smallest negatively charged particles. It turned out that they are not. But that did not prevent these physicists from making true claims about electrons.

These views are versions of what we may call *moderate moral error theory*. Like the standard and non-standard versions we encountered previously, moderate moral error theory attributes the doxastic error of systematically false beliefs to ordinary moral thinking, but it is moderate in that it does not take this doxastic error to render false all moral judgements, or some significant subset thereof, and neither to give rise to a presupposition failure.

One might object that what I call moderate moral error theory is too moderate to deserve the label 'error theory'. If the view that moral thinking involves systematically false beliefs suffices to motivate the label 'error theory', the category of (moral) error theory becomes a lot more inclusive than it is commonly taken to be.

In response, I agree that recognizing moderate moral error theory alongside standard moral error theory significantly widens the category of (moral) error theory. But how inclusive a philosophical category like moral error theory is does not seem a philosophically interesting question. The interesting question is whether the categorization marks a philosophically interesting distinction. There is indeed a philosophically interesting distinction to make between metaethical views on which ordinary moral thinking involves systematically false beliefs, and metaethical views on which ordinary moral thinking does not involve systematically false beliefs—either because the folk's metaethical beliefs about moral properties and facts are largely correct, or because the folk have no or very few such beliefs. My proposal is to mark the distinction by categorizing the first kind of views as versions of moral error theory.

Let me add, however, that in order for a theory to be a version of moderate moral error theory, the doxastic error it attributes to ordinary moral thinking must be sufficiently pervasive as opposed to peripheral. I have no theory to offer about what counts as a sufficiently pervasive error; I can only mention two examples that will be discussed more carefully in the coming chapters. The first is the view that ordinary moral thinking involves the belief that moral properties and facts are objective although they are in fact mind-dependent. The second is the view that ordinary moral thinking takes moral judgements to purport to attribute objective moral properties and report objective moral facts although they in fact express non-cognitive attitudes. Both these views seem to me clear-cut examples of views that attribute errors to ordinary moral thinking that are sufficiently pervasive to make the label '(moderate) moral error theory' apt.

As we shall see in Section 2.3, Mackie endorsed standard moral error theory.[14] Since Mackie's theory and arguments for and against it are the central topics of Parts II and III of the book, I shall in those parts focus mostly on standard moral error theory. Note, however, that many versions of moderate moral error theories are reliant on something like the argument from queerness, since they maintain that ordinary moral thought and discourse involve systematic errors about the nature of moral properties and facts. The discussion in Part II is therefore equally relevant to moderate moral error theory as to standard moral error theory.

Standard moral error theory: the problem of formulation

Let us now consider a problem concerning the formulation of standard moral error theory. According to moral error theory, first-order moral claims are uniformly false. A first-order moral claim is a claim that entails that some agent morally ought to do or not to do some action; that there are moral reasons for some agent to do or not to do some action; that some action is morally permissible; that some institution, character trait, or what have you, is morally good or bad; and the like. So, for example, the claim that that torture is wrong is false. This raises the question of what to say about the truth-values of negated first-order moral claims, such as the claim that torture is not wrong. This latter claim appears to be a moral claim and since it is the negation of a claim that standard moral error theory deems false, it appears that the theory should deem the negated claim true. Yet we know that according to standard moral error, moral judgements are uniformly false.

This leads to two worries: First, is standard moral error theory a coherent theory?[15] Second, can it be maintained that moral error theory lacks first-order moral implications? It is immediately obvious that the standard formulation of moral error theory has implications for first-order moral

[14] For a reading of Mackie that dissents from the majority's reading, see ch. 13 of Sobel (ms). According to Sobel, Mackie propounded an error theory according to which moral judgements are uniformly neither true nor false rather than false.

[15] This problem has been discussed by, e.g., Pigden (2007); Sinnott-Armstrong (2006); Sobel (ms); Tännsjö (2010). Pigden calls the problem of formulating moral error theory the *Doppelganger Problem* and his solution is in some respects similar to the one I am going to offer.

theory since it implies that first-order moral judgements are uniformly false. But the worry we shall now address is whether the standard formulation of moral error theory has implications that are themselves moral.

Mackie insisted that his error theory is purely a second-order view and as such logically independent of any first-order moral view.[16] But this can be doubted. According to the standard interpretation of Mackie's error theory, a first-order moral claim like 'Torture is morally wrong' is false. According to the law of excluded middle it follows that its negation, 'Torture is not morally wrong', is true. That torture is not morally wrong would seem to imply that torture is morally permissible. More generally, then, the apparent upshot is that contrary to Mackie's contention moral error theory does have first-order moral implications. And rather vulgar ones at that; if moral error theory is true, any action turns out to be morally permissible!

But it seems that we can also derive an opposite conclusion. According to moral error theory, 'Torture is morally permissible' is false. According to the law of excluded middle it follows that torture is not morally permissible, which seems to entail that torture is morally impermissible. More generally, then, the apparent upshot is that any action is morally impermissible! This may not be a vulgar first-order moral implication, but it is surely absurd. It also transpires that the standard formulation of moral error theory leads to a straightforward logical contradiction since we have derived that it is true that, e.g., torture is morally permissible (since any action is morally permissible) and that it is false that torture is morally permissible (since any action is morally impermissible).

One way out of the predicament is to adopt the non-standard version of moral error theory according to which all first-order moral claims are neither true nor false, due to a failure of presupposition. But this non-standard version of error theory can be questioned. In general, I take claims that predicate non-instantiated properties of some individual or individuals to be false.[17] For instance, a claim to the effect that some person

[16] Mackie 1977: 15–17.

[17] I assume a liberal account of properties according to which there is a property *F* if there is in some natural language a meaningful predicate that purports to pick out *F* (see Schiffer 1990). The predicate 'morally wrong' fits this description, so there is a property of moral wrongness but error theorists maintain that this property is not instantiated. I take it that most moral error theorists maintain that moral properties are necessarily uninstantiated they are simply too queer to be instantiated in any possible world. A more theoretically motivated reason for this view is that fundamental moral facts, e.g., that inflicting pain is *pro tanto*

is a witch (where being a witch involves being a woman with magical powers) is false. The same goes for a claim to the effect that acts of torture are morally wrong.

Moreover, the claim that it is not the case that torture is wrong seems, from the perspective of moral error theorists to be true, since, on their view, nothing has the property of being wrong. In contrast, the negation of the claim that the present king of France is bald seems to be neither true nor false, since there is no present king of France. This suggests that while claims about the present king of France *presuppose* that there is a present king of France, first-order moral claims, like the claim that torture is wrong, *entail* that there are moral properties.[18]

Walter Sinnott-Armstrong has suggested another way out of the predicament according to which the scope of moral error theory is to be restricted, to the effect that only *positive* first-order moral claims are deemed uniformly false.[19] A positive first-order moral claim is defined as a claim that entails something about what some agent morally ought to do or not to do, what there is moral reasons for some agent to do or not to do, and so on and so forth; or what would be morally good or bad, or morally desirable or undesirable, and so on. Importantly, it says nothing about mere permissibility.

Restricting moral error theory to positive first-order moral claims only, rids moral error theory from incoherence and from the absurd implication that anything is morally impermissible. But one may object that it

morally wrong, would be necessary facts. But since there are no such facts in the actual world, there is no possible world in which there are moral facts. Correlatively, there is no possible world in which moral properties are instantiated. By way of comparison, atheists might hold that there is a property of being God and that this property involves being a necessary being that is omnipresent, omniscient, omnibenevolent, and that created the universe. However, since there is, according to the atheist, nothing in the actual world that instantiates this property, there is no possible world in which this property is instantiated. The point that there is no possible world in which moral properties are instantiated refutes Christian Coons's recent attempt to establish that there are at least some moral facts (Coons, 2011). Coons's argument involves as a crucial premise the claim that there is a possible world in which there are moral facts. But since moral error theorists hold that there are no instantiations of moral properties in the actual world, and since moral facts are necessary facts, they also hold that that there is no possible world in which there are moral facts, i.e., that there is no possible world in which moral properties are instantiated. This point on behalf of moral error theorists is spelled out in more detail in Wielenberg (ms).

[18] Cf. Lycan 2000: 196.

[19] Sinnott-Armstrong 2006: 34–6.

remains the case that a negative first-order moral claim such as 'Torture is not morally wrong' entails 'Torture is morally permissible' since it appears to be a platitude that any action that is not morally wrong is morally permissible. In other words, moral error theory would still imply vulgar first-order moral nihilism, according to which anything is morally permissible. But Mackie's contention that his error theory is purely a second-order view and as such logically independent of any first-order moral view must be taken to include the first-order moral view that anything is morally permissible. In other words, Mackie's moral error theory holds that all first-order moral claims are false and claims about moral permissibility are no exception.

A better way out is to deny that the implications from 'not wrong' to 'permissible' and from 'not permissible' to 'wrong' are conceptual and maintain instead that they are instances of generalized conversational implicature. To illustrate, 'not wrong' conversationally implicates 'permissible' because normally when we claim that something is not wrong we speak from within a system of moral norms, or moral standard for short. According to most moral standards, any action that is not wrong according to that standard is permissible according to that standard.[20] General compliance with Gricean maxims that bid us to make our statements relevant and not overly informative ensures that we do not normally state explicitly that we speak from within some moral standard when we claim that something is not wrong.[21] But the implicature from 'not wrong' to 'permissible' is cancellable. The error theorist can declare that torture is not wrong and go on to signal that she is not speaking from within a moral standard. She might say something like the following: 'Torture is not wrong. But neither is it permissible. There are no moral properties and facts and consequently no action has moral status.' This would cancel the implicature from 'not wrong' to 'permissible'. (Analogous reasoning of course demonstrates why the error theorist's claim that torture is not morally permissible does not commit her to the view that torture is morally impermissible and hence morally wrong.) On this view, error theory has neither the vulgar implication

[20] Some moral standards allow for moral dilemmas, in which one and the same action token is simultaneously not wrong and impermissible, or simultaneously not wrong and wrong.

[21] See Grice 1989: 26ff.

that anything is permissible nor the absurd implication that anything is impermissible.

But one might object that the problems remain. The law of excluded middle entails that if 'Torture is wrong' is false, then 'Torture is not wrong' is true. If the latter claim is a first-order moral claim, the standard formulation of moral error theory still has first-order moral implications, i.e. implications that by its own lights are false.

In response, recall that according to the definition above, first-order moral claims are claims that entail that some agent morally ought to do or not to do some action; that some action is morally permissible; that some institution, character trait, or what have you, is morally good or bad; and so on. Now, according to the view on offer, a negated claim like 'Torture is not wrong' does not *entail* that torture is permissible; it merely conversationally implicates that it is, since the implicature from 'not wrong' to 'permissible' is cancellable. Likewise, 'Torture is not morally permissible' does not entail that torture is impermissible and hence wrong; it merely conversationally implicates that torture is impermissible and hence wrong. Thus negated atomic claims involving moral terms are not strictly speaking first-order moral claims, but some such claims conversationally implicate first-order moral claims.[22] Since claims like 'Torture is not wrong' are true we cannot derive that their negations (such as 'Torture is wrong') are true. This saves the standard formulation of moral error theory from the threat of incoherence and from implausible first-order moral implications. I shall continue to say, then, that according to standard moral error theory first-order moral claims are uniformly false.

Alternative routes to moral error theory

Just as my aim in Part I is not to give a complete historical inventory of moral error theory and its advocates, my aim in Part II is not to give a complete account of all ways in which one might arrive at moral error theory. As I have already noted, the focus in Part II is on Mackie's argument from queerness. Of course, this is not to suggest that there are no alternative interesting routes to moral error theory.

One might argue that judgements about moral rightness and wrongness, duty and responsibility, and so on, presuppose that agents have free

[22] Some, but not all. For example, the claim that it is not the case that Dick believes that torture is wrong does not conversationally implicate a first-order moral claim.

will. But since agents do not have free will, there are no true moral judgements. There are several possible grounds on which to reject free will and one might take such arguments to support either an error theory about all moral concepts or an error theory that is restricted only to certain moral concepts. For example, one might argue that attributions of moral responsibility presuppose that agents are the ultimate causes of their own actions. However, many philosophers take such a notion of agent-causation to be metaphysically untenable and hold that there is no such thing.[23] Consequently, one might argue, there are no true attributions of moral responsibility, but other kinds of moral judgements, for example about moral goodness and badness, may be true.

Another possible way to arrive at moral error theory may be to adopt a Nietzschean critique of morality, according to which morality is an invention of the inferior herd, or Marxist critiques of bourgeois morality. But first of all, Nietzschean and Marxist critiques of morality may be read as substantively normative rather than metaethical. Nietzsche's project is often to revaluate commonly held values and in particular to subvert Christian morality and replace it with a system of values fit for the *Übermensch*. This project seems clearly substantively normative rather than metaethical. Similarly, Marxist critiques of moralities that prevail in capitalist societies are often based, implicitly or explicitly, on the view that, for example, exploitation and alienation of workers are morally unjust or morally bad, which seems clearly a first-order moral view.

On the other hand, there are indeed some arguments in Nietzsche that seem more metaethical than substantively normative and some that suggest moral error theory. But Nietzsche's metaethical position remains a matter of controversy among Nietzsche scholars.[24] Similarly, there are versions of Marxism that reject the very notion of justice rather than, say, take exploitation to be unjust or communist society to be required by justice.[25]

I mention these alternative routes to moral error theory just to set them aside. As before, one needs to be selective. A thorough treatment of the free will problem and its relevance to moral error theory lies far beyond the scope of this work, and contributing to the already vast literature on

[23] See, e.g., Pereboom (2005) and Strawson (1994).

[24] For readings of Nietzsche as moral error theorist and fictionalist, see Hussain (2007) and Pigden (2007). For a response to Hussain, see Leiter (2011).

[25] For an introductory discussion, see Kymlicka 2002: Ch. 5.

Nietzschean and Marxist critiques of morality requires scholarly competence that I do not possess.

Finally, a note on the structure of this book. Many books that defend a specific metaethical position proceed by eliminating alternative views and end up defending what is supposedly the only, or the most, plausible view that survives the elimination process. Or in the words of David Enoch, the view that scores highest in plausibility points.[26] That is not the structure of this book. The main contending views in this book are moral error theory and non-naturalist moral realism. I do not say enough about alternative views, such as moral naturalism and non-cognitivism, to refute them conclusively. Such a project would require a different book. I would very much like to offer conclusive refutations of these views, but I doubt that it is a possible feat.

I do, however, discuss and develop some of Mackie's arguments against moral naturalism and non-cognitivism. I am inclined to believe that moral error theory is ultimately more plausible than alternative views in metaethics and I am quite certain that it is more plausible than is usually acknowledged. I hope that parts II and III demonstrate this and that they be seen as contravening the commonly held view that moral error theory is an unattractive last resort in metaethics that deserves serious consideration only if and when all alternatives have been shown to fail.

[26] Enoch 2011.

PART I
History

2

Hume: Projectivist, Realist, and Error Theorist

Commentators have attributed to Hume a wide variety of metaethical views. The main questions to be considered in this chapter are whether Hume is a moral projectivist and whether he is a moral error theorist. I shall argue that Hume is a moral projectivist, and I shall identify two senses in which Hume might be labelled a moral error theorist. This involves distinguishing between Hume's *descriptive* metaethics and his *revisionary* metaethics. The former is his account of actual or vulgar moral thought and talk, that is to say, the moral thought and talk of ordinary people; the latter is his account of how actual or vulgar moral thought and talk could be reformed so as to no longer involve error. We can then say that in descriptive metaethics, Hume is indeed a projectivist and an error theorist, and in revisionary metaethics, Hume is a projectivist and a subjectivist realist but not an error theorist.[1]

In the previous chapter, we considered four theses commonly associated with moral projectivism. The next section considers which of these theses Hume endorses and argues that Hume is a moral projectivist and an error theorist in descriptive metaethics and a projectivist but not an error theorist in revisionary metaethics. Although error theorist readings of Hume have found some supporters over the years, they are currently rather unpopular. Sections 2.1 and 2.2 consider why this is and respond to objections to error theorist readings. The moral error theories of Hume and Mackie are compared in Section 2.3.

[1] In calling Hume's account of moral properties subjectivist, I mean only that he takes moral properties to be mind-dependent, in the sense defined in Section 1.2. I do not mean to deny that Hume predicts that convergence in moral opinions will occur when we take up the perspective of an impartial spectator.

Before moving further, a caveat is in place. Since my project in this chapter is to bring Hume's work into conversation with modern metaethical debate, there is a clear risk of anachronistic interpretations. Let us first note that modern metaethical debate focuses much more on semantic analyses of moral judgement than did eighteenth-century debate. Hume and his contemporaries tended to discuss moral semantics only in passing and took greater interests in moral epistemology, psychology, and ontology. Importantly, however, many of these issues are still at the forefront of the metaethical debate. We can, therefore, hope to advance our understanding of Hume's views by discussing them in the terminology of modern metaethics and by applying to them modern metaethical categories. Doing so enables us to understand how Hume might both embrace the reality of moral distinctions and moral properties and maintain that the moral judgements of ordinary people involve systematic error.

Let us also note that while the four theses discussed in the previous chapter are useful tools in understanding moral projectivism and its relation to moral error theory, they call for some further comments in the context of interpreting Hume. The four theses, recall, are formulated in terms of wrongness, and an initial worry is that this makes them problematic as tools in interpreting Hume's ethics. Hume focuses mainly on virtue and vice rather than on rightness and wrongness, and takes people's characters to be the primary bearers of moral properties. One might also question whether the metaethical questions that arise with respect to rightness and wrongness arise also with respect to virtue and vice.

I will respond to these two worries in turn. First, to allay the worry about anachronism, it is worth noting that although Hume is chiefly concerned with virtue and vice, he occasionally speaks in terms of rightness and wrongness. For example, in the opening of the second *Enquiry*, Hume says, '[l]et a man's insensibility be ever so great, he must often be touched with the images of RIGHT and WRONG'[2], and he goes on to speak about 'sentiments of

[2] EPM 1.2; SBN 170. In referring to Hume's works I follow the format adopted in the journal *Hume Studies*. References to the *Treatise* are to David Hume, *A Treatise of Human Nature*, ed. David Fate Norton and Mary J. Norton (New York: Oxford University Press, 2000), hereafter cited as 'T' followed by Book, part, section, and paragraph numbers; and to *A Treatise of Human Nature*, ed. L. A. Selby-Bigge, revised by P. H. Nidditch, 2nd ed. (Oxford: Clarendon Press, 1978), hereafter cited as 'SBN' followed by page number. 'Abs.' stands for Abstract. References to the second *Enquiry* are to David Hume, *An Enquiry concerning the Principles of Morals*, ed. T. L. Beauchamp (Oxford: Oxford University Press, 1998), hereafter cited as 'EPM' followed by section and paragraph numbers; and to *An Enquiry Concerning the Principles of Morals*, ed. L. A. Selby-Bigge, revised by P. H. Nidditch, 3rd ed. (Oxford: Clarendon Press,

right and wrong'.[3] Similarly, when Hume criticizes moral rationalism in the *Treatise*, he follows some of his rationalist opponents and speaks in terms of rightness and wrongness.[4]

Second, it is noteworthy that some of Hume's rationalist contemporaries also theorized about virtue and vice. John Balguy and Richard Price, for example, defended theories according to which virtue and vice are mind-independent properties, and truths about them are accessible via the understanding, or abstract reasoning, alone.[5] This suggests that the kinds of metaethical questions that are of interest in this book arise regardless of whether we focus on rightness and wrongness or on virtue and vice. Regardless of whether we take rightness and wrongness or virtue and vice to be the central moral concepts, we can ask whether moral properties are mind-independent, in the sense explained in Section 1.2, and whether the vulgar take moral properties to be mind-independent.

In light of these and previous comments, we can now reformulate Joyce's theses (1)–(4) to make them more applicable to Hume's moral theory.

Phenomenological	We experience moral properties, for example, the rightness and wrongness of acts or the virtues and vices of persons, as mind-independent.
Psychological	This experience has its origin in some non-perceptual faculty; in particular, upon observing certain actions and characters, and so on, we have an affective attitude (for example, the sentiment of approbation or disapprobation) that brings about the experience described above.
Ontological	In fact, moral properties do not exist in the world.
Semantic	When we utter sentences of the form 'X is morally right/wrong' and 'X has a moral virtue/vice', we purport to ascribe properties to X, but our beliefs about these properties are systematically in error in ways that may render moral judgements uniformly false.

1975), hereafter 'SBN' followed by page number. 'App.' stands for Appendix. References to Hume's essays are to David Hume, *Essays, Moral, Political, and Literary*, ed. D. F. Miller (Indianapolis: Liberty Fund, 1985), hereafter cited as 'EMPL' followed by page number

[3] EPM 9.10; SBN 276, see also T 3.2.2.23; SBN 498.

[4] See, for example, T 3.1.1.4, 3.1.1.14, 3.1.1.18; SBN 456, 460, 463.

[5] See Raphael (ed.), 1991: 387–408, esp. 392–96; Price (1948/1758): esp. 15–17, 233–36.

2.1. Hume's Metaethics: Descriptive and Revisionary

Hume on the phenomenological and psychological theses

An important basis of my interpretation is Hume's famous comparison of sensory qualities to moral and aesthetic properties. Hume makes this comparison in the *Treatise*[6] and repeats it in the essays 'The Sceptic'[7] and 'Of the Standards of Taste'.[8] Paying close attention to the comparison can help to throw light on which of the four projectivist theses Hume accepts. There is evidence that Hume accepts the phenomenological thesis as an accurate description of moral phenomenology. In the *Treatise*, Hume states that '[v]ice and virtue [...] may be compar'd to sounds, colours, heat, and cold, which, according to modern philosophy, are not qualities in objects, but perceptions in the mind' and he immediately adds that 'this discovery in morals, like that other in physics, is to be regarded as a considerable advancement in the speculative sciences'.[9]

The fact that this discovery in morals is a significant advancement suggests that it is not what most people already think: it is advancement precisely because most people believe pre-reflectively that moral properties are in external objects and not that they are perceptions in the mind.[10] That is, ordinary moral phenomenology is such that moral properties are experienced as mind-independent features of the world in the sense explained in Section 1.2, just as the phenomenological thesis says, and this gives rise to the mistaken belief about moral properties.[11] Further evidence that this is Hume's view can be mounted. In 'The Sceptic' Hume writes,

> even when the mind operates alone, and feeling the sentiment of blame or approbation, pronounces one object deformed and odious, another beautiful and

[6] T 3.1.1.27; SBN 469.

[7] EMPL 163–65.

[8] EMPL 230, 233–34.

[9] T 3.1.1.26; SBN 469.

[10] Mackie makes the same point in a footnote (Mackie 1980: 158, n. 5).

[11] See Section 2 and Section 1.2. I shall eventually argue that Hume takes moral properties to be mind-dependent because he takes them to depend on psychological responses of spectators. Note that Hume's view that mental objects, such as people's characters, are the primary bearers of moral properties does not commit him to the view that moral properties are mind-dependent. The view that characters are the primary bearers of moral properties is consistent with the view that moral properties do not depend on the psychological responses of *observers*.

amiable; I say that, even in this case, those qualities are not really in the objects, but belong entirely to the sentiment of that mind which blames or praises. I grant, that it will be [. . .] difficult to make this proposition evident, and, as it were, palpable, to negligent thinkers (EMPL 163).

Why would it be difficult to make this proposition evident and palpable to negligent thinkers? Presumably, because negligent thinkers are prone to rely on their experiences of moral properties as mind-independent features. Note that on my reading, Hume does not deny that the vulgar think that moral properties depend on minds in the sense that whether an agent or action is virtuous or vicious depends on the agent's mental qualities, or character. Hume holds that the vulgar think of moral virtue and vice as mind-independent in the sense defined in Section 1.2, that is, as properties that do not depend on the psychological responses of evaluating observers.

A few pages later, there is more of the same: 'with regard to beauty, either natural or moral, the [. . .] agreeable quality is thought to lie in the object [evaluated]; not in the sentiment [of the evaluating observer]'.[12] Although Hume does not discuss ordinary moral phenomenology directly and explicitly, these passages support attributing to him the phenomenological thesis.[13]

Attributing to Hume the psychological thesis that our experiences of moral properties as mind-independent are brought about, and hence explained, by affective attitudes should find little resistance. The passages already considered indicate that he accepts it. In the opening paragraphs of the second *Enquiry*, Hume contrasts rationalist and sentimentalist accounts of morality and goes on eventually to offer support for the latter and to argue against the former.[14] This is, of course, also among his main concerns in Book 3 of the *Treatise*. Here Hume famously

[12] T 3.1.1.27; SBN 469.

[13] There is some evidence that Hume's contemporary and philosophical ally Adam Smith accepted a similar picture of moral phenomenology. References to Adam Smith are to his *The Theory of Moral Sentiments*, ed. D. D. Raphael and A. L. Macfie (Indianapolis: Liberty Fund, 1982), cited as 'TMS' followed by part, section (where appropriate), chapter, and paragraph numbers. Smith says at one point that when we sympathize entirely with another agent, '[h]is actions seem . . . to *demand*, and . . . to *call aloud* for proportionable recompense' (TMS 2.1.4.2, emphases added). It is plausible that Smith intends the terms 'demand' and 'call aloud' to capture experiences of objective mind-independent moral relational properties.

[14] EPM 1.1; SBN 169.

asks the reader to consider wilful murder and to see if he (the reader) 'can find that matter of fact, or real existence, which [he] call[s] *vice*'.[15] Hume predicts that the vice will entirely escape the reader until he turns his reflection inwards and finds 'a sentiment of disapprobation which arises in [him], towards this action'.[16] Indeed, Hume thinks that '[t]o have the sense of virtue is nothing but to feel a satisfaction of a particular kind from the contemplation of a character'.[17] This feeling of satisfaction gets mistaken for a perception of an objective moral feature 'because [the feeling of satisfaction] is not so turbulent and violent as to distinguish itself, in an evident manner, from the perception of the object'[18] and because of 'our common custom of taking all things for the same, which have any near resemblance to each other'.[19] In cases where we approve of people on account of their virtues, say, benevolence or wit, our sentiments of approbation are often not turbulent and violent and, therefore, they have a near phenomenological resemblance to our perceptions of those character traits. Hence, we apprehend as a perception of a mind-independent moral feature what is really a moral sentiment. This is Hume's account of how affective attitudes explain moral phenomenology.

So far I have argued that Hume endorses projectivism (see Section 1.2). It is important to note that this does not yet commit him to error theory, subjectivism, expressivism, or some other competing metaethical view. The more controversial questions are whether Hume accepts the ontological and semantic theses.

Hume on the ontological and semantic theses

Let us first consider the semantic thesis and whether Hume accepts it, and let us put discussion of the ontological thesis on hold for a moment. Much of what was said in support of the claim that Hume accepts the phenomenological thesis supports attributing to Hume the semantic thesis as well. We noted that Hume repeatedly compares moral properties to sensory qualities, which according to the modern philosophy are perceptions in the mind. We also saw that Hume thinks of these doctrines as considerable advancements in morals and in physics, and that these would hardly be

[15] T 3.1.1.26; SBN 468, Hume's emphasis. [16] T 3.1.1.26; SBN 469.
[17] T 3.1.2.3; SBN 471. [18] EMPL 165. [19] T 3.1.2.1; SBN 470.

advancements if ordinary people accepted them all along. Commenting on Thomas Reid's work, Hume remarks that to deny that ordinary people believe that sensory qualities are in objects rather than in the minds of perceivers is to imagine 'the Vulgar to be Philosophers & Corpuscularians from their Infancy.'[20] Hume emphasizes '[the] pains it cost Malebranche & Locke to establish [the] Principle [that sensory qualities are not] really in the Bodies,' and he notes that 'Philosophy scarce ever advances a greater paradox in the Eyes of the People, than when it affirms that Snow is neither cold nor white; Fire hot nor red'.[21]

Hume's comparison of moral properties to sensory qualities and his claims about what the vulgar believe about the latter provide evidence that he would say that ordinary people believe that moral properties are in the evaluated objects rather than in the minds of perceivers. I concede, however, that the claim that Hume attributes mistaken beliefs about moral properties to the vulgar is open to a challenge. Another interpretive possibility is that Hume thinks that the vulgar have no metaethical beliefs, including beliefs about whether moral properties are mind-independent. While Hume's texts do not conclusively rule out this possibility, the textual evidence I have mounted make my interpretation more than plausible.[22]

One might argue that if Hume holds that ordinary people believe that moral properties are mind-independent, he also holds that these common beliefs affect the meaning of moral terms, with the result that, in verbalizing moral beliefs, ordinary speakers make assertions that attribute mind-independent moral properties to objects, such as people's characters. But since there are no such properties, in making moral judgements ordinary speakers are, indeed, systematically misdescribing the world; they are in error in the sense that they make false judgements. This would be to attribute to Hume a version of what we have called standard moral error theory (see Section 1.3).

[20] Wood 1986: 416. See T 1.4.2.12–13 (SBN 192–3) for a similar point.

[21] Wood 1986: 416.

[22] A general project in the *Treatise* is to trace the origins of ideas central to human thinking, such as ideas about causation, personal identity, the persistence of material objects, morality, and so on. On Hume's view, many of these ideas do not have the origins the vulgar tend to think that they have. My reading of Hume's metaethics is in line with this general project and Hume's pursuit of it. However, in this book I remain non-committal on whether it is defensible to attribute to Hume error theories in areas other than morality.

There is another possibility, however, that brings us back to the nature of the error highlighted in the semantic thesis and the difference between standard moral error theory and moderate moral error theory (see Section 1.3). When an ordinary speaker comes to believe that Cicero is virtuous, she has a pleasing sentiment of approbation, which she mistakes for an impression of a mind-independent property. A copy of this sentiment gives rise to the idea that Cicero is virtuous, so when she has the lively idea (that is, the belief) that Cicero is virtuous, she believes that Cicero has the mind-independent property of being virtuous. The popular belief that moral properties are mind-independent and non-relational is false, but on this view, it does not affect the meaning of moral terms, such as 'virtuous' and 'vicious'. Therefore, when an ordinary speaker claims that Cicero is virtuous, the *meaning* of her utterance might not involve anything to the effect that Cicero has a mind-independent property of being virtuous. On this view, the false popular belief that moral properties are mind-independent does not render moral judgements false. It is thus a version of moderate moral error theory.

This view resembles Mark Sainsbury's reading of Hume.[23] Sainsbury has argued that in making first-order moral claims—for example, in claiming that Cicero is virtuous or that wilful murder is vicious—we *use* the concepts of virtue and vice, and this is not to engage in reflection on the concepts of virtue and vice. Therefore, says Sainsbury, there are, according to Hume, no 'first-order' errors in ordinary moral discourse.[24] The error that occurs is second-order and incidental to the meaning of ordinary moral terms. James Baillie has argued, in a similar vein, that Hume holds that one is not committed to ontological falsehoods merely in employing moral concepts.[25] But, he adds, 'when we don our philosophers' caps to *theorize* about morality itself, we run the (avoidable) risk of falling into deep error, such as positing these mind-independent moral properties'.[26]

The view I have sketched above differs in two ways from Sainsbury's and Baillie's. First, Sainsbury and Baillie both seem to suggest that on Hume's view, the mistaken belief that moral properties are mind-independent emerges from philosophical theorizing. While this is a possible

[23] Sainsbury (1998). [24] Sainsbury 1998: 141–42.
[25] Baillie (2000). [26] Baillie 2000: 15 (Baillie's emphasis).

interpretation, I have defended the interpretation on which Hume thinks it is the vulgar, that is, ordinary people, who pre-reflectively take moral properties to be mind-independent and non-relational. This belief is implicit in ordinary moral thinking, just as the belief that colours are properties in objects rather than in the minds of perceivers is implicit in ordinary thinking about colours. On this interpretation, the conception of moral properties as mind-independent is not a philosophers' fancy. It is ingrained in ordinary moral thinking, or 'implanted by nature,' as Hume might say. Rather than lead into error, philosophical theorizing about the ontological status of moral properties can help debunk this error.

Second, although on this view ordinary people's false beliefs about moral properties do not render moral judgements false, the account still deserves to be called a (moderate) moral error theory. It maintains, after all, that when ordinary speakers judge that a character is virtuous or vicious, or an action right or wrong, they believe that the character or action possesses mind-independent properties of being virtuous or vicious, right or wrong. Hence, ordinary speakers are systematically in error when they predicate moral properties of an object, since they then have false beliefs about the object. Ordinary moral thought thus involves systematic errors, but these errors may not render the moral assertions of ordinary speakers systematically false.

Here is an analogy meant to shed light on this idea: prior to Einstein, many people believed that motion is absolute rather than relative. In other words, they had false beliefs about movement. It would be implausible, however, to maintain that prior to Einstein people's assertions about motion, for example, the assertion that the Earth moves, were all false. We might say, instead, that people were systematically in error in the sense that they had false beliefs about motion, but that these false beliefs did not determine the meaning of the term 'motion'. This allows us to say that some of their assertions about motion, for example, that the Earth moves, were indeed true, albeit accompanied by false belief.

So, depending on whether and how background beliefs about moral properties are taken to affect the meaning of moral terms, we have two versions of moral error theory attributable to Hume: standard moral error theory, according to which the popular belief that moral properties are mind-independent affects the meaning of moral terms with the result that moral judgements are uniformly false, and moderate moral error theory, according to which this popular belief does not affect the meaning of moral terms and, hence, does not render moral judgements uniformly false. Which of the two versions is the more defensible reading of Hume is a thorny question to which I shall not venture an answer. Choosing between the two requires determining whether and to what extent background beliefs about the ontology of moral properties affect the meaning of moral terms.[27] This task is difficult enough in its own right, and I offer no speculations on what Hume's view on the matter might have been. As previously mentioned, Hume and his contemporaries did not offer detailed theories of moral semantics.[28]

Many commentators want to resist the view that Hume attributes errors to ordinary moral thought or discourse.[29] Rachel Cohon, for example, remarks that in the second *Enquiry*, when Hume says that it is the 'office of taste' to gild and stain 'all natural objects with the colours, borrowed from internal sentiment [and raise], in a manner, a new creation',[30] Hume makes no explicit attribution of error to ordinary speakers.[31] But it is unsurprising that Hume does not attribute error in this passage, since he is here concerned neither with the semantics of moral discourse nor with our pre-reflective beliefs about the ontology of moral properties; he is discussing a psychological mechanism, namely, the functions of taste, which he

[27] See the concluding discussion in Joyce 2010: 53.

[28] According to Walter Ott, Hume is silent on the topic of reference (Ott, 2006: 242). This is in line with the observation that Hume did not have much to say about moral semantics, or about how moral terms refer. Ott's positive proposal is that Hume understood the meaning of words (at least of nouns, adjectives, and verbs) to be their functions of indicating ideas in the speaker and reviving ideas in hearers (Ott, 2006: 245). There is some textual evidence for this interpretation (see, e.g., T 1.1.7.7–1.1.7.15; SBN 20–4). On this view, the primary bearers of truth-values are not utterances or token sentences, but vivid ideas (that is, beliefs or judgements) that words and sentences give rise to. This interpretation of Hume's view on meaning is consistent with attributing to him moderate moral error theory: Since many people have false background beliefs about moral properties, moral terms and sentences give rise to false beliefs, but they need not do so *uniformly*. They need not give rise to false beliefs in those who have come to believe that moral properties, like sensory qualities, are mind-dependent. It should be noted that commentators disagree deeply on how to interpret Hume's views on meaning. The opening sentence of Ott's paper states that 'Nearly everything written on Hume's philosophy of language is false' (233). That gives some indication of how largely interpretations diverge.

[29] Kail, who defends a variant of the projectivist error theorist reading, notes that it is currently not a popular one (Kail 2007: 148). Notable defenses of other versions of this reading are found in Stroud (1977) and Mackie (1980). I discuss two objections to error theorist readings in Section 2.2.

[30] EPM App. 1.21; SBN 294.

[31] Cohon 2008: 123.

contrasts with the functions of reason.[32] Cohon also notes that projectivist (which she seems to take to imply error theorist) interpretations often rely for support on Hume's projection metaphor regarding causation (the mind's 'great propensity to spread itself on external objects'[33]) rather than on Hume's explicit claims about morality.[34] My interpretation, however, relies not on Hume's claims about causation but on his comparisons between sensory qualities and moral properties.

Cohon concedes that in 'The Sceptic,' Hume makes the attribution of error we have considered, that is, that natural and moral beauty are commonly thought to lie in objects rather than in sentiments. But she remarks that 'this is simply the mistake of thinking a relational property is an intrinsic quality'.[35] We may add, however, that if our foregoing discussion is on the right lines, it is also the mistake of thinking that a mind-dependent property is a mind-independent property. Cohon seems to consider these mistakes negligible, but the belief that a character or an action has a non-relational and mind-independent moral property is true if and only if the character or the action has such a property. And on Hume's view, it does not. Hence, it remains a plausible conclusion that Hume attributes systematic error to ordinary moral thought or discourse, either in the form of false moral judgements or merely in the form of false beliefs about the ontology of moral properties that accompany moral judgements, some of which may be true.

There are some well-known passages in which Hume seems to commit himself to a subjectivist naturalist account. This account is also realist in that it holds that moral judgements are truth-apt and that some are true. These passages may seem difficult to square with any error theorist interpretation. In the second *Enquiry*, Hume says, '[t]he hypothesis we embrace is plain. It maintains, that morality is determined by sentiment. It defines virtue to be *whatever mental action or quality gives to a spectator*

[32] It is true, though, that there are fewer explicit attributions of error to moral thought and discourse in the second *Enquiry* than in Hume's earlier writings. Howard Sobel made the intriguing proposal that Hume was here motivated by pragmatic concerns, to avoid propagating '[t]ruths which are *pernicious* to society' and combating 'errors which are salutary and *advantageous*' (EPM 9.14; SBN 279, Hume's emphases). See Sobel 2009: 98–101. So, while it is *philosophically* important to highlight and correct the errors in vulgar moral thought and discourse, it might not be *pragmatically* well advised to do so.

[33] T 1.3.14.25; SBN 167.

[34] Cohon 2008: 122.

[35] Cohon 2008: 123.

the pleasing sentiment of approbation; and vice the contrary'.[36] It is far from obvious, however, that Hume is here making a semantic claim. He does use the word 'define', but since the passage appears in a context in which he is arguing against the rationalist view that there are mind-independent moral relations discoverable by reason, it is natural to take him to be offering real definitions, which tell us what virtue and vice are, rather than merely verbal definitions that tell us what the terms 'virtue' and 'vice' mean.[37] Hume's hypothesis that morality—that is, moral properties like rightness and wrongness, and being virtuous or vicious—is determined by sentiment concerns ontology. To have a moral property is to be the object of a distinctively moral sentiment of approbation or disapprobation of an impartial spectator. Importantly, Hume does not here advance a semantic hypothesis concerning ordinary moral discourse.

What we have just said answers the question whether Hume accepts the ontological thesis that moral properties, for example, wrongness and viciousness, do not exist in the world. On this interpretation, Hume thinks that moral properties do indeed exist in the world, but they are not what they are thought to be by ordinary speakers and thinkers. Moral properties as they are commonly conceived do not exist in the world, but given Hume's hypothesis that morality is determined by sentiment, moral properties do exist in the world. We will return to Hume's moral ontology in Section 2.3.

There is another well-known passage in which Hume seems to endorse subjectivism. This is where Hume says that 'when you pronounce any action or character to be vicious, you *mean* nothing but that from the constitution of your nature you have a feeling or sentiment of blame from the contemplation of it'.[38] Here Hume seems clearly to be making a claim about the meaning of moral judgements. However, the simplistic subjectivism he seems to advocate is an implausible account of the meaning of ordinary moral judgements. On grounds of charity, commentators have been unwilling to attribute this simplistic view to

[36] EPM App. 1.10; SBN 289, Hume's emphasis. Two clarifications: by 'a spectator' Hume means an impartial spectator, and by 'the pleasing sentiment of approbation' he means approbation of a peculiar kind (T 3.1.2.4; SBN 472; EPM 5.1n17; SBN 213n1).

[37] In support of this reading, it is worth noting here Hume's disparaging attitude to analytic definitions. Hume says that giving 'a synonimous term *instead* of a definition' (T 1.3.2.10; SBN 77, emphasis added) is philosophically unilluminating. See also T 1.3.14.4 (SBN 157).

[38] T 3.1.1.26; SBN 469, emphasis added.

Hume. In this vein, A. E. Pitson suggests that Hume is here guilty of rhetorical exaggeration.[39] It might be thought that Pitson's reading gains support from Hume's famous letter to Hutcheson in which he asks whether his formulations on this score are not 'laid a little too strong.'[40] But in the letter, Hume declares himself uncomfortable with the conclusion he considers himself intellectually compelled to accept. He gives no indication that he has made a rhetorical exaggeration, deliberate or not. It is, therefore, preferable to interpret Hume in a way that avoids making the accusation of rhetorical exaggeration. On my interpretation, Hume is talking about what we could, or perhaps should, mean by 'vicious' in a reformed moral discourse.[41]

The context of the passage is the one in which Hume asks the reader to consider some vicious action, such as wilful murder, and see whether he can find that matter of fact, which he calls vice. The vice, says Hume, entirely escapes him, as long as he considers the object. He cannot find it 'till [he] turn[s] [the] reflection into [his] own breast and find[s] a sentiment of disapprobation, which arises in [him] towards this object'.[42] Hume then immediately goes on to make the claim quoted above: 'So that when you pronounce any action or character to be vicious, you mean nothing but...' The '[s]o that' is important since it suggests that the claim about meaning is grounded in the preceding psychological and ontological claims. This makes it natural to interpret Hume as saying something like, 'insofar as you say or believe something that is not false, you mean nothing but...' The suggestion, then, is that Hume gives an account of the psychology of moral judgements and, on that basis, suggests a revisionary, error-free account of moral thought and discourse.[43] This revision may involve merely debunking the popular, but false, belief that moral properties are mind-independent and non-relational. But if this belief partially

[39] Pitson 1989: 66.

[40] Greig 1969: 39–40.

[41] Mackie also suggests that we read Hume 'as intending to say that this is what you ought to mean because that is all that, on reflection, you could maintain' (1980: 58). But this raises the question of what, on Mackie's view, Hume meant by 'ought' here. I take it that Mackie means that, on Hume's view, this is all you could maintain without saying or believing something that is false.

[42] T 3.1.1.26; SBN 468–69.

[43] It is noteworthy that claims similar to Hume's seeming commitment to subjectivist naturalism are found in Adam Smith. For example, Smith says that '[t]o be the *proper* and approved object either of gratitude or of resentment can *mean* nothing but to the object of

determines the meaning of moral terms, it requires revising our moral discourse, too.[44]

For Hume, the fundamental metaethical insight is that morality is a matter of sentiment. How we verbalize these sentiments is a contingent matter. According to Hume's descriptive metaethics, either the vulgar do it by attributing to objects mind-independent moral properties, and this is, as we have seen, an error, or they do it by attributing to objects properties that they believe are mind-independent, and this is also an error. Alternatively, we could verbalize the moral sentiments by expressing them or, as I claim Hume suggests, by *reporting* them. Since moral judgements are causally explained by sentiments, Hume might suppose that the transition to a subjectivist discourse in which moral judgements report sentiments would be natural and smooth. In the light of what Hume goes on to say later,[45] we could take him to suggest that on a more refined version of reformed moral discourse, moral claims would report sentiments of approbation and disapprobation that are peculiarly moral, partly in that we have them only when we put ourselves in the position of an impartial sympathetic spectator.[46]

that gratitude, and of that resentment, which naturally *seems* proper and *is* approved of' (TMS 2.1.2.1, emphases added). As with Hume's claim in the second *Enquiry* considered above, it is plausible to take Smith to be offering a real definition, that is, an account of *what it is* to be the proper object of gratitude or resentment. Smith also says that '[t]he very words, right, wrong, fit, improper, graceful, unbecoming, mean only what pleases or displeases those [i.e., the moral] faculties' (TMS 3.5.5). Like Hume, Smith is here concerned to reveal the psychological reality of moral judgements, so it might be plausible to take him to offer a revisionary account of ordinary moral discourse. But it is more difficult to find evidence in Smith that he took ordinary moral thought and discourse to involve systematic error, so in the case of Smith, this interpretation lacks strong textual support.

[44] However, I find no recommendation in Hume that we actually make the transition from ordinary, error-ridden moral thought and discourse to reformed moral thought and discourse free of error. On my reading, Hume's project is merely to sketch what an error-free moral discourse might look like. There is even some indication in Hume that he thinks it advisable on pragmatic ground to stick to ordinary error-ridden moral thought and discourse. See Note 31 and Section 9.2.

[45] For example, T 3.1.2.4, 3.3.1.15; SBN 472, 581–2.

[46] In order further to support the interpretation that at T 3.1.1.26 (SBN 469), Hume is not talking about what 'vicious' means in *actual* moral discourse, it is worth considering his claim about force and energy in the abstract of *Treatise*: 'either we have no idea at all of force and energy, and these words are altogether insignificant, or they can *mean* nothing but that determination of the thought, acquir'd by habit, to pass from the cause to its usual effect' (T Abs. 26; SBN 657, emphasis added). Here Hume can be taken to make a point parallel to the one I claim he makes at T 3.1.1.26 (SBN 469), namely, that in a reformed discourse about force and energy, the terms 'force' and 'energy' would be used to signify 'that determination of the thought, acquir'd by habit, to pass from the cause to its usual effect.' This is because we realize, on reflection, that this is all these words could signify. But it would be implausible to suggest this as an analysis of how 'force' and 'energy' are used in actual discourse. See, also, Craig (2007).

Hume is clear that the discovery that moral properties, like sensory qualities, are mind-dependent has 'little or no influence on practice';[47] it 'takes off no more from the reality of [moral properties] than from that of [sensory qualities]' and gives no 'umbrage either to critics or moralists'.[48] This is because '[n]othing can be more real, or concern us more than our own sentiments'[49] and because '[t]here is a sufficient uniformity in the senses and feelings of mankind [for them] to have the greatest influence on life and manners'.[50] Our negative sentiments vis-à-vis vicious actions, such as wilful murder, will not be affected by the discovery that our verbalizations of these sentiments, or our beliefs about the ontology of vice, are in error. The same types of characters and actions will be condemned and praised in reformed moral thought and discourse, free of these errors, as in ordinary, error-ridden moral thought and discourse. This might well be another reason for supposing that the transition from ordinary, error-ridden moral thought and discourse to reformed, subjectivist moral thought and discourse can be made smoothly. Since the transition does not require that we make substantively different moral judgements, the error can be peacefully debunked.[51]

2.2. Two Objections: Hume's Friendly Attitude to Virtue and the Motivating Power of Moral Judgement

The view I attribute to Hume explains why his friendly attitude to virtue is not a strong objection to error theorist readings.[52] The thought that there is

[47] T 3.1.1.26; SBN 469.

[48] EMPL 166n3.

[49] T 3.1.1.26; SBN 468.

[50] EMPL 166n3.

[51] The case is analogous to ordinary thought and discourse about sensory qualities, for example, colour. According to Hume, the vulgar think that colours are mind-independent qualities of objects. But there are no such properties, so either vulgar colour judgements are false, or what the vulgar believe when they accept such judgements is false. However, the vulgar use of colour terms is extensionally equivalent with the use of the enlightened 'Philosophers & Corpuscularians' (Wood, 416) who have seen through the error and think of colours as secondary properties (that is, as powers or as properties in the mind); both the vulgar and the philosophically enlightened hold that the sky is blue, that grass is green, ripe tomatoes red, and so on. So ordinary thought and discourse about colors need not be greatly upset. This error, too, can be peacefully debunked.

[52] Kail notes that this is a consideration sometimes mounted against projectivist and error theorist readings of Hume (Kail 2007: 148). But, as already noted, Kail himself favours a variant of the projectivist reading.

an objection here has, perhaps, been fuelled by the notion that error theorists must somehow be opposed to morality or at least to engaging in erroneous moral thought and to using ordinary erroneous moral discourse.[53] But this is a misunderstanding, and it is no less so in Hume's case. Hume, after all, thinks that there are moral properties;[54] it is just that they are not in objects, as the vulgar think, and that the error embodied in ordinary moral thought is contingent and peacefully debunkable.

Nicholas Sturgeon finds 'little to challenge' in the suggestion that when Hume gives a subjectivist definition of the term 'vicious' in the *Treatise*, he is making a reform proposal.[55] Sturgeon, nevertheless, rejects projectivist error theorist readings both because they have as much trouble accommodating 'Hume's many suggestions that moral facts are about our sentiments' as non-cognitivist readings, and because they have as much trouble as Sturgeon's own favoured reductive realist interpretation accommodating Hume's 'insistence that moral judgements themselves motivate.'[56] The first point presents no problems for our reading, according to which Hume thinks that moral facts are facts about mind-dependent, relational properties, whereas the vulgar think, mistakenly, that they are facts about mind-independent properties. The second point might seem to be a more serious worry, since on our reading, moral judgements express beliefs, and on a popular reading of Hume, beliefs are motivationally inefficacious.

There is a weaker and a stronger version of the claim that beliefs are motivationally inefficacious. Both versions agree that motivation requires a suitable pair of belief and desire; beliefs alone cannot motivate. The difference is that the weaker version allows that beliefs, a species of what Hume calls *ideas*,[57] can *generate* desires, a species of what Hume calls

[53] See Chapter 9.

[54] When Hume ranks among 'disingenuous disputants' those who deny 'the reality of moral distinctions' (EPM 1.1; SBN 169), he has in mind philosophers like Hobbes and Mandeville who denied that humans have, and are motivated by, genuinely moral or other-regarding concerns and affections, as opposed to egoistic or self-regarding considerations. There is a similar critique of 'licentious systems' in moral philosophy in Smith, TMS 7.2.4.

[55] Sturgeon 2001: 7–8.

[56] Sturgeon 2001: 69n33. Sturgeon also says that projectivist and error theorist readings are often taken to gain support from Hume's is-ought passage, and Sturgeon takes this support to be undermined by his readings of the is-ought passage and others, which, he claims, fit better with his reductive realist interpretation.

[57] According to Hume's phenomenological conception of belief, 'belief is nothing but an idea, that is different from a fiction, not in the nature, or the order of its parts, but in the

impressions. On this view, beliefs are directly motivationally inefficacious, but beliefs can be indirectly motivationally efficacious by giving rise to desires. The stronger version denies both the direct and the indirect motivational efficacy of beliefs: beliefs cannot motivate directly and cannot give rise to desires. There is evidence that Hume endorses the weaker but rejects the stronger version.[58] For example, here is Hume's sketch of how hedonic beliefs, ideas of pleasure or pain, generate desire:

> An impression first strikes upon the senses, and makes us perceive heat or cold, thirst or hunger, pleasure or pain, of some kind or other. Of this impression there is a copy taken by the mind, which remains after the impression ceases; and this we call an idea. This idea of pleasure or pain, when it returns upon the soul, *produces the new impressions of desire and aversion, hope and fear*, which may properly be called impressions of reflection, because derived from it (T 1.1.2.1; SBN 7–8, emphasis added).[59]

Hume might say something similar about the moral case: upon observing, or contemplating, certain actions or characters, we get impressions of virtuousness or viciousness, of praise or blame. To have such impressions is to experience the pleasing sentiment of moral approbation, or the displeasing sentiment of moral disapprobation. Of these impressions there are copies taken, which we call ideas of virtue and vice, praise and blame. And these pleasing and displeasing ideas produce new desires. The belief that some action or character is virtuous or vicious can thus produce a desire to perform or not to perform that action, or to emulate or not to emulate that character.[60] Note that were Hume to say that an agent's ideas of virtue and vice, praise and blame, are ideas *of* his own pleasure and pain and that these ideas are what generate new desires, the position would look like a version of psychological egoism. It is more plausible to read Hume as saying that it is the ideas *themselves*, or the having of them, that are pleasing and displeasing. The objects of ideas of virtue and vice, praise

manner of its being conceiv'd' (T 1.3.7.7; SBN 628, Hume's emphasis). See, also, T 1.3.7.2–8 (SBN 94–8).

[58] For similar points, see Cohon 2008: 18–19, 42–3; Kail 2007: 181–2, 190–2; Sturgeon 2001: 21–2.

[59] Later on in the *Treatise*, Hume says, 'we find by experience, that the ideas of those objects, which we believe either are or will be existent, produce in a lesser degree *the same effect* with those impressions, which are immediately present to the senses and perception. The effect, then, of a belief is to raise up a simple idea to an equality with our impressions, and bestow on it a like influence on the passions' (T 1.3.10.3; SBN 119, emphasis added).

[60] See Garrett 1997: 202.

and blame, are certain actions and characters, rather than pleasure and pain. What generates desires is the *pleasant thought* of virtue and praise (or the *unpleasant thought* of vice and blame), not the thought *of* pleasure and pain.

But even if it should turn out that the most plausible reading of Hume is one on which he denies that moral belief can generate desires, the point about the motivating force of moral judgements is a weak objection to error theorist readings. Hume seems not to commit himself to the view that there is a necessary connection between making a moral judgement and being motivated to act accordingly.[61] What he does say are things like '[m]orals excite passions, and produce or prevent actions',[62] not that morals do so *necessarily*, and that 'men are *often* govern'd by their duties'.[63] This is easily explained on error theorist readings, for recall that the psychological thesis says that our experiences of moral properties as mind-independent are causally explained by affective attitudes, and recall, also, the suggestion above that ideas of virtue and vice are copies of pleasing sentiments of moral approbation and displeasing sentiments of moral disapprobation. In other words, moral judgements are causally explained by motivationally efficacious attitudes. The correlation between making moral judgements and being motivated to act is therefore strong but contingent. The view allows for cases in which the lively idea that some action is virtuous or vicious fails to produce a desire or some other motivating attitude. Since this latter implication is, in itself, plausible, and since the general view that the

[61] One might, perhaps, think that Hume does commit himself to a necessary connection between making a moral judgement and being motivated to act accordingly when he argues that moral rationalists who maintain that moral facts are 'eternal and immutable' relations must show that 'the[se] [relations] have no less, or rather a greater, influence in directing the will of the deity, than in governing the rational and virtuous of our own species' (T 3.1.1.22; SBN 465). But he is not here claiming a necessary connection between making a moral judgement and being motivated to act accordingly. Note that he only speaks about morally righteous individuals, such as the deity and rational and virtuous human beings. He is arguing against the existence of mind-independent (relational) moral facts discoverable by reason, as postulated by moral rationalists. The premise is that such (relational) moral facts would necessarily influence the wills of morally righteous individuals and Hume's point is that 'it has been shewn, in treating of the understanding, that there is no connexion of cause and effect, such as this is suppos'd to be, which is discoverable otherwise than by experience, and of which we can pretend to have any security by the simple consideration of objects' (T 3.1.1.22; SBN 466). Furthermore, as Hume says, '"[t]is one thing to know virtue, and another to conform the will to it' (T 3.1.1.22; SBN 465).

[62] T 3.1.1.6; SBN 457.

[63] T 3.1.1.5; SBN 457, emphasis added.

connection between moral judgement and motivation is strong but contingent fits well with other aspects of Hume's position, it is defensible to attribute it to Hume.

2.3. Moral Error Theories: Hume's and Mackie's

We saw in the previous section that Hume thinks there are moral properties. This gives some vindication to realist readings of Hume.[64] But crucially, this is not at the expense of error theorist readings. Hume is a realist about moral properties in the sense that he thinks that there really are mind-dependent moral properties; to have a moral property is, as we have seen, to be the object of a distinctively moral sentiment of approbation or disapprobation of an impartial spectator. On this account, moral properties are relational properties, so this interpretation rejects Hume's claim that moral properties are perceptions in the minds of perceivers.[65] On this account, what is in the mind of perceivers is one *relatum* rather than the moral (relational) property itself.[66] Despite this mismatch, on balance this is still the best interpretation of Hume's view.[67] Two considerations support it. First, Hume's main concern was the negative one of denying that moral properties are in external objects rather than the positive one of affirming that they are perceptions in the

[64] Such realist readings must, of course, not make mind-independence a necessary condition of realism, since, as we have seen, Hume thinks that moral properties are mind-dependent. For an influential realist reading of Hume, see Norton (1982).

[65] T 3.1.1.25; SBN 469.

[66] In one sense, Hume thinks that both *relata* are in minds, for he thinks that mental qualities are the primary bearers of moral properties: 'If any *action* be either virtuous or vicious, 'tis only as a sign of some [mental] quality or character' (T 3.3.1.4; SBN 575, Hume's emphasis). But this does not mean, of course, that both *relata* are in the mind of a perceiver (though it might be, for instance, when one takes pride in one's own mental qualities).

[67] Hume is not altogether consistent in his treatment of the ontology of moral properties. For instance, he claims that 'these two particulars are to be consider'd as equivalent, with regard to our mental qualities, *virtue* and the *power* of producing love or pride, *vice* and the *power* of producing humility or hatred' (T 3.3.1.3; SBN 575, second and fourth emphases added), but as we have already seen, he also 'defines virtue to be *whatever mental action or quality gives to a spectator the pleasing sentiment of approbation*; and vice the contrary' (EPM App. 1.10; SBN 289). In the *Treatise*, he also states that '[t]he *pain or pleasure*, which arises from the general survey or view of any action or quality of the mind, *constitutes* its vice or virtue' (T 3.3.5.1; SBN 614, emphases added, Hume's emphasis omitted). I try, in the main text, to provide what seems, on balance, the most consistent and faithful interpretation of Hume's apparently conflicting claims about the ontology of moral properties.

mind. He might therefore have been speaking loosely when he claimed that moral properties are perceptions in the minds of perceivers. Secondly, our interpretation squares well with other claims Hume makes, for example, that '[moral] attributes *arise* from the particular constitution and fabric of human sentiment and affection'[68] and that 'objects *acquire* [moral] qualities from the particular character and constitution of the mind which surveys them'.[69]

On my interpretation, Hume is, therefore, a subjectivist realist, but he is also an error theorist in that he thinks that ordinary moral thought embodies error. It is a common and natural assumption that projectivist and error theorist readings conflict with subjectivist realist readings, but I have suggested a way in which these readings can be reconciled.[70] Error theorist readings are a plausible interpretation of Hume's account of ordinary moral thought and discourse, his *descriptive* metaethics, while subjectivist readings are a plausible interpretation of his positive account of moral ontology on which he bases his reform proposals for moral thought and discourse, his *revisionary* metaethics.

It is illuminating to compare Hume's error theory and overall metaethical view with Mackie's. A striking difference is that while Mackie thinks that moral judgements are necessarily false because, necessarily, there are no moral properties,[71] the view we have attributed to Hume has it that there are moral properties, but ordinary speakers are systematically mistaken about them in ways that may render their moral judgements uniformly false. This difference in ontologies reflects different views on how the nature of moral properties is determined. Mackie takes the nature of moral properties to be

[68] EMPL 162, emphasis added.

[69] EMPL 171, emphasis added.

[70] A reconciling interpretation of Hume's metaethics is also offered in Garrett 1997: Ch. 9. My interpretation of Hume's metaethics has some affinities with Garrett's, but our reconciliation projects are different. Garrett's main aim is to offer an interpretation that reconciles cognitivist and non-cognitivist (or 'propositional' and 'non-propositional') readings of Hume (Garrett 1997: 199–204), while my main aim is to reconcile error theorist and subjectivist realist readings.

[71] As I read Mackie, his view is that there are no instantiated moral properties, and that this is not just a contingent truth about the actual world: it is metaphysically impossible for there to be instantiated moral properties. This follows from a version of strong moral supervenience, which I believe Mackie endorses, and which is independently plausible. See Sections 1.3 and 5.1. In attributing to Mackie the view that there are no moral properties, I attribute to him the view that it is metaphysically impossible for moral properties to be instantiated. It should be clear that in attributing to Hume the view that there are moral properties, I attribute to him not only the view that moral properties are possibly instantiated but also the view that moral properties are instantiated in the actual world.

determined by ordinary speakers' conception of moral properties. He thinks reflection on this common conception tells us that moral properties and facts are objectively (mind-independently) prescriptive and intrinsically motivating, that they supervene on other properties and facts, and that we could come to know of them only by intuition.[72] In short, Mackie thinks objectivist intuitionists like Samuel Clarke, Richard Price, G. E. Moore, and W. D. Ross were essentially right about the nature of moral properties and the semantics of moral judgement, but he rejects their view that there are any moral properties or moral facts.

Hume, by contrast, takes the nature of moral properties to be determined by the psychological attitudes that causally explain our moral judgements. There are no moral properties as the vulgar ordinarily and pre-reflectively think of them, but once we reflect properly on what goes on when we make moral judgements, we can come to see the true nature of moral properties and also that there are, indeed, moral properties. In contrast to Mackie, Hume did not have much sympathy with his contemporary intuitionists' conceptions of moral properties. Probably with something like Clarke's view of moral fittingness as a brute and unanalysable relation in mind, Hume remarks that he does not know what to respond, 'till some one be so good as to point out to me this new relation'.[73] It is likely that Clarke would respond that Hume is asking for the impossible; the relation of fittingness can be 'pointed out' only in the sense that it can be intuited. Mackie would probably accept this response, with the crucial caveat that there is nothing to intuit.

A final difference between Hume and Mackie concerns whether ordinary moral thought and discourse are *essentially* error-ridden.[74] Mackie maintains that they are, since he thinks it is of the essence of moral judgements to be about objectively prescriptive, intrinsically motivating, supervenient properties, knowable by intuition. He might have said, then, of Hume's subjectivist reform proposal for moral thought and discourse that it would be thought and discourse about (a special type of) sentiments but not recognizably moral thought and discourse.[75] Hume, on the other

[72] Mackie 1977: Ch. 1.

[73] T 3.1.1.20; SBN 464. For Samuel Clarke's view, see Raphael 1991: 197–99.

[74] *Cf.* Joyce 2010: 53 and Sobel 2009: 51–2.

[75] Howard Sobel has noted that if Mackie's view is that moral discourse is essentially error-ridden, he cannot say what he evidently did say, namely that '[a] man [can] hold strong *moral* views... while believing that they [are] simply attitudes and policies with regard to

hand, maintains that what is essential for moral judgements is not primarily a matter of content. What is essential is that the judgement be caused by peculiarly moral kinds of sentiments of approbation and disapprobation. This is why, as we have already mentioned, Hume thinks the error in ordinary moral thought and discourse is contingent.

We may conclude that Hume, unlike Mackie, is no moral sceptic. According to Hume, there are moral properties, we can make true moral judgements, and we can have moral knowledge.[76] According to Mackie, by contrast, there are no moral properties, moral judgements are (necessarily) false, and hence, we cannot have moral knowledge.

To summarize this chapter, I have argued that in interpreting Hume's metaethics, we should distinguish between a descriptive and a revisionary project. Hume's descriptive metaethical analysis is plausibly read as error theorist. Two versions of moral error theory attributable to Hume have been identified: standard moral error theory according to which ordinary speakers believe falsely that moral properties are mind-independent and non-relational, which renders moral judgements uniformly false, and moderate moral error theory according to which this popular, but false, belief does not determine the meaning of moral terms and hence does not render moral judgements uniformly false.

Unlike contemporary moral error theorists, Hume is no ontological anti-realist about moral properties and no sceptic regarding moral knowledge. Based on his subjectivist realism about moral properties, Hume proposes a revisionary account of moral thought and discourse according to which moral judgements report attitudes. Since we are able to know what these attitudes are, we are able to have moral knowledge. This interpretation has the important implication that error theorist, subjectivist, realist, and non-sceptical readings of Hume's ethics can all be reconciled.

conduct.' Sobel 2009: 52, quoted from Mackie 1977: 16, Sobel's emphasis. To give Mackie a defensible view here, we could take him to be saying that a man can subscribe to both views, but that he cannot attend to both views simultaneously. He must compartmentalize his thoughts and avoid entertaining both thoughts at one and the same time. See Section 9.2.

[76] Hence, my reading of Hume accommodates Norton's point that on Hume's view, we have moral knowledge, and consequently, we need not 'succumb to the moral sceptics,' see Norton 1982: 150.

3

Hägerström: Projectivist, Non-Cognitivist, and Error Theorist

The Swedish philosopher Axel Hägerström was in many respects a metaethical pioneer. He was one of the first to elaborate and defend a non-cognitivist theory and several of his arguments and claims predate or anticipate arguments and claims that other metaethicists made a few decades later and that became highly influential. In the early twentieth century, Hägerström was a major figure in Scandinavian philosophy and jurisprudence and his work had considerable influence both in academia and in public intellectual debate. In spite of this, Hägerström's work remains largely unknown in the contemporary debate. This is mostly due to the fact that he wrote in Swedish and German and also to the fact that his work is not very reader-friendly. C. D. Broad noted that Hägerström 'had steeped himself in the works of German philosophers and philosophical jurists,' and Broad aptly remarked that 'his professional prose-style [...] had been infected by them so that it resembles glue thickened with saw-dust.'[1] Still, Broad thought that the high reputation Hägerström enjoyed in Scandinavia was well-deserved and he evidently considered it worthwhile to introduce his work to the Anglophone philosophical community.[2]

Hägerström's work is of interest to us because he endorsed different versions of moral error theory that he combined with non-cognitivism. Apart from its purely historical interest, studying his work also brings the

[1] Broad 1951: 99.

[2] Broad published a survey of Hägerström's metaethics (Broad 1951) and he also translated some of Hägerström's work (Hägerström 1953).

benefit of further enhancing our understanding of moral error theory and how it might be developed and combined with other views. Some of Hägerström's ideas and arguments—in particular his sociopsychological explanations of how and why we come to believe in objective moral properties—are reminiscent of the arguments and explanations Mackie and other error theorists offered some decades later. Moreover, one of Hägerström's colleagues and critics, the Swedish philosopher and sociologist Einar Tegen, wrote a critical article on Hägerström's work in which he offered a very early formulation and defence of moral error theory as we know it today.

Hägerström made various revisions of his metaethical theory at several points during his career. Some of the revisions are available in manuscripts and lectures published posthumously and yet others are available only in unpublished manuscripts. There are, however, helpful commentaries that allow us to track the development of his theories.[3] In this chapter we shall look at two different versions of a non-cognitivist metaethical theory, one 'pure' and one 'mixed', both of which involve elements of error theory.

3.1. Some Background

Hägerström's most famous defence of non-cognitivism is in his inaugural lecture as professor at Uppsala University. This lecture was delivered in 1911, about a quarter of a century before the emotivist theories of Ayer and Stevenson first appeared in print.[4] Ayer and Stevenson based their metaethical theories on different theories of meaning, logical positivism in the case of Ayer and a distinction between descriptive and emotive meaning in the case of Stevenson. In contrast, Hägerström took a more psychologistic route to non-cognitivism and in his early work he comments only occasionally and in passing on moral semantics. This is no doubt a result of the influence from Franz Brentano and his Austrian and German followers.

[3] Hägerström died in 1939. For posthumous publications, see, e.g., Hägerström 1952, 1953, and 1987. For commentaries, see Petersson 1973 and 2011, and Mindus 2009. My understanding of Hägerström's metaethics has been greatly informed by Petersson's work.

[4] Ayer 1946 [1936]: Ch. 6; Stevenson 1937. Hägerström was thus an early non-cognitivist, but the history of the view goes back at least to the philosophers in the tradition inaugurated by Franz Brentano, such as Christian von Ehrenfels, Alexius Meinong, and Anton Marty in the nineteenth century. Hägerström read and was influenced by many of these philosophers. However, not all of them were as careful as Hägerström was in distinguishing between subjectivism and non-cognitivism. For a history of non-cognitivism, see Satris (1987).

This is not the place for a detailed exploration of Hägerström's intricate theories of philosophical psychology, but in order to understand his metaethical theory some key notions and distinctions need to be explained.[5] Fundamental to our understanding of Hägerström's metaethics is his division between *ideas* and *feelings*. These are two fundamentally distinct psychological states or, as Hägerström says—taking the cue from Brentano and Meinong—*psychological acts*. The basic distinction between ideas and feelings is in terms of their content. In the case of the former, the content is something that has or can have real existence. For something to have real existence is for that thing to exist independently of minds. Ideas are only about things that can have this kind of existence, independently of being experienced by a mind. In saying that the content of ideas is something that can have real existence, the 'can' should be understood as indicating epistemic rather than metaphysical possibility. Ideas can be of objects that lack real existence, such as centaurs and disembodied minds; and of objects whose real existence is metaphysically impossible, such as a necessary being who is the creator of the universe and that exists in isolation from the spatiotemporal realm but still intervenes in that realm. The ontological status of the contents of such ideas is often unclear in Hägerström's writings. We shall not delve deeper into this matter.

Let us note instead that according to Hägerström's theory of judgement, to judge that something is the case is to have an idea that the content of another idea is objectively real.[6] To judge that there is a coffee cup on my desk is to have the idea that the content of the idea of a coffee cup on my desk is objectively real. Conversely, to judge that there is no coffee cup on my desk is to have the idea that the content of the idea of a coffee cup on my desk is not objectively real. In the case of the aforementioned example of the idea of a necessary being who is the creator of the universe, Hägerström seems to hold that it lacks determinate content. This idea is in fact a 'simultaneous association' of separate and in this case incompatible ideas, e.g., that of an entity, or being, isolated from the spatiotemporal realm and that of an entity or being that intervenes in the spatiotemporal realm.[7] What the atheist judges as not objectively real, then, is not the content of one idea but a conglomerate content of distinct ideas united

[5] See Petersson 1973: 30–72 for a general discussion of Hägerström's psychological theory.
[6] Petersson 1973: 50.
[7] Hägerström 1953: 142. *Cf.* Petersson 1973: 54.

by the association of ideas that theists express when they use expressions like 'the necessary being who is the creator of the universe' or 'God'. It is quite possible that Hägerström held that the simultaneous association that constitutes the theist's idea about God lacks determinate content and is therefore neither true nor false, and that, correspondingly, the statements that express this simultaneous association are also neither true nor false. The atheist, then, would seem to judge the theist's ideas about God not only as not objectively real but as too confused to rise to the level of truth or falsity. We shall come back to this point presently, as it parallels some of Hägerström's claims about moral judgement.

Let us now return to the contrast between ideas and feelings. The content of feelings, such as pleasure, pain, hunger, thirst, fear, sadness, etc., is something essentially phenomenological, something that exists only as an experiential quality. The content of feelings is thus dependent for its existence on a mind experiencing the content. We can of course have an idea of a feeling of, e.g., hunger, but as is the case with all psychological acts, the act, in this case the feeling, is different from its content, i.e. the experiential quality.[8] The content of a feeling is not even imaginable as the content of an idea. In other words, it is epistemically impossible for the content of a feeling to be the content of an idea. This is another point that has some relevance for the understanding of Hägerström's metaethics and to which we shall return presently.

Now that we have some basic grasp of Hägerström's notions of ideas, judgements, and feelings, we can begin to discuss his account of moral judgement and to examine whether it involves endorsement of theses (1)–(4) that we encountered in Chapter 1.

3.2. Hägerström's Early and Later Metaethical Views

Hägerström on the phenomenological and psychological theses

Hägerström focuses mainly on ought judgements and judgements about duty, and occasionally on judgements about goodness. Such judgements are neither pure ideas of things that are objectively real, nor are they pure

[8] Petersson 2011: 56.

feelings. Moral judgements are complex psychological acts. Just as the idea of God as a necessary being who is the creator of the universe is a simultaneous association of separate ideas, the idea that some action is a duty is a simultaneous association of the idea of an action and a feeling of conative impulse. The judgement that an action is a duty is likewise a simultaneous association of a judgement concerning some real property the action has or is thought to have, and a feeling of conative impulse. For example, a person's judgement that she has a duty to return a borrowed book to the library is a simultaneous association of the idea of returning the book (and perhaps the idea that intentionally not to return it would be theft) and a feeling of conative impulse actually to return it.

What we have said so far invites some terminological awkwardness. We have said that Hägerström takes moral judgements to be psychological acts of simultaneous associations of ideas and feelings, but given Hägerström's theory of judgement these simultaneous associations are strictly speaking no judgements. In one sense, then, Hägerström holds that there are no moral judgements. But for reasons of simplicity I shall continue to talk about moral judgements. Henceforth when I attribute views about moral judgement to Hägerström I attribute to him views about what it is to hold that some course of action is good, wrong, dutiful, etc.

What exactly is the nature of the associative connection between the idea or judgement and the feeling of conative impulse? This is not clear. As Petersson notes, it is a natural interpretation that in the case of moral judgements, the judgement is the psychological cause of the feeling.[9] But as he also points out, interpreting all associations between psychological acts as causal connections is problematic. In the case of the idea of God, for example, it doesn't seem that the idea of a being, existing in isolation from the spatiotemporal realm causes or is caused by the idea of a being that intervenes in that realm.[10] It is perhaps an interpretive possibility, however, that associative links can be understood as causal in the specific case of moral judgements, even if this is not a tenable understanding of the nature of associative links between psychological acts quite generally.

It is clear that Hägerström holds that we experience and think of moral properties as mind-independent features of the world. He thinks that this is reflected in moral language, in which moral terms such as 'duty' and

[9] Petersson 1973: 56. [10] Petersson 1973: 57.

'wrong' are used in inferential reasoning in ways that suggest that they are predicates that ascribe properties to objects.[11] We shall also see that he gives a detailed debunking explanation of how the idea of objective moral properties comes about and takes root in human thought.[12]

This suggests the quick conclusion that Hägerström endorses both the phenomenological and the psychological theses. Recall that the former thesis says that we experience moral properties, for example, the rightness and wrongness of acts or the virtues and vices of persons, as mind-independent, and the latter says that this experience has its origin in some non-perceptual faculty; in particular, upon observing certain actions and characters, and so on, we have an affective attitude that brings about the experience of moral properties as mind-independent.

While I think the quick conclusion is justified regarding the phenomenological thesis, matters are more complicated regarding the psychological thesis. Hägerström thinks that the presence of affective attitudes, or conative impulses, is one component of the explanation but it is certainly not the only component and arguably not the most central one. In order to understand Hägerström's explanation of moral phenomenology we need to revert to his theory of moral judgement as a simultaneous association of a judgement and feeling of conative impulse.

The explanation has both intrapersonal and interpersonal or social aspects. Hägerström begins with the latter and invites us to consider the role of a mentor trying to foster a disciple. The mentor aims to affect the disciple's behaviour by making her internalize certain norms and values. In so doing, the mentor states that some actions are such that they *must not* be performed, while others *may* be performed and she attaches to these statements declarations of sanctions to punish disobedience. These commands are meant to arouse in the disciple conative impulses to perform certain actions and to refrain from performing certain others.[13] The thought is that in making her imperatival statements, the mentor 'has a feeling of conative impulse associated with the idea of a certain action on the part of the recipient'[14] and that such speech acts are 'effective in producing in the recipient of the order a corresponding state of consciousness'.[15]

[11] Hägerström 1953: 136.
[12] See, e.g., Hägerström 1987 (1911): 34–46; 1952 (1917): 48–54, 120–3; 1953: 153–6.
[13] Hägerström 1952: 48; 1953: 124–5.
[14] Hägerström 1953: 124.
[15] Hägerström 1953: 125; cf. 1952: 48.

This dual role theory of the meaning of imperative statements anticipates C. L. Stevenson's account of the emotive meaning of moral terms, according to which moral judgements report or express certain favourable or unfavourable attitudes and encourage others to share these attitudes.[16]

The mentor realizes that she may sooner or later lose her authoritative influence on the disciple and she therefore introduces the idea of a superhuman power or God who condones and condemns the same type of actions. The psychological upshot of this process of inculcation is that the disciple eventually associates certain courses of behaviour with 'imperatival images'; the disciple eventually *sees* certain types of action as 'not to be done' or as something that 'must be done'. The ideas of the authorities' commands are reified and transformed into ideas of objective features of not-to-be-doneness or must-be-doneness.[17] When this has happened, the mentor and the idea of a superhuman power or God have become otiose. But this is in fact part of the mentor's intended aim. The most reliable means to secure that the disciple sticks to a certain course of behaviour is precisely to get her to believe that the reified imperatival phrases pick out objective properties of actions.[18]

Note that if we think of the mentor not as an agent acting intentionally, but in terms of processes of development of social custom or natural selection and their shaping of moral belief, this aspect of Hägerström's debunking explanation of moral phenomenology is well in line with important aspects of contemporary debunking explanations of morality. We shall return to such explanations in Chapter 7. Note also that the idea of certain 'modes of action [having] this "must be done" bound up with them *from their very nature*'[19] is highly reminiscent of Mackie's claim that according to ordinary moral thinking, certain actions have a property of 'to-be-pursuedness somehow built into [them]'.[20]

The intrapersonal aspect of Hägerström's debunking explanation of moral phenomenology has to do with his moral psychology, which holds, as we have seen, that moral judgements are simultaneous associations of

[16] According to one well-known scheme of Stevensonian analysis, the statement that an action is morally good means 'I like this, do so as well!' See Stevenson 1937 and 1944.

[17] Hägerström 1952: 49–51. Cf. 1953: 153–5 and the discussion in Broad 1951.

[18] Hägerström 1952: 53. This is reminiscent of a point we shall return to in Chapter 4 and in Section 6.2.

[19] Hägerström 1953: 155, emphasis in original. Cf. Hägerström 1953: 158.

[20] Mackie 1977: 40.

ideas and feelings of conative impulses. These simultaneous associations find their natural expressions not in imperative or optative statements, but in assertions, i.e., expressions of indicative sentences.[21] This is because 'the cognitive element predominates in determining the expression and forces the expression for the feeling in among the expressions for the objective properties of presented objects'.[22] The 'indicative form of the expression for the simultaneous association [is the] ground for the objectification'[23] that gives rise to the idea of objective moral properties. In this way the suggestive surface grammar of moral language, in particular the indicative form of moral sentences, is part of what prompts the idea of objective moral properties and the idea that moral judgements are genuine judgements about such properties, rather than simultaneous associations of ideas and feelings.

More generally, Hägerström holds that 'every apprehended sentence in the indicative form, provided that it is not a mere conglomeration of words [...] carries with it [...] an actual experience of judging'.[24] But again, moral judgements have no determinate content. A moral property is experienced as 'a certain something regarded as present in the thing or the action of which one is thinking, without being able to form an idea of what that property is.'[25] But this lack of a clear idea in no way prevents us from using moral terms as predicates in indicative sentences.

This should suffice to make plausible an affirmative answer to the question whether Hägerström endorses the psychological thesis. We have seen that his explanation of moral phenomenology involves not merely the claim that we mistake a feeling for a perception of a mind-independent property; it involves also broadly linguistic considerations of both the interpersonal and the intrapersonal kind. Since we have seen already that Hägerström also endorses the phenomenological thesis we can attribute to him moral projectivism. Let us now move on to inquire whether he also endorses the ontological and semantic theses and thus whether he is a moral error theorist.

[21] It is perhaps a bit misleading to call this aspect of Hägerström's theory wholly intrapersonal, for what makes it natural for a speaker to express her moral judgements in indicative form are the conventions of the 'social linguistic community' (1953:138) of which the speaker is a member.

[22] Hägerström 1953: 138.

[23] Hägerström 1953: 138.

[24] Hägerström 1953: 141; cf. 159.

[25] Hägerström1953: 141.

Hägerström on the ontological and semantic theses

Recall that according to the ontological thesis, moral properties and facts do not exist in the world. Due to Hägerström's psychologistic approach to metaethics, ontological questions about moral properties and facts are not at the forefront of his discussions. Hägerström advocated a naturalistic ontology and his view on moral ontology was probably that if we can establish that moral judgements are simultaneous associations of the kind described above, and if we can explain psychologically how they come about, there is no need to postulate moral properties and facts. Nevertheless, Hägerström did offer some arguments that target moral properties directly. In particular, he argued that no sense can be made of the idea that moral properties are objective properties of objects.

Consider the predicate 'good' in a statement like 'Socrates is a good man'. Hägerström asks whether 'good' here refers to an objective property in the object, in the same way he thinks 'tall' and 'temperate' do in statements like 'Socrates is tall' and 'Socrates is temperate'. He responds that whenever we judge of a human being or some item that she or it is good, we have in mind some objective property or properties in virtue of which she or it is good, or in virtue of which we think she or it is good. We might for example judge that Socrates is a good man in virtue of his temperance. If Socrates's goodness were an objective property, we would then be judging that Socrates is temperate and that he has the additional distinct property of being good.[26] But Hägerström claims that no sense can be made of evaluative properties like goodness as distinct from and additional to the properties in virtue of which they obtain. He also rejects the view that the goodness of a person or item is identical to the properties in virtue of which it is good on the ground that we can imagine a person or item having these properties but lacking the property of being good.

This has some resemblance to G. E. Moore's open question argument.[27] But as an argument for the view that moral properties, like goodness, are not identical to natural properties, it is no more compelling than the open question argument. The fact that I can imagine, or believe I can imagine, a person having certain natural properties and lacking goodness might simply be due to the fact that I have mistaken beliefs about goodness.

[26] Hägerström 1952: 114.
[27] Moore 1903. Petersson (2011: 67–8, n. 4) also notes this.

Moreover, goodness might be identical not to the properties in virtue of which a person or an item is supposedly good, but to some natural property like being what we desire to desire or being what a naturalistically specified ideal observer would desire. Hägerström's argument has no force against such naturalist accounts of goodness.[28] Our main aim here, however, is not to assess the force of Hägerström's arguments but to argue that the ontological thesis is attributable to him.

It is interesting to note that Hägerström's puzzle about goodness and its dependence on natural properties is reminiscent of the one Moore struggles with in his essay 'The Conception of Intrinsic Value'.[29] In this essay, Moore tries to articulate the way in which the property of intrinsic goodness depends on natural properties without itself being a natural property.

Many contemporary non-naturalists would say that the solution to the puzzle is that non-natural properties like intrinsic goodness necessarily supervene on natural properties. Many contemporary critics of non-naturalism will of course respond that invoking supervenience fails to solve the puzzle or introduces a new one. We shall consider some versions of such worries in Section 5.1. Hägerström, however, thought that the difficulties here lead to an insoluble dilemma for the view that there are objective moral properties. We may suppose that goodness is an objective property but then it turns out to be impossible to identify a distinct property of goodness in addition to the properties in virtue of which it obtains. The statement that Socrates is temperate 'determines' Socrates as temperate, but the statement that Socrates is a good man because he is temperate is not a further determination of Socrates since we can make no sense of this goodness as distinct from the temperance.[30] The dilemma is

[28] As far as I am aware, Hägerström never considered such sophisticated subjectivist accounts. He did consider autobiographical versions of subjectivism, according to which moral statements report the speaker's attitudes and communal versions, according to which moral statements report the prevailing attitudes in the speaker's society. He swiftly rejected such accounts, saying that that is simply not what we mean when we make moral judgements (1952: 116, 124). It is quite possible that he would say the same about the more sophisticated versions of subjectivist naturalism.

[29] Moore 1993 (1922).

[30] Hägerström 1953: 123. *Cf.* Moore: '[Natural intrinsic properties] seem to *describe* the intrinsic nature of what possesses them in a sense in which predicates of value never do' (1922: 274, Moore's emphasis). Moore repeats this claim in his (1942: 585) and goes on to say that '[p]roperties which are intrinsic properties, but *not* natural ones [e.g., the property of being intrinsically good], are distinguished from natural intrinsic properties, by the fact that, in ascribing a property of the former kind to a thing, you are not describing it *at all*, whereas,

that we can make no sense of moral properties as distinct from the properties on which they depend, but neither is it the case that moral properties are identical to the properties on which they depend.[31] Hägerström must have held that this dilemma becomes apparent only when we reflect carefully on the nature of moral properties, for he also held that ordinarily when we make moral judgements we intend to predicate objective moral properties. This brings us to his view on the semantic thesis, which, to recall, says that when we utter sentences of the form 'X is morally right/wrong' and 'X has a moral virtue/vice', we purport to ascribe properties to X, but our beliefs about these properties are systematically in error in ways that may render moral judgements uniformly false.

The question whether Hägerström endorsed the semantic thesis requires a more complicated response than the previously discussed question whether he endorsed the ontological thesis. This is because Hägerström made some revisions to his theory after he had first presented it in his inaugural lecture in 1911. These revisions concern the nature of moral judgement. Some of the revisions are most clearly stated only in unpublished manuscripts, but they are available in Bo Petersson's work on Hägerström. Some revisions also appear in the 1952 collection of manuscripts written in 1917, 1921, and 1930. Let us begin with Hägerström's early view.

We have already seen that according to Hägerström's psychological theory of moral judgement, a moral judgement is a kind of psychological act that consists in a simultaneous association of an idea of some course of action and a feeling of conative impulse to action. Importantly, moral judgements are not beliefs that predicate moral properties of objects. There are no moral beliefs and no moral properties. In the inaugural lecture Hägerström concludes from this that since such simultaneous associations of ideas and feelings are neither true nor false, moral judgements lack truth-value.[32] However, social factors and surface features of moral

in ascribing a property of the latter kind to a thing, you are always describing it *to some extent*' (1942: 591, Moore's emphases). Moore here seems to endorse some kind of non-cognitivism. But his endorsement is strikingly undecided (see, e.g., 1942: 554) and after Moore's death, A. C. Ewing published a note in which he reports that Moore had retracted. Ewing reports Moore's declaration 'that he still held to his old view [i.e., non-naturalist realism], and further that he could not imagine what in the world had induced him to say he was almost equally inclined to hold the other view [non-cognitivism à la Stevenson]' (Ewing 1962: 251).

[31] Hägerström 1953: 116.

[32] Hägerström 1987: 45–6.

discourse give rise to an idea of 'a certain alleged moral authority' that explains why ordinary speakers and thinkers tend to believe that there are moral beliefs and moral properties and facts, and why they tend to believe that moral judgements can be true or false.[33]

What actually goes on in our minds when we make a moral judgement, i.e., that an idea of a course of action is associated with a feeling, is introspectively closed off to us. We apprehend the simultaneous association of idea and feeling as a perception of an objective moral property in an object.[34] Petersson concludes that Hägerström's early theory attributes to us ordinary speakers false beliefs about what we are up to when we make moral judgements; we mistakenly believe that in making moral judgements we attribute moral properties to objects when in reality we are doing no such thing.[35] In other words, Hägerström's early theory is a form of error-theoretic non-cognitivism.[36] Many years later Ayer endorsed a similar view. He maintained that although moral judgements are in fact expressions not of beliefs but of non-cognitive attitudes, 'many people do believe that [in making moral judgements] they are reporting objective ethical facts.'[37]

So much for the early theory. In his work after 1911, Hägerström introduces a distinction between '*primary*' and '*secondary*' moral judgements.[38] The former typically appear in engaged situations when we deliberate about what to do and are about to act, whereas the latter typically appear in detached and contemplative situations. An aforementioned example can serve to illustrate the difference: Imagine that I pick up from my desk a book on overdue loan from the library. I ponder whether to return the

[33] Hägerström 1987: 46.

[34] Petersson 1973: 123–4. Cf. the discussion of Hume in Section 2.2.

[35] Petersson 1973: 125; 2011: 57–8.

[36] Petersson says that 'there seems to be no error theory in [Hägerström's] texts in 1911' (2011: 58). But this is because Petersson assumes that according to moral error theory, moral judgements are uniformly false (1973: 131). This conception of moral error theory is narrower than mine. How to use the term 'moral error theory' is of course a matter of stipulation and the usage suggested by Petersson is certainly not uncustomary. However, I have suggested in the previous chapters that there is reason to broaden the ordinary usage of the term and recognize moderate moral error theory alongside standard moral error theory. In my view, Hume's and Hägerström's theories illustrate why this is apt. Hägerström's early metaethical theory is a version of moderate moral error theory.

[37] Ayer 1984: 31.

[38] Petersson calls them 'primary and secondary valuations' (2011: 59, see also his 1973: 132–62). I take moral judgements to be a subcategory of valuations.

book or to keep it. As we saw, my idea of keeping the book, and possibly my idea that doing so would be theft, in association with a conative impulse to return the book constitute my moral judgement that I ought to return the book (or that it would be wrong not to, or that I have a duty to return it). This is a primary moral judgement. Like before, Hägerström holds that these are simultaneous associations of ideas and feelings.

But he now contrasts this with the kinds of moral judgement one might make in more detached and contemplative situations, e.g., universal or general judgements to the effect that happiness is good, that stealing is normally wrong, that there is a duty to keep one's promises, that Socrates was virtuous, etc. Such judgements need not involve any feeling of conative impulse to act and that is precisely what makes them detached and unengaged. These are secondary moral judgements, or moral norms. Note that the distinction between primary and secondary moral judgements is not a distinction between first-order moral judgements and second-order or metaethical judgements. Primary and secondary moral judgements are different kinds of first-order moral judgements. Unlike primary moral judgements, secondary moral judgements are not simultaneous associations, but genuine judgements that do attribute properties to objects, namely the properties we mistakenly believe we attribute in making primary moral judgements.[39] In a manuscript from 1913, Hägerström says the following:

> Hence, if a secondary valuation is a real value judgement, in which I reflect [on] the object's value, it also claims theoretical truth. Thus, [it is] a subsumption under the concept of reality. This is so, notwithstanding that in all value determinations we are not thinking of what is, but of what ought to be. *Therefore all secondary valuations are false*, even if they result from a certain psychological necessity. For it is not possible to reflect on the purported values without subsuming them under the concept of reality. And it is not possible to refrain from reflecting on the values.[40]

This passage may seem to confirm Broad's description of Hägerström's prose-style, quoted in the opening of this chapter. It is not entirely clear what the psychological necessity amounts to, but here is an interpretation: For the sake of illustration, return to the example in which I ponder

[39] Petersson 2011: 59. Note that what Hägerström calls secondary judgements are a kind of first-order moral judgements, they are not second-order or metaethical judgements

[40] The first four sentences are cited in Petersson (2011: 60, Petersson's translation and emphasis). The last two sentences are cited in Petersson (1973: 130, my translation).

whether to return a book on overdue loan. In normal circumstances, when I make the primary valuation that I ought to return the book, I cannot avoid also to make, implicitly or explicitly, the more reflective secondary valuation that stealing is generally wrong, or that there is a duty to return borrowed items, or the like. It might well be an exaggeration to call this a 'psychological necessity', but it does seem to be a plausible generalization of what goes in normal cases when primary valuations are made.

Hägerström's later theory is thus a mixture of non-cognitivism and error theory in that it endorses non-cognitivism about primary moral judgements and error theory about secondary moral judgements.[41] In subsequent writings, Hägerström complicates his theory further in various ways, e.g., by distinguishing between kinds of secondary moral judgements whose contents are concrete and whose contents are abstract. These niceties need not detain us here, however.[42] The points most relevant to our concerns are that two versions of moral error theory appear in Hägerström's work and are in different ways combined with non-cognitivism. The first, as we have seen, is a kind of error-theoretic non-cognitivism according to which we ordinary speakers are systematically mistaken about what we are up to when we make moral judgements. The second is a mixed theory that considers a certain kind of moral judgements (i.e., secondary judgements) uniformly false.[43]

Needless to say, neither of these theories is moral error theory in precisely the form with which we are familiar from the work of J. L. Mackie, although we saw that some of Hägerström's arguments and claims resemble some of Mackie's. As we shall see next, however, one of Hägerström's critics, the Swedish philosopher Einar Tegen, did anticipate Mackie's version of moral error theory.

3.3. Tegen's Critique

Tegen's article, 'The Basic Problem in the Theory of Value', was published in 1944. The problem alluded to in the title is that value seems at once to be

[41] As far as I know, Petersson (1973) was the first to highlight this mixed nature of Hägerström's later theory.

[42] For thorough discussions, see Petersson 1973: 126–63 and 2011: 59–66. See also Mindus 2009: Ch. 3.

[43] Two other general features of Hägerström's work on metaethics are worthy of notice. First, Hägerström thought that the belief that there is a unique moral truth that one has

both objective and subjective.[44] Tegen agrees with Moore and Ross that we tend to speak, think, and dispute as if there are objective values.[45] He also agrees with them that value is conceptually indefinable. But the best explanation of our evaluative judgements, including our moral judgements, is not that we apprehend objective evaluative properties. We value an object only if the perception or thought of the object elicits certain reactions in us or answers to certain interests. Tegen is not specific about what these reactions and interests are. He says rather metaphorically that upon observing certain objects, events, people, etc., we experience a certain 'feeling colour'.[46] Experiences of such feeling colour get apprehended as perceptions of objective evaluative properties, i.e., as properties 'it is possible to dispute about'.[47] This is what he calls 'the subjective element' in his analysis of value and he concludes that

> [t]here are no such things [as objective values]. But the values *appear* as objective in immediate consciousness. [...] [But] the values are just [...] subjective qualities transferred to objects I am attending to, but without my knowing or recognizing this fact. Hence their appearance of objectivity (1944: 44, Tegen's emphasis).

What Tegen sketches here is a projectivist theory of moral belief, of the kind we are familiar with from the discussion of Hume in Chapter 2 and to which we shall come back in subsequent chapters.

come by tends to lead to fanaticism (1987: 47–8). He seems to have thought or hoped that his unmasking of (primary) moral judgements as neither true nor false (and later of secondary moral judgements as uniformly false) would lead to a kind of liberating humanism in that it would promote toleration and understanding of other people's beliefs and customs. It is therefore ironic that Hägerström's theory came to be regarded by its opponents as objectionably relativistic and as a severe threat to humanistic values. Nevertheless, Hägerström's optimistic attitude about the liberating effects of his metaethical theory may well have been shared by other non-cognitivists and error theorists in the twentieth century (see Section 9.1). Secondly, Hägerström claimed that an implication of his view was that the moral philosopher's task is to study the logical, conceptual, psychological, sociological, and historical aspects of normative and evaluative judgements. But importantly, it is not a task for the moral philosopher to prescribe how people ought to act since this is an area in which there is no truth to be found (1987: 48–50). This view, with its disparaging attitude to normative ethics is familiar from the work of the logical positivists and other non-cognitivists and set the tone for much of analytic moral philosophy in the twentieth century.

[44] Tegen 1944: 37–8. Similarly, Hägerström says at one point that ordinary evaluative judgements suggest that 'goodness is a non-objective but yet objective property' (1952: 120, my translation).

[45] Tegen 1944: 36.

[46] Tegen 1944: 38–9.

[47] Tegen 1944: 39.

As we have seen, a projectivist theory also appears in Hägerström's work and like Hägerström, Tegen also emphasises that social factors help inculcate and effectuate the appearance of objectivity of evaluative and moral properties.[48] There is thus considerable agreement between Tegen and Hägerström. But there is also notable disagreement. Tegen concludes his article by offering an alternative to Hägerström's theory, one he claims to be 'decidedly a more natural, direct and uncomplicated' explanation of the apparent objectivity of evaluative and moral properties.[49]

Recall that on Hägerström's early view there are strictly speaking no moral *judgements*. Thoughts to the effect that a person is good or that an action is a duty, or the like, are simultaneous associations of ideas and feelings or conative impulses. As Hägerström sometimes puts it, to have such simultaneous associations is to 'glide' between the idea and the feeling; it is to not clearly separate two distinct psychological acts.[50] The natural expression of a simultaneous association in which a person is apprehended as a good person, is according to Hägerström an interjection like 'Oh, what a noble man!'[51] However, for various reasons—because the cognitive element 'predominates',[52] because we are socially conditioned to see moral properties as objective, and not least because we need to make inferences about, and dispute about, value and morality—verbalizations of our evaluations take indicative rather than interjectional form.

Tegen objects that we never observe the kind of gliding between ideas and feelings that Hägerström's theory involves.[53] Hägerström would perhaps respond that this is no surprise since the gliding is normally introspectively closed off to us; we are systematically mistaken about what we are up to in making moral judgements. But Tegen might well have countered that the alleged gliding should be introspectively recognizable once the theory has been laid out and properly explained. His alternative theory, as I understand it, is that evaluative terms are used as predicates signifying objective evaluative properties and that evaluations are strictly speaking judgements expressed in indicative form, due to our misapprehension of

[48] Tegen 1944: 44–5, 48–9.
[49] Tegen 1944: 49.
[50] See, e.g., Petersson 1973: 56.
[51] Hägerström 1952: 35.
[52] See Section 3.2.
[53] The target of Tegen's criticism is Hägerström's early theory. Tegen does not mention Hägerström's distinction between primary and secondary moral judgements or his mixed theory.

certain feelings as perceptions of objective evaluative and moral properties. This theory is comparatively simpler in that it does not postulate a kind of gliding between distinct psychological acts that is not introspectively recognizable and it is less complicated in that what gets verbalized in indicative form are indeed judgements proper.[54]

So we come to make judgements about objective evaluative and moral properties. But as we have seen, Tegen holds that there are no such properties. The implication is that 'all (positive) judgements of value are *false*'.[55] This might be the first published statement of moral error theory in the form in which we are familiar with it in the contemporary metaethical debate, chiefly through Mackie's work, which first appeared in print two years later.[56] Tegen's restriction that only positive evaluative and moral judgements are false shows that he is aware of the logical problems of how to formulate standard moral error theory (see Section 1.2). Apart from his brief discussion of this complication, Tegen presents his conclusion with remarkably little ado. For example, he does not seem worried about the radical and counterintuitive implications of moral error theory.

Let us finally comment on the strength of Tegen's position. Like Hägerström, Tegen is not primarily concerned with moral ontology but he clearly holds that there are no moral properties. I speculated above that Hägerström may well have thought that once he had given his psychological and sociological explanations of why we tend to speak as if there are objective moral properties it would simply be superfluous to include in our ontology objective moral properties. Tegen may well have thought something similar and this may explain why he gave no direct arguments against objective moral properties, but still stated with confidence that there are none. Hägerström's and Tegen's projectivist theories may indeed make objective moral properties superfluous in explaining our moral judgements, but it does not follow that there are no objective moral properties. We have seen in Section 1.2 and Chapter 2 that projectivism and realism are compatible. What would strengthen a position like Tegen's,

[54] Tegen also criticises Hägerström's concept of feeling. I set this criticism aside, however, since it seems for our purposes less noteworthy than the criticism I consider in the main text. Moreover, it has been argued that Tegen's critique in this respect is based on a misreading of Hägerström (Petersson 1973: 38–40).

[55] Tegen 1944: 50, Tegen's emphasis.

[56] Mackie (1946). The similarities between Tegen's and Mackie's views are noted in Petersson 1973: 164.

then, are arguments pointing to something specifically problematic about objective moral properties. This is the task that Mackie's queerness arguments are meant to fulfil. We will examine these arguments in Part II but before we come to that we shall in Chapter 4 consider some other precursors of moral error theory in the twentieth century.

4

Other Precursors of Moral Error Theory

In the early twentieth century, moral error theory was in circulation in different regions of the philosophical world. We saw in the previous chapter that the Swedish philosopher Axel Hägerström defended a variant of the theory and that possibly the first defence of moral error theory, as we are familiar with it in the contemporary metaethical debate, appeared in Einar Tegen's article 'The Basic Problem in the Theory of Value' (1944). In this chapter we shall consider some other prominent precursors that predate Mackie's canonical statement and defence of moral error theory in *Ethics: Inventing Right and Wrong* (1977). In particular, we shall see that Bertrand Russell, Ludwig Wittgenstein, and Richard Robinson at different times all defended metaethical theories and used arguments that are rather similar to Mackie's. At the same time defenders of moral realism began to take moral error theory seriously and to offer arguments against it.

We shall see that what prompted some philosophers in the early and middle twentieth century to be attracted to moral error theory was variations on a common theme, *viz.* a general dissatisfaction with the ontological and epistemological commitments of the non-naturalistic theories of Moore and Ross. In Section 4.4 we shall consider Mackie's own early statement and defence of moral error theory in his article 'A Refutation of Morals' (1946), which in some respects differs from his later statement and defence in *Ethics: Inventing Right and Wrong.*

4.1. Russell

Bertrand Russell was in many ways a metaethical pioneer and renegade. In the early twentieth century he was quite persuaded by Moore's arguments in *Principia Ethica* (1903), but he subsequently came to endorse a version of emotivism. In between this change of views, he briefly formulated and defended a version of moral error theory.[1] He did so in the lecture 'Is There an Absolute Good?', which he delivered in 1922 and which remained unpublished in his lifetime.[2] Anticipating Mackie, Russell holds that 'ethical judgements claim objectivity; but this claim, to my mind, makes them all false'.[3]

Taking the cue from Moore, Russell focuses on the predicate 'good' and the property of goodness.[4] According to Russell, when we judge that something is good we judge that this thing has a property that is common to all good things and absent from all things that are not good. Russell holds that such judgements involve a claim to objectivity because he agrees with Moore that when we judge that something is good we do not merely report our positive attitudes to that thing.[5] Hence, we mean to ascribe to all good things a common objective—i.e., mind-independent—property that all things that are not good lack.

Russell maintains that there is no such property common to all and only good things that we mean to ascribe by using the term 'good'. He gives a projectivist explanation of how we come to believe falsely that there is such a property. The things we judge to be good are things towards which we have positive emotions of approval. We mistake the similarity of our emotions towards these things for a perception of an objective quality common to all and only these things, and we call this supposed property 'good'.[6] This projectivist view about how and why we come to believe that there are objective moral properties is strikingly similar to the one we

[1] For an exposition of the metaethical positions Russell advocated at different times and some speculations about the reasons for his changes of views, see Pigden 1999: 8–23.

[2] This brief lecture is now available in Pigden (1999).

[3] Russell 1999: 123. Russell explicitly compares his analysis of moral judgements to his famous analysis of statements like 'The present King of France is bald'. See Russell (1905).

[4] Pigden notes that Russell rather confusingly called properties 'predicates' (Pigden 1999: 119). So did Moore occasionally in *Principia Ethica*.

[5] Russell 1999: 123.

[6] Russell 1999: 123.

attributed to Hume in Chapter 2 and that we have also encountered in Hägerström and Tegen in Chapter 3.

It is notable that Russell does not argue explicitly that the property common to all and only good things is non-natural and simple. There is no explicit argument to the effect that moral properties are metaphysically queer. Russell's main argument against a property common to all and only good things consists in an appeal to theoretical economy.[7] More exactly, Russell claims that such a property is explanatorily superfluous since we can account for 'the facts'—for example, the persistence of moral disagreement and the reliable links between people's judgements about goodness and badness and their motivation to act—without assuming that there is such a property that we purport to pick out by the term 'good', and a corresponding property common to all and only bad things that we purport to pick out by the term 'bad'. Russell concludes that 'Occam's razor demands that we should abstain from assuming [these properties]'.[8]

Moral realists could respond by granting that moral properties are indeed explanatorily superfluous in the ways Russell suggested, but that we are nevertheless justified in assuming that there are (instantiated) moral properties since the upshot that moral judgements are uniformly false is so wildly counterintuitive.[9] This is a kind of Moorean argument for moral properties that we will return to later in the book. As we shall see in Chapter 7, a Humean projectivist story of the kind Russell sketches about how and why we come to believe in objective moral properties goes some way to undermine the Moorean argument.

It seems to me, however, that further arguments are required in order to cast serious doubt on objective moral properties. Moral realists may query why theories that assume only positive and negative attitudes that we mistake for perceptions of objective moral properties are more economical than theories that assume perceptions of instantiated objective moral properties, especially when we take into consideration the fact that

[7] Russell also notes that the theory he sketches is not vulnerable to the objections Moore levelled at rival views in *Principia Ethica* (Russell 1999: 123). To maintain this, however, Russell must hold that the property we mean to attribute to all and only good things is non-natural. Otherwise his position will be vulnerable to Moore's open question argument. Whether the open question argument is a strong argument, however, is a further issue.

[8] Russell 1999: 124. Cf. Pigden 1999: 117.

[9] See Chapter 5. Pigden speculates that one reason why Russell eventually abandoned the error theory may have been that he found it intolerably out of joint with his strongly held moral and political views (Pigden 1999: 20).

some moral judgements seem obviously true. In response, critics of moral realism need to point to some particular problematic feature or features of moral properties. In other words, they need to appeal to something like the queerness of moral properties and facts.

4.2. Wittgenstein

Wittgenstein's 'A Lecture on Ethics' was prepared in 1929 or 1930, but not published until 1965. It contains some obscurities, but interestingly it also contains arguments that resemble some of the queerness arguments that Mackie offered in 1977. Equally interesting is the fact that Wittgenstein ends up with a theory according to which moral judgements are uniformly meaningless, rather than uniformly false.

Wittgenstein accepts Moore's characterization of the discipline of ethics as 'the general enquiry into what is good.'[10] He then goes on to distinguish attributive uses of the term 'good' from predicative uses. 'Good' is used predicatively in sentences like 'Happiness is good'; it is used attributively in sentences like 'X is a good chair' and 'X is a good philosopher'. Wittgenstein calls this latter sense the 'relative sense' of 'good.' To say of some object that it is good in this relative sense is simply to say that it meets 'a certain predetermined standard.'[11] Such statements, Wittgenstein thinks, are philosophically unproblematic.[12] But the attributive, or relative, use of 'good' is not the one that is central in moral discourse. Wittgenstein illustrates this with an example of a tennis player who intentionally plays badly. When it is pointed out to the player that his play is no good, he responds that he does not want to play any better. In such a case there is, according to Wittgenstein, nothing more to say. A contrasting case is one in which

[10] Wittgenstein 1965: 4. See Moore 1903: Ch. 1.

[11] Wittgenstein 1965: 5. At about the same time, W. D. Ross made the same distinction between what he called attributive and predicative uses of 'good' (Ross 2002 [1930]: 65–8). Unlike Wittgenstein, Ross of course held that judgements involving predicative uses of good are perfectly meaningful and sometimes true. P. T. Geach famously argued that predicative uses of 'good' are illegitimate, or meaningless. As we shall see presently, Wittgenstein concurs, but whereas Geach seems to think that the predicative use of 'good' is an invention by certain philosophers (namely the ones he calls 'Objectivists'), Wittgenstein seems to hold that the predicative use of 'good' is central in ordinary moral discourse (see Geach 1956: 35–6; Wittgenstein 1965: 5–6).

[12] Wittgenstein 1965: 5.

a person has told a preposterous lie, and is criticized for it. Wittgenstein imagines the liar responding along the following lines:

> 'I know I behave badly, but then I don't want to behave any better,' could [his critic] then say 'Ah, then that's all right'? Certainly not; he would say 'Well, you *ought* to want to behave better.' Here you have an absolute judgement of value, [in contrast with] a relative judgement (1965: 5, Wittgenstein's emphasis).

This passage suggests that Wittgenstein accepts what we in Chapter 6 will call 'the conceptual claim', namely the claim that moral facts entail facts about irreducibly normative reasons, and correspondingly that moral claims entail claims about irreducibly normative reasons.[13] Insofar as Wittgenstein holds that irreducible normativity is metaphysically queer, his view resembles Mackie's fourth queerness argument, which we will also discuss in Chapter 6. As we shall see presently in this section, however, when Wittgenstein explains why there are and can be no moral facts he focuses on motivation rather than normativity. As we shall see in the next chapter, Mackie tended to oscillate between issues concerning motivation and issues concerning normativity in his discussions of why moral facts are queer.

According to Wittgenstein, judgements of absolute value cannot be inferred from non-evaluative judgements or from judgements about relative value.[14] This is of course reminiscent of Hume's Law, and a further resemblance with Hume appears when Wittgenstein imagines a book containing the total description of the world, as it is presently and as it has been and will be. Such a book would contain no moral judgements. Descriptions of murders, for example, would only describe the physical and mental processes involved in the events. This is reminiscent of Hume's claim that when we contemplate a case of wilful murder in all its respects recognizable by our perceptual and intellectual faculties, we find nothing that corresponds to the term 'vice'.[15]

[13] The notion of irreducible normativity will also be explored in chapter 6.

[14] Wittgenstein 1965: 6. In fact, Wittgenstein seems to hold that judgements about relative value are not genuinely evaluative judgements (1965: 5–6).

[15] 'Take any action allow'd to be vicious: Wilful murder, for instance. Examine it in all lights, and see if you can find that matter of fact, or real existence, which you call *vice*. In which-ever way you take it, you find only certain passions, motives, volitions and thoughts. There is no other matter of fact in the case. The vice entirely escapes you, as long as you consider the object' (T 3.1.1.26; SBN 468).

According to Wittgenstein, there can be no book on ethics.[16] One has to assume here that he means to say that there can be no book which is genuinely about substantive ethics, for he would probably agree that Moore's *Principia Ethica*, for example, is a book on ethics, but that it belongs to the branch of ethics we now call metaethics. Wittgenstein says quite dramatically that 'if a man could write a book on Ethics which really was a book on Ethics, this book would, with an explosion, destroy all other books in the world.'[17] This claim must be sorted among the lecture's obscurities. Why would a book on ethics have such disastrous effects?

Let us ask instead why Wittgenstein held that his imagined world-book that contains the total description of the world would contain no propositions about ethics. One might think that the reason is that Wittgenstein is attracted to some kind of non-cognitivism about ethics, according to which there are no ethical propositions. But the lecture does not contain much evidence that this was his rationale. When Wittgenstein explains why there are and can be no moral facts, he says the following:

> [T]he *absolute good*, if it is a describable state of affairs, would be one which everybody, independent of his tastes and inclinations, would *necessarily* bring about or feel guilt for not bringing about. And I want to say that such a state of affairs is a chimera. No state of affairs has, in itself, what I would like to call the coercive power of an absolute judge (1965: 7, Wittgenstein's emphases).[18]

Moral judgements are '*similes*' in that they resemble, on their face, judgements involving attributive or relative uses of 'good', 'right', etc.[19] As we saw, Wittgenstein considers judgements of the latter kind unproblematic. But when we drop the similes and try to describe the moral facts directly, we find that it cannot be done. This is because 'there are no [moral] facts.'[20] Wittgenstein concludes that 'what first appeared to be a simile [i.e. an ordinary moral judgement] now seems to be mere nonsense.'[21]

[16] Wittgenstein 1965: 7.

[17] Wittgenstein 1965: 7.

[18] Cf. Mackie: 'An objective good would be sought by anyone who was acquainted with it, not because of any contingent fact that this person, or every person, is so constituted that he desires this end, but just because the end has to-be-pursuedness somehow built into it' (1977: 40). *Cf.* also the discussion of Hägerström in Section 3.2.

[19] Wittgenstein 1965: 8.

[20] Wittgenstein 1965: 10.

[21] Wittgenstein 1965: 10. The same holds for religious discourse, according to Wittgenstein (1965: 9–12).

Whence the conclusion that moral judgements are nonsensical rather than meaningful but false? The explanation seems to be that when we use moral language we try '*to go beyond* the world and that is to say beyond significant language.'[22] The view that we can speak meaningfully only about what there is or could be in the world is familiar from Wittgenstein's *Tractatus* (1922), according to which thoughts that we express by uttering sentences are pictures of facts. Since there are and could be no moral facts—facts which everybody, independent of his tastes and inclinations, would *necessarily* bring about or feel guilt for not bringing about—there can be no pictures of moral facts and so we cannot speak meaningfully about such facts. That is why the imagined world-book would contain no moral propositions.

Note finally that this is further evidence that Wittgenstein did not rely implicitly on a non-cognitivist view when he claimed that the imagined world-book would contain no ethical propositions. For if moral judgements were to express non-cognitive states rather than purport to describe facts, it is difficult to see in what sense we would try to go beyond the world in using moral language. It seems that in exclaiming 'Boo!' or 'Hooray!' I am sticking firmly within the world.

Hence, Wittgenstein's theory says that ordinary moral judgements involve the error of trying to go beyond the world by purporting to describe something that there is not and could not be in the world. On Wittgenstein's view, this is to speak nonsense. But note that this metaethical theory stands and falls with the claim that there are and could be no moral facts. The only argument to this effect that Wittgenstein offers in the lecture is the one that involves the premise that moral facts would be of a kind that everybody, independently of individual tastes and inclinations, would necessarily bring about, or be motivated to bring about, or at least feel guilty for failing to bring about. As we shall see when we discuss Mackie's motivational queerness argument, it is highly questionable whether this premise coheres with the ordinary conception of moral facts, as it appears in everyday moral thought and discourse.

[22] Wittgenstein 1965: 11 (Wittgenstein's emphasis).

4.3. Robinson

Richard Robinson formulated a kind of moral error theory in a contribution to a symposium on emotivism in 1948. Robinson's main concern is to get clear about what we should mean by the phrase 'the emotive theory of ethics'. He defined emotive meaning as 'the power of a word to express and arouse feeling, as opposed to its power to express and arouse the thought of an object'.[23] It is clear that Robinson did not think of the emotive theory of ethics quite as we think of it today. Emotivism today is normally thought of as a rival view to the moral realism of W. D. Ross and the moral error theory of Mackie. But Robinson took the emotive theory of ethics to be compatible both with a theory like Ross's or with a theory like Mackie's.[24] The reason is that emotive theories of ethics must tell us something about the descriptive function of moral terms, and the descriptive function might be to ascribe a non-natural property of goodness or rightness. Another possibility for advocates of the emotive theory at this point is to say—as R. M. Hare did a few years later—that the descriptive function of moral terms is to refer to those (natural) properties on the basis of which an object or an action is commended.[25]

Robinson in fact thought that Ross was very nearly right about the descriptive functions of ethical terms.[26] Unlike Ross, however, Robinson thought that there are no non-natural properties, so the descriptive function of ethical terms commits us to a systematic error.[27] The suggestion that this attribution of error may be a component of the emotive theory of ethics is another aspect that distinguishes Robinson's formulation from emotivism as we know it today. As noted in Section 1.2, contemporary emotivists and non-cognitivists, known as expressivists, typically deny that moral thought and discourse commit us to systematic errors.[28]

According to Robinson's version of the emotive theory, moral judgements, such as '*x* is good' have two functions. First, they function *emotively* to express a favourable attitude to *x* and to invite others to share

[23] Robinson 1948: 79.
[24] Robinson 1948: 84, 86.
[25] Hare (1952), cf. Robinson 1948: 91.
[26] Robinson 1948: 83–4.
[27] Robinson 1948: 84.
[28] We shall return to this point briefly in Chapter 7. Cf. the discussion of Hägerström's later metaethical view in Chapter 3.

this evaluation of *x*; secondly, they function *descriptively* to attribute a non-natural property of goodness to *x*.[29] Robinson notes that the idea that moral judgements involve systematic error is not unprecedented. He refers to Mackie's 1946 article and he also highlights the not very commonly known fact that Ross defended a view of judgements about beauty according to which they involve systematic error. According to Ross, an object's property of being beautiful is its mind-dependent property of having the power to produce aesthetic enjoyment in those who perceive the object. However, when we judge that *x* is beautiful, we ascribe to *x* a mind-*in*dependent property:

> [We] do not *mean* by 'beautiful' an attribute having [...] reference to a mind, but something entirely resident in the object, apart from relation to a mind. [...] [W]e are deceived in thinking that beautiful things have any such common attribute over and above the power of producing aesthetic enjoyment (Ross, 2002 [1930]: 128n, Ross's emphasis).[30]

Ross's fellow intuitionist, E. F. Carritt, suggested a similar view, albeit a bit more tentatively, in the course of criticizing Ayer's emotivism:

> Aesthetic judgements, assertions, i.e. that things are beautiful [...] generally *mean* to attribute to the thing a quality independent of anybody's thoughts or feelings. But so far as they do assert this, there are reasons for thinking that perhaps none of them are true in the sense in which they are thus meant. But whether these reasons for denying the truth of aesthetic judgements, except as statements of feeling, are sound or no, they do not apply to moral judgements (1938: 132, Carritt's emphasis).

Neither did Ross apply this kind of analysis to moral judgements. In his later work, however, he considered an error theoretic analysis to be the most plausible contender to non-naturalist moral realism.[31] As we shall see presently, however, he rejected this kind of theory rather swiftly.

[29] Robinson 1948: 94. It is notable that A. C. Ewing, in his later work on metaethics, defended a mixed view according to which moral judgements express non-cognitive attitudes and also ascribe non-natural properties of meriting or justifying the non-cognitive attitude in question. Robinson refers frequently to Ewing's work, but in 1948 Ewing had not yet published his 'second thoughts' on what he called 'a middle way in ethics'. See Ewing (1953, 1959). Unlike Robinson, Ewing did not take moral judgements to involve systematic error. See Olson and Timmons (2011) for discussion of Ewing's views. In this article we argue that Ewing's 'middle way' view can hardly avoid commitment to error theory.

[30] Cf. the analysis of moral judgements we attributed to Hume in Chapter 2.

[31] Ross 1939: 261. Ross's term for subjectivism here was 'the relational view'.

Robinson speculates about the possible consequences that might ensue if his theory were commonly accepted. Would people care less about morality? Must advocates of the theory repudiate all values and stop making moral judgements? In the end, however, Robinson is not greatly worried. Like Hume, he thinks that 'the effect of changing from an objectivist to a subjectivist view, upon one's moral feelings and one's obedience to them, seems to be upon the whole very slight.'[32] He also makes the optimistic psychological speculation that '[w]hen and where such an effect occurs, it seems nearly always to consist in a slight strengthening of those moral feelings that are thought to accord with sympathy and benevolence'.[33]

Robinson is adamant that his analysis is metaethical and should not be 'mistaken for that peculiar evaluation which consists in repudiating all values'.[34] There is no imperative for advocates of the analysis to stop making moral judgements. Robinson is concerned to promote moral feelings, such as commitments to truth-telling and sincerity. He maintains that thanks to the 'practical force', i.e., the emotive function, of moral judgements, one can hope to achieve this by making moral judgements.[35] We will return to a similar idea in Chapter 9.

We know already that Robinson accepted Ross's analysis of the descriptive function of moral judgements. But how do we know that the descriptive function commits us to falsehoods? Robinson says at one point that there is 'no evidence' for non-natural properties.[36] This is a bit curious since he actually considers two arguments to the effect that there are such properties. One argument, which he finds in Ross and Ewing, is that we could not form the idea of an unanalysable notion of, e.g., goodness or obligation, unless we had encountered this notion in experience.[37] Since we have these ideas, there must be unanalysable properties of being good or obligatory, of which we are aware.[38]

[32] Robinson 1948: 98. Cf. the discussion of Hume in Section 2.2.
[33] Robinson 1948: 98.
[34] Robinson 1948: 93.
[35] Robinson 1948: 89–90, 93, 98.
[36] Robinson 1948: 96.
[37] Ross 2002 [1930]: 82; Ewing 1944: 135.
[38] Note, however, that we would need to add further premises in order to reach the conclusions that these properties are unanalysable and *non-natural*.

Robinson's response is that this argument 'rests upon a false empiricism'.[39] In Chapter 2, we saw that Hume offered an explanation of how such ideas may arise: a feeling of satisfaction gets mistaken for a perception of an objective moral feature 'because [the feeling of satisfaction] is not so turbulent and violent as to distinguish itself, in an evident manner, from the perception of the object'.[40] Robinson also accepts Mackie's point that the mistaken belief that there are non-natural properties serves to make moral judgements more effective in altering people's attitudes and thereby in affecting their behaviour. Moral judgements will be more effective in this respect if they are not simply taken to report or express the speaker's attitudes, but also to report mind-independent, irreducibly normative, facts. This is because of 'the greater authority of the objective language'.[41] This is part of the explanation why the error persists and why it is difficult to detect.

A second argument for non-natural properties is found in Ross's swift rejection of moral error theory. Ross considers the possibility that all there is are favourable or disfavourable attitudes, such as approval and disapprovals, and that on the basis of these attitudes we mistakenly ascribe non-natural properties to objects.[42] He responds that there are some things that are *worthy* of approval. He admits that

> [n]o one can *prove* that they are, but then *nothing* could be proved unless there were truths which are apprehended without proof; and we apprehend that conscientiousness or benevolence is good with as complete certainty, directness, and self-evidence as we ever apprehend anything (1939: 262, Ross's emphases).

We can take this line of reasoning to be a kind of Moorean argument (see Chapter 7): the proposition that conscientiousness or benevolence is good is quite simply more credible than its negation. We realize this *a priori*, by intuition. Robinson, however, will have none of this. For him, believing in intuitionism in ethics is 'repugnant'.[43] He does not object to non-inferential beliefs and knowledge based on perception, or to *a priori* beliefs and knowledge based on rules of logic and semantic definitions. But he rejects

39 Robinson 1948: 100.

40 EMPL 165, see Section 2.2.

41 Robinson 1948: 102; Mackie 1946: 82. Cf. the discussion of Hägerström in Section 3.2. We will return to this point in the following Section 4.4 and in Chapters 6 and 7.

42 Ross 1939: 261. What Ross sketches is thus a kind of projective error.

43 Robinson 1948: 103.

ethical intuitions, which are supposedly based on neither of these. At this point, non-naturalists can respond by appealing to companions in guilt. We shall consider such arguments in Chapter 6.

What of Robinson's positive arguments against non-natural properties? The sole argument here seems to be that Robinson's version of the emotive theory is ontologically more economical.[44] If we can explain why there are such things as moral thought and discourse without appeal to non-natural properties and apprehension of them, but simply in terms of human attitudes of approval and disapproval, and the social need to coordinate behaviour, it is superfluous and therefore implausible to postulate instantiations of non-natural properties. It is notable that Robinson does not point to any distinctively queer features of non-natural properties and facts. The implicit assumption seems to be that since such properties and facts conflict with naturalistic ontologies and since they are explanatorily superfluous, they can be dismissed for Occamist reasons. As we shall see in the Chapter 5, error theories in various areas are often based on this kind of reasoning.

4.4. Mackie in 1946: the Argument from Relativity

Mackie's argument from queerness against moral realism has been at the centre of metaethical debates for more than three decades. Mackie first discussed the queerness of moral facts in his article 'A Refutation of Morals' (1946) but it wasn't until the arrival of his book *Ethics: Inventing Right and Wrong* (1977) that the debate on queerness caught on. Mackie's main thesis in the article is the same as in the book, namely that moral discourse is not nonsensical but that it, as a result of projection—or as Mackie sometimes preferred to say, 'objectification'—of feelings and non-cognitive attitudes, involves implausible ontological commitments that render moral judgements uniformly erroneous.[45]

While Mackie's main metaethical thesis did not change, he did change his mind regarding the status of the argument from queerness. In the early article he thought another argument, the argument from relativity, 'more

[44] Robinson 1948: 103. [45] Mackie 1946: 90.

convincing',[46] whereas in the book he described the argument from queerness as 'more important' and 'certainly more generally applicable'.[47] The argument from queerness will be scrutinized in chapters 5 and 6; here we shall focus on the argument from relativity.

The well-known argument from relativity starts out from the empirical claim that there are significant variations in moral views between groups of people that are temporally, geographically and socially divided, as well as significant variations in moral views within groups and societies. One may think that the moral realist could take issue already with this premise and deny that the variations in moral views are in the end significant (whatever that means exactly). I shall put this response aside, however, as the anti-realist could easily respond that human biology, psychology, and social conditions—in short, the human predicament—are uniform enough to give rise to some uniform moral views across cultures and times. Significant and widespread moral agreement at some fundamental level need not favour moral realism over anti-realism.[48]

The next step of the argument is to ask how the variations in moral views are best explained. The best explanation, according to the anti-realist is that variations in moral views are consequences of variations in living circumstances and cultural patterns of behaviour. It is these variations that explain variations in moral views, rather than the other way around.[49]

Why could not the realist accept this explanatory hypothesis? Why exactly is the anti-realist explanation better? Well, according to Mackie, 'if we have a moral faculty, it must be an extremely faulty one, liable not only to temporary illusions, as sight is, but to great and lasting error'.[50]

But perhaps it is no surprise that our so-called 'moral faculty' is extremely faulty. As Mackie noted in his later work, we need not think of the moral faculty as a separate organ of the mind, but simply as the capacity to reflect on and grasp certain necessary truths and make inferences from these necessary truths and the relevant non-moral truths.[51] Most philosophers agree that we have these capacities and also that they

[46] Mackie 1946: 78.
[47] Mackie 1977: 38.
[48] In Mackie's words, 'perhaps there are a few feelings so natural to man that they are found everywhere' (1946: 78).
[49] Mackie 1977: 36.
[50] Mackie 1946: 78.
[51] Mackie 1980: 147; see Section 5.2.

are highly fallible. The deep and pervasive disagreements in virtually all branches of philosophy bear witness to its fallibility. Since moral theorizing is a philosophical discipline it is no surprise to find deep and pervasive disagreements here too. Moreover, since common moral views are formed by a kind of pre-philosophical moral theorizing, which may of course be highly influenced by variations in living circumstances and cultural patterns of behaviour, it is not surprising to find significant variations in moral views across and within groups and societies. Perhaps there are moral truths that, like philosophical truths quite generally, are very difficult to come by. Moral truths may well be especially difficult to come by, since our moral thinking is liable to be biased by cultural heritage, social codes, and the like.

In this way, moral realists can explain why most people are, most of the time, mistaken about moral facts. When these factors are taken into account, it is no longer obvious that anti-realism is better placed to explain variations in moral views. Mackie recognizes that moral realists may take this tack in response to the argument from relativity.[52] At this point in the dialectic, Mackie thinks we can be 'legitimately [...] influenced by the "queerness" of the alleged moral facts, their striking differences from most of the other objects of knowledge and belief'.[53]

Significant variation in moral views may of course be a challenge when it comes to justifying moral beliefs epistemically, but it seems not to be an insurmountable challenge for the moral realists' ontological view that there are moral properties and facts.[54] It is the latter, ontological, view that Mackie is mainly concerned to discredit in his article as well as in his later work on metaethics. The argument from relativity on its own seems not to take us very far in achieving this. Perhaps it was this realization that

[52] Mackie 1946: 85–6.

[53] Mackie: 1946: 86.

[54] Note that substantive moral disagreement need not undermine the epistemic justification of the belief that there are moral properties and facts. There might be widespread agreement that there are moral properties and facts. Substantive moral disagreement may undermine the epistemic justification of first-order moral belief. To be sure, there is a lot more to be said about the metaethical relevance of moral disagreement than can be said here. For an elaboration of the argument from disagreement that differs from Mackie's, see Schiffer (1990: 608–9). For a recent book-length challenge to moral realism and cognitivism based on the phenomenon of moral disagreement, see Tersman (2006). For a recent defence of non-naturalist moral realism against such challenges, see Enoch (2011: Ch. 7).

lead Mackie eventually to describe the argument from queerness as more important and more generally applicable.

* * *

We have seen that the precursors and early proponents of moral error theory tended to focus on phenomenological and psychological issues, arguing that ordinary moral judgements in one way or another involve projection of attitudes. But as we know from Chapter 1, while moral projectivism is congenial to moral error theory, it does not entail that there are no moral properties, or that ordinary moral thought and discourse involve systematic errors. Neither does variability in moral judgements between individuals and between and within groups establish these conclusions.

Some precursors and early proponents of moral error theory offered cursory arguments to the effect that since moral projectivism is true, moral properties and facts are not needed as components in the best explanations of how and why we make moral judgements. Moral properties and facts can therefore be discarded on Occamist grounds. But such appeals to ontological simplicity are not very forceful in the absence of an argument to the effect that moral properties and facts are ontologically problematic or mysterious in ways that make recognition of them theoretically costly. The missing component in the early arguments for moral error theory is therefore an argument that directly targets moral properties and facts by explaining in what way or ways they are ontologically mysterious, and not just superfluous for the purpose of explaining moral judgements. Such an argument must also establish that ordinary moral thought and discourse involve attributing mysterious properties and reporting mysterious facts. Mackie's queerness arguments are designed to fit this bill. Part II of the book is devoted to a critique of these highly influential arguments.

PART II

Critique

5

How to Understand Mackie's Argument from Queerness (I)

Albeit well-known, the argument from queerness is not always adequately understood and it is sometimes discarded on insufficient grounds. No doubt, this is in part due to Mackie's own opaque presentation, ranging over no more than four compressed pages. My aim in this chapter and Chapter 6 is to sort out how the argument from queerness is best understood and to assess even-handedly its strengths and weaknesses. This involves some, but not only, exegesis. It also involves drawing a distinction between *the argument from queerness* and *the queerness arguments*.

There are four distinct queerness arguments, focusing on supervenience, knowledge, motivation, and irreducible normativity.[1] This chapter deals with the first three. In my view, these arguments are ultimately unsuccessful. The conclusions reached in this chapter, then, are all ultimately negative. The fourth queerness argument, concerning irreducible normativity, is more forceful. That argument is the topic of Chapter 6.

In the course of explaining the distinction between the queerness argument and the argument from queerness I shall also discuss why anyone should be worried bout the alleged queerness of moral properties and facts. But the first question concerns *who* should be worried. The first task of this chapter is, in other words, to get in clear view the target of the argument from queerness. This will eventually help to explain why some extant well-known responses are inadequate.

[1] For a four-fold disentanglement different from mine, see Shepski (2008).

Mackie's targets

Mackie held that intuitionist non-naturalists like Richard Price, G. E. Moore, and W. D. Ross, were essentially right about the semantics of ordinary moral discourse but that the metaphysical and epistemological commitments of their views were untenable. According to Mackie,

> it was an extravagance for Moore to say that 'good' is the name of a non-natural quality, but it would not be so far wrong to say that in moral contexts it is used as if it were the name of a supposed non-natural quality, where the description 'non-natural' leaves room for the peculiar evaluative, prescriptive, intrinsically action-guiding aspects of this supposed quality (1977: 32).[2]

Talk of non-natural properties is the philosopher's reconstruction of ordinary moral discourse.[3] Mackie held that non-cognitivist and naturalist analyses fail in various respects to give adequate reconstructions of ordinary moral discourse. Against the former, Mackie claims that the 'ordinary user of moral language means to say something about whatever it is that he characterizes morally [that is not] simply expressive of his, or anyone else's, attitude or relation to it'.[4]

Needless to say, this assertion is far too swift to cast serious doubt on non-cognitivism but Mackie's brief discussion is nevertheless reminiscent of an old argument against non-cognitivism that has come back in vogue recently. The argument is that non-cognitivist accounts do not fit well with how ordinary speakers use, or intend to use, moral terms.[5] The idea is roughly that when using moral vocabulary, ordinary speakers typically intend to make moral assertions, i.e., to attribute moral properties to objects and individuals. If this is right it is also plausible that this is what they believe they are doing. But if non-cognitivism is right, this is in fact *not* what ordinary speakers are up to in using moral terms: in making moral judgements, they are merely or primarily expressing non-cognitive attitudes like desires, or prescriptions, plans, and the like.[6] The implication

[2] What Mackie meant by 'prescriptive, intrinsically action-guiding aspects' will be discussed in Section 5.3.

[3] Mackie 1977: 34.

[4] Mackie 1977: 33.

[5] For an early anticipation, see Reid 1991 [1788]: esp. 305. For recent developments, see Cuneo (2006); Olson (2010); Streumer (2014). Olson and Timmons (2011) discuss the argument as it appears in Ewing (1947).

[6] Some versions of non-cognitivism hold that moral judgements are primarily expressions of non-cognitive attitudes or prescriptions and secondarily descriptive assertions.

is that non-cognitivism attributes to ordinary speakers systematically false beliefs about what they are up to when they make moral judgements. Non-cognitivists would then be committed to a version of moderate moral error theory of the kind we attributed to Hägerström in Chapter 3. We saw in that chapter that in opposition to Hägerström, Tegen defended the simpler view that moral judgements are straightforward assertions based on mistaken beliefs about moral properties and facts.

The view that ordinary speakers are systematically mistaken about what mental states they express, or what speech acts they perform, in using moral terms seems far-fetched. It is certainly more far-fetched than Tegen's simpler view that ordinary speakers are systematically mistaken about whether there are mind-independent moral facts and properties.[7] As Mackie observed already in his paper from 1946: 'Many refutations of the "boo-hurray" theory have been worked out, but they all depend upon and illustrate the fact that we think that we are doing things of quite different sorts when we say "right" and when we say "ow"'.[8]

Against naturalism, Mackie claims that the ordinary user of moral language means to say something that 'involves a call for action or from the refraining from action, and one that is absolute, not contingent upon any desire or preference or policy or choice, his own or anyone else's'.[9] As he

But the objection is that in using moral terms, ordinary speakers typically intend to make assertions with moral content and that they typically believe that this is in fact what they are doing. It is notable that some non-cognitivists acknowledge that there seems to be more to moral judgements than merely or primarily expressions of non-cognitive attitudes. At one point when he accepted emotivism, Bertrand Russell remarked that if someone were to advocate introduction of bull-fighting in his country he would oppose the proposal and he reported that in doing so he would feel not only that he was expressing his desires, but also that his desires in the matter are right (Russell 1946: 742, also quoted in Mackie 1977: 34). Expressivist Simon Blackburn recognizes the 'nagging feeling that on [the non-cognitivist's] metaphysic "there are no obligations, and so on, *really*"' (Blackburn 1993a: 157, Blackburn's emphasis). Blackburn may agree that it *seems* to ordinary speakers that in using moral terms they are typically making moral assertions and attributing moral properties, but he may deny that this is also what they *believe* they are doing (*cf.* Section 1.2).

[7] A related objection will be made against Finlay's relativist analysis in Section 6.2.

[8] Mackie 1946: 81. Non-cognitivist views of course face many problems that Mackie did not develop and that will not be considered here. Elsewhere I have argued that non-cognitivism has trouble accounting for degrees of moral and normative belief (Bykvist and Olson 2009, 2012). For a state of the art discussion of problems and prospects for non-cognitivism, see Schroeder (2010).

[9] Mackie 1977: 33.

also says, naturalistic analyses leave out 'the categorical quality of moral requirements.'[10]

Again, Mackie's claims are far from conclusive criticism, but they are certainly reminiscent of a complaint against naturalism that is quite common in the contemporary debate. This complaint is often labelled 'the normativity objection.'[11] It can be illustrated by a familiar critique of divine command theories that reduce rightness and wrongness to God's will. Suppose we are told that for an act to be right is for that act to be willed by God. If God is good then whatever he wills is good or right. But as Richard Price and other British moralists argued in the eighteenth century, this presupposes that the objects of his will are good or right already.[12] If we are told merely that some act is willed by God we haven't been told anything normative. What needs to be added is the claim that God is good and that, as a consequence, whatever he wills is good or right. Hence, reducing rightness and wrongness to God's will leaves out the crucial element of normativity.

Very similar objections apply to contemporary naturalism in metaethics. Some versions of naturalism reduce moral properties to natural properties. So for instance, goodness might be reduced to what we desire to desire,[13] and rightness might be reduced to what our fully rational selves would desire our actual selves to do[14] or to a complex disjunctive property picked out by the term 'right' in 'mature folk morality.'[15] On yet other versions of naturalism, moral properties are functional properties identified as those properties that 'bear upon the maintenance and flourishing of human organisms.'[16] On this latter view, different natural properties may realize the functional role and if disjunctive properties are not allowed it will not be possible to reduce moral properties to natural properties. The view guarantees, however, that every instance of a moral property is an instance of a natural property. This is why this view is sometimes called non-reductive naturalism.

[10] Mackie 1977: 33.

[11] See, e.g., Dancy 2006: 131–42; Parfit 2011: 324–7.

[12] Mackie cites Price and other British moralists approvingly at many places in his 1977 and 1980.

[13] Lewis 1989. Pigden traces this analysis of goodness to Russell's work, see Pigden 1999: 12–13; 71–3.

[14] Smith 1994: Ch. 5.

[15] Jackson 1998: Chs. 5, 6.

[16] Brink 1984: 121–2.

Now, the normativity objection against naturalist views maintains that they all leave out the irreducible normativity of moral facts. We haven't been told anything normative until we are told that what we desire to desire is *good*, or that what our fully rational selves would desire our actual selves to do is *right*, or that the complex disjunctive property picked out by the term 'right' in mature folk morality is in fact had by all and only *right* actions. For all we know, our second order desires and the desire of our fully rational selves might be pathological, and mature folk morality could turn out all or partly misguided.[17] Similarly, the mere fact that some property bears upon the maintenance and flourishing of human organisms is not normative. What needs to be added is that there are *irreducibly normative reasons* to promote the maintenance and flourishing of human organisms. An irreducibly normative reason is a fact that counts in favour of some course of behaviour, where the favouring relation is irreducibly normative. This will be further developed in Chapter 6.

As critics of moral naturalism are well aware, these brief points will not suffice to convince their opponents. Moral naturalists are likely to respond that they are *explaining* normativity rather than *explaining it away*. The point of describing this possibly deadlocked controversy here is not to resolve it but to get into clear focus the target of the argument from queerness, which is moral realism of the intuitionist non-naturalist brand à la Price, Moore, and Ross. Importantly, moral naturalism is not one of the targets. Mackie certainly argued that naturalism is defective but as we have seen in this section, he did not use the argument from queerness to this end. In the argumentative structure of Mackie's 1977 book, he had, by the time he presented the argument from queerness, already discarded naturalism and non-cognitivism. Intuitionist non-naturalism was then the only remaining rival view, to be attacked on metaphysical and epistemological grounds. Keeping in mind this structure of the dialectic facilitates assessment of some extant responses to the argument from queerness, as we will see in Section 5.1 when we consider briefly one popular naturalist response to Mackie's argument that realists are committed to a queer relation of supervenience.

[17] Cf. Allan Gibbard's emendation of G. E. Moore's open question argument in Gibbard 2003.

Now that we have a clearer view of Mackie's targets, we can introduce the distinction between the argument from queerness and the queerness arguments.

The Argument from queerness and the queerness arguments

After having argued that moral properties and facts are queer in various ways, Mackie went on to say that

> [c]onsiderations of these kinds suggest that it is in the end less paradoxical to reject than to retain the common-sense belief in the objectivity of values, *provided* that we can explain how this belief, *if* it is false, has become established and is so resistant to criticism (1977: 42, emphases added).

It is in the end 'less paradoxical' to reject than to retain the common-sense belief in moral properties and facts because a metaethical theory that rejects moral properties and facts is ontologically and/or epistemologically simpler and less mysterious than a theory that admits them, in that the former admits fewer properties and facts that are queer. This is the conclusion of the argument from queerness. On the simpler and less mysterious theory, then, there are no moral properties and facts. Given that moral judgements purport to refer to moral properties and facts, moral judgements are uniformly false.

The argument from queerness is thus profitably seen as having two steps. The first is to identify ways in which moral properties and facts are queer and therefore ontologically suspicious. This is the purpose of the queerness arguments, of which there are four, and which will be scrutinized in this chapter and the next. Moral non-naturalists can attempt to rebut the queerness arguments in various ways. One is to deny that moral properties and facts have the queer feature in question. We shall see in Section 5.3 that this response is effective against the third queerness argument. Another is to appeal to companions in guilt, i.e., to argue that there are other properties and facts that share the allegedly queer features of moral properties and facts and that the queerness arguments therefore overgeneralize. We shall see in Sections 5.1. and 5.2 that this kind of response has force against the first and second queerness arguments. In Section 6.3 and Chapter 8 we shall consider whether it also has force against the fourth queerness argument. A third way of rebutting the queerness arguments is to appeal to a kind of Moorean argument according to which we hold some of our moral beliefs with great confidence, much greater in fact than the confidence with which we hold the beliefs that appear as premises in the queerness arguments. This kind of response will be discussed in Chapter 7.

Step two of the argument from queerness is to offer explanations of our moral practices and beliefs that make no use of the assumption that there are moral properties and facts. Here moral projectivism, as discussed in Part I, is congenial to moral error theory in that it gives a phenomenological and psychological explanation of why we tend to think and speak as if there are moral facts and properties when in fact there are none. In Chapter 7 we shall discuss debunking explanations of how and why this way of thinking and speaking has become established.

Let us now consider what could be meant by the claim that moral properties and facts are queer. In his first discussion of the queerness of moral facts, Mackie said that

> [o]ne of [the moral sceptics'] main arguments is that moral facts would be "queer", in that unlike other facts they cannot be explained in terms of arrangements of matter, or logical constructions out of sense-data, or whatever the particular theorist takes to be the general form of real things (1946: 78).

We can take this to suggest that one kind of moral sceptics—who, in Mackie's view, are 'often of a scientific and inductive turn of mind, and less devoted than some others to the clear light of intuition or the authority of reason'[18]—hold that moral properties and facts are fundamentally different from anything else in the natural world in the sense that they cannot be exhaustively explained or construed out of whatever the naturalist takes to be the general form of real things. In this sense, moral properties and facts are ontologically fundamental additions to a scientifically based naturalistic worldview.[19] Such a worldview takes current natural science to provide the most accurate guide to what there is in the world. In being ontologically fundamental additions to such a worldview, moral properties and facts appear queer.

[18] Mackie 1946: 80.

[19] I disagree with Shepski's interpretation that Mackie objects to the 'degree of differentness' of moral and normative facts and properties. I suspect that, in many cases, comparing degrees of differentness makes little sense. Richard Garner's point that '[m]oral facts are unusual in an unusual way—they demand' (Garner 1990: 143) is a better interpretation of Mackie. We will say more about this particular unusualness in Chapter 6.

This suggests that the argument from queerness presupposes a naturalistic ontology. There is no doubt that Mackie and many other error theorists, not only moral error theorists, have been attracted to a naturalistic ontology.[20] But there is no necessary connection between the argument from queerness and naturalistic ontologies. Even philosophers who are not naturalistically inclined and endorse ontologies inclusive of things like Cartesian souls, Leibnizian monads, irreducible qualia, or abstract entities existing outside the spatiotemporal realm may agree that moral properties and facts are queer because of the way in which they supervene on other properties and facts, or because of our peculiar way of knowing about them, or because of their motivating power, or because of their irreducible normativity.[21] In short, one need not endorse ontological naturalism in order to find Mackie's argument from queerness compelling or attractive.[22]

Sometimes when philosophers judge something to be queer or mysterious, they mean to say, among other things, that it is inexplicable. But not everything that is inexplicable is queer in the sense of giving rise to puzzlement. At a basic level, some entities, relations, laws, etc., may be inexplicable, and depending on the relevant theoretical framework, this need not give rise to puzzlement. It is difficult to define queerness or say what queerness is in general. What we need to do is consider specific examples of allegedly queer features and assess whether they are queer enough to

[20] Two cases in point are Paul Boghossian and David Velleman's error theory about colours and Hartry Field's error theory about numbers. Boghossian and Velleman defend the Galilean view that 'the property an object appears to have, when it appears to have a certain colour, is an intrinsic qualitative property which, as science teaches us, it does not in fact possess. [...] The best interpretation of colour experience [therefore] ends up convicting it of widespread and systematic error' (1989: 81–2). Field defends a theory on which there are no mathematical entities (1989: 228). One of his main arguments is that 'a realist view of mathematics involves the postulation of a large variety of aphysical entities—entities that exist outside of space-time and bear no causal relations to us or anything we can observe—and there just doesn't seem to be any mechanism that could explain how the existence and properties of such entities could be known' (1989: 230). He also appeals to a methodological principle that recommends that we 'view with suspicion any claim to know facts about a certain domain if we believe it impossible in principle to explain the reliability of our beliefs about that domain [e.g., if we believe that the reliability of our beliefs about that domain is simply a brute fact]' (1989: 233).

[21] Mackie suggested at one point that if God exists, objective prescriptivity could be accounted for in a 'non-mysterious way' (1977: 231, see also 1982: 118). However, as we saw above, reducing moral facts to God's will fails to account for the normativity of moral facts.

[22] I am much indebted to Ruth Chang, Jens Johansson, and Henrik Rydéhn for helpful comments and discussions here.

motivate rejection of the entities that possess them. The queerness arguments discussed in Chapters 5 and 6 are attempts at identifying what is specifically queer about moral properties and facts.

Some philosophers have wondered why anyone should worry about moral facts and properties being queer. After all, there are many things that many of us find queer in one way or other. Mark Platts mentions, among other things, neutrinos, aardvarks, and impressionist paintings.[23] But no one would suggest that since these things are so queer, they are ontologically suspicious, or that there are no such things. On this basis, Platts offers a quick dismissal of what has been called the 'sheer queerness' objection.[24]

The point that the argument from queerness has a bipartite structure, comprising at least one queerness argument and debunking explanations of moral beliefs, serves to illustrate why Platts's quick dismissal is too quick. Neutrinos, aardvarks, and impressionist paintings may strike us as *prima facie* queer, but when we reflect on how they fit into the natural order of things it is unlikely that we will continue to view them as queer. On reflection, we realize that they are actually parts of the best explanations of some of our observations and beliefs. At this point they no longer seem *ontologically* suspicious, although we may find them queer in other ways. They may, for example, appear utterly different from most other things we encounter. Error theorists are unlikely to maintain that debunking explanations of our beliefs about neutrinos, aardvarks, and impressionist paintings are more plausible than explanations that imply or presuppose the existence of such entities. By contrast, moral properties and facts do not in this way fit into the natural order of things, and they are not parts of the best explanations of our observations and beliefs. Moral properties and facts are both metaphysically queer and explanatorily redundant.

Moral non-naturalists typically agree that moral properties and facts are not parts of the causal order, in particular moral properties and facts do not appear in the best explanations of our moral beliefs.[25] But moral non-naturalists may of course refuse to recognize anything queer about moral properties and facts. They might argue on Moorean grounds that there are moral properties and facts, or at least that the opposite view is

[23] Platts 1980: 72. [24] Enoch 2011: 134–6.

[25] See, e.g., Ewing 1959: 55; Enoch 2011: 7, 159–60, 177, 219.

a lot less credible. At this point in the dialectic, error theorists can invoke Occam's razor and appeal to considerations of parsimony. We shall return to these matters in Chapter 7. Let us now proceed to consider the first queerness argument.

5.1. The First Queerness Argument: Supervenience

Most metaethicists accept that the moral supervenes on the natural. Unfortunately, however, there is no uncontentious definition of what it is for a property to be natural. As indicated in the previous section, we can say that broadly speaking a philosophical naturalist is someone who takes current natural science to provide the best picture of what there is in the world and who does not add anything ontologically fundamental to that picture. Naturalists who want to accommodate moral facts and properties, then, must claim that moral facts and properties are no ontologically fundamental additions to such a worldview. To allow supernatural or non-natural properties and facts would be to make such additions and allowing them is therefore intolerable to naturalists. Let us say, then, that for a property to be natural is for it to be of a kind that 'fit[s] into a scientifically based, naturalistic view of the world'[26], i.e., one that is not an ontologically fundamental addition to that view of the world.[27] This characterization is admittedly vague but still useful in that it gives some grasp of what we are after, and as it is commonly accepted as a starting point of metaethical debate it does not beg the question against non-naturalism or indeed other forms of realism.

[26] Sturgeon 2006a: 92. See also Kitcher 2011: 3–4.

[27] See Darwall, Gibbard, and Railton (1992) for a discussion of the contrast between 'continuity' and 'discontinuity' views concerning the relation between moral properties and scientifically based naturalistic worldviews. Proponents of the former maintain that moral properties and facts are no ontologically fundamental additions to scientifically based naturalistic worldviews, whereas proponents of the latter maintain that they are. See also David Enoch's recent discussion of naturalism. Enoch takes facts and properties to be natural 'if and only if they are of the kind the usual sciences invoke' (2011: 103). He takes naturalism about *Fs* (for example, normative or mental properties and facts) to be the view that *Fs* are 'nothing over and above' natural properties and facts (101–2). I have nothing to object to this, but notice that one can deny that normative properties and facts are nothing over and above the natural without being a non-naturalist, for one might hold with some theists that the normative is reducible to the supernatural.

It is also important not to beg the question against supernaturalist views, according to which moral properties supervene on supernatural properties like being commanded by an omnipotent and omnibenevolent creator. For brevity, let us say that a natural* property is one that is either natural or supernatural. We can then say, without begging important questions, that virtually all metaethicists in all camps accept that the moral supervenes on the natural*.[28] But how to account for the supervenience relation remains controversial. Mackie famously argued that non-naturalists have trouble explaining supervenience and that in order to do so they must postulate a metaphysically queer relation. In order to assess these claims, let us look at a non-naturalist account of moral supervenience.

First, it is plausibly a necessary truth that whatever has a moral property, e.g., wrongness, ultimately has this property *in virtue of* or *because of* some natural* property, e.g., the property of being a lie or the property of being an infliction of pain. Second, it is plausibly a necessary truth that any two items that are exactly alike in natural* respects are exactly alike in moral respects. Note that in order not to trivialize this latter claim we need to exclude purely numerical properties from the set of relevant natural* properties.[29] Note also that the natural* properties of an item include both the intrinsic and relational properties of that item. This gives us the following two supervenience theses:

(S_1) Necessarily, for any item, *x*, that has a moral property, M, *x* ultimately has M in virtue of some natural* property.

(S_2) Necessarily, for any two distinct items, *x* and *y*, if *x* and *y* are exactly alike in natural* respects, *x* and *y* are exactly alike in moral respects.

It is plausible to take the necessities in S_1 and S_2 to be *conceptual*. We can imagine a speaker violating one or both of S_1 and S_2, claiming for example that some action is wrong but not in virtue of or because of some natural* property it has, but simply plain wrong. We can also imagine a speaker claiming about two actions that they are exactly alike in all natural* respects but the one nevertheless wrong and the second not wrong. I submit that hearers would be deeply puzzled by such claims and would judge that the speaker misuses moral terms. This is evidence that such claims

[28] For recent discussions of this topic, see Smith (2000) and Sturgeon (2009).

[29] Cf. Mackie 1977: 83–90.

manifest failure to grasp the meaning of moral concepts, such as wrongness, and that S_1 and S_2 are conceptual truths.[30]

However, our main aim here is not to defend S_1 and S_2 or their status as conceptual necessities. The thing to note here is that insofar as S_1 and S_2 are conceptually necessary, non-naturalists have no trouble *explaining* this.[31] Like with any conceptual necessities, it is the meaning of our terms, in this case our moral terms, that commits us to S_1 and S_2. And in order to support the conceptual status of S_1 and S_2 non-naturalists can appeal to what I claim would be a natural reaction to a speaker who flouts one or both of the theses, namely that such a person has failed to grasp our moral concepts adequately. This is because for some course of behaviour to have a moral property is for it to be, e.g., morally required, forbidden, or permitted, and courses of behaviour can be morally required, permitted, or forbidden only on the basis of natural* properties.[32] We realize this when we reflect on the nature of moral properties, just as when we reflect on the property of being a rectangle we realize that rectangles can have no more and no less than four corners.

Perhaps the trouble for non-naturalists gets more serious when we shift focus from concepts to properties and look at the ontological implications of S_1 and S_2. Imagine a non-naturalist realist who is also a hedonistic utilitarian, i.e., someone who thinks that actions are right if and only if they maximize happiness. Critics like Mackie demand an *explanation* of

[30] Smith (2000: 91); Dreier (1992); Zangwill (1995). The intuitive insights behind S_1 and S_2 can be traced back to Sidgwick (1981 [1907]: 208–9, 379); Moore 1993 [1922]); and Hare (1952: 80–1, 131, 145). Unlike Hare, however, Sidgwick and Moore did not use the term 'supervenience' in this context.

[31] For a much discussed argument that non-naturalists have trouble explaining supervenience, see Blackburn 1984: 181–7, and 1993b.

[32] Notice how similar this is to Blackburn's quasi-realist explanation of moral supervenience: '[Moral] supervenience can be explained in terms of the constraints upon proper projection. Or purpose in projecting value predicates may demand that we respect supervenience. If we allowed ourselves a system (schmoralizing) which was like ordinary evaluative practice, but subject to no such constraint, then it would allow us to treat naturally identical cases in morally different ways. This could be good schmoralizing. But that would unfit schmoralizing from being any kind of guide to practical decision-making (a thing could be properly deemed schbetter than another although it shared with it all the features relevant to choice or desirability)' (Blackburn 1984: 186). Similarly, the non-naturalist could say, reflecting on schmoral properties we recognize that they do not supervene on natural* properties, whereas when we reflect on moral properties, we realize that they supervene necessarily on natural* properties. Matthew Kramer responds to Blackburn's supervenience worry along somewhat similar lines.(Kramer, 2009: 352–3). I do not share Kramer's view that the supervenience relation is ontologically uncostly for non-naturalism. However, as we shall see below, it is not dialectically forceful to press this point against non-naturalism.

the necessary covariance between the property of maximizing happiness and the property of rightness. In response, the non-naturalist hedonistic utilitarian can appeal to her fundamental moral principle, which says that there is an asymmetric dependence relation between rightness and maximizing happiness and also that it is in some sense necessary that rightness depends on happiness-maximization: necessarily, the property of maximizing happiness has the further property of *making* actions morally right.[33] Importantly, however, the necessity in question is not conceptual, since that would amount to a version of moral naturalism. The necessity is of some other, non-conceptual, kind. Let us call it *normative necessity*.[34] Beyond this, our non-naturalist hedonistic utilitarian will say, it is not possible to give further explanations.

Now, in response to our non-naturalist hedonistic utilitarian's claim that an action is right in virtue of or because of its being happiness-maximizing, Mackie famously asks 'just what *in the world* is signified by this "because"?'[35] The answer is, as we have seen, the asymmetric dependence relation of normative necessity that obtains between the action's rightness and its property of maximizing happiness; it is necessary that the latter property makes the action right. Mackie obviously finds such a relation metaphysically queer. But why? He doesn't elaborate in *Ethics: Inventing Right and Wrong* (1977). In *The Miracle of Theism* (1982), Mackie points out that non-naturalists are committed to what he calls 'necessary synthetic connections' (what we have called normative necessities) between distinct properties. He concludes that 'there would be something here in need of explanation'[36] and he considers whether theistic assumptions could provide such explanations.[37]

We shall come back presently to the urge for non-naturalists to explain the allegedly brute connection between natural* properties and moral properties, but let us first try to substantiate the worry that the relation of normative necessity is queer.

[33] Cf. Enoch 2011: 140–8; DePaul (1987); Suikkanen (2010).

[34] See, e.g., Moore (1993 [1922]); Fine (2005); Enoch (2011: 146). Fine argues that normative necessity is a *sui generis* modal relation distinct from metaphysical necessity. But we can remain neutral on whether this is so or whether normative necessity is a species of metaphysical necessity. What is important is that normative necessity, like metaphysical necessity but unlike, e.g., causal or physical necessity, holds across possible worlds. See n. 38.

[35] Mackie 1977: 41 (Mackie's emphasis).

[36] Mackie 1982: 118.

[37] Mackie 1982: 114–18.

Hume's Dictum

We have already seen that according to moral non-naturalists, normative necessities obtain between distinct properties. This means that according to hedonistic utilitarians, there is a relation of necessary coextension between the property of maximizing happiness and the property of being right. Non-naturalists who are pluralists about right-making properties are committed to the view that a, possibly highly complex, disjunctive natural* property is necessarily coextensive with the property of being right.

However, according to a common view of property identity—an instance of a thesis that has become known as *Hume's Dictum*—there can be no relations of necessary coextension between distinct properties; such relations are queer. Necessary coextension between properties across possible worlds implies property identity.[38] We can now formulate the first queerness argument as follows:

(P1) Moral properties and natural* properties are distinct properties.
(P2) Moral properties supervene necessarily on natural* properties.
(P3) Relations of necessary coextension between distinct properties are queer.
(C1) Hence, supervenience relations between moral and natural* properties are queer.
(P4) If supervenience relations between moral properties and natural* properties are queer, moral properties are queer.
(C2) Hence, moral properties are queer.

Let us now assess the argument. As we have seen, (P1) is endorsed by Mackie's targets and (P2) is widely endorsed. (P4) seems a reasonable premise, but it may be possible to reject it and thereby to block the conclusion (C2). But the intermediate conclusion (C1), which follows from (P1)–(P3) is troubling

[38] For a recent discussion of *Hume's Dictum* as a general thesis in metaphysics, see Wilson (2010). Wilson formulates *Hume's Dictum* in terms of metaphysically necessary connections between distinct entities. Note that it is no solution for non-naturalists simply to claim that normative necessity is distinct from metaphysical necessity. Normatively necessary connections too are supposed to hold across possible worlds, and that suffices to generate a challenge to non-naturalism based on *Hume's Dictum*. *Hume's Dictum* is the basis of Bart Streumer's case against irreducibly normative properties (Streumer 2008). Streumer claims that his case for moral error theory does not rely on a queerness argument but, as I argue in this section, appeals to *Hume's Dictum* in this context are plausibly seen as one way of explicating Mackie's queerness argument concerning supervenience.

enough for moral non-naturalists. The key premise is (P3). But note that this means that the argument generalizes beyond the moral and the normative. *Hume's Dictum* casts doubt on necessarily coextensive distinct properties quite generally and the argument therefore fails to demonstrate that there is something uniquely queer about moral properties. This is significant since *Hume's Dictum* is far from uncontroversial. It is not clear whether there is a compelling argument in its favour.[39] Some philosophers take *Hume's Dictum* to be intuitively plausible but not everyone shares this intuition. Let us consider some examples, some of which are sometimes offered as compelling counterexamples to *Hume's Dictum*.

It is an implication of *Hume's Dictum* that 'impossible properties', i.e., those that necessarily lack extension, turn out identical. For example, the property of being a round square and the property of being an even prime larger than 2 are one and the same property. This seems clearly counterintuitive.

A standard counterexample to *Hume's Dictum* is being an equiangular triangle and being an equilateral triangle. To support the intuition that these are distinct although necessarily coextensive properties, we can follow Elliot Sober and imagine a machine that is sensitive to equiangular triangles only; the machine is programmed to give a signal just in case it is exposed to such figures.[40] Such a machine also gives a signal each time it is exposed to an equilateral triangle, but since we imagine the machine to be constructed so as to respond only to equiangular triangles, it is intuitive that it is the property of being an equiangular triangle and not the property of being an equilateral triangle that is causally responsible for the machine giving its signal.[41] Whether such counterexamples work remains controversial, but if they do, the non-naturalists can employ a companions-in-guilt strategy to respond to Mackie's argument.[42]

There are many other suggested counterexamples to *Hume's Dictum*. Consider being the number 2 and being the positive square root of 4.[43] It might be argued that these are distinct properties, since the latter property

[39] See Wilson (2010) for an extensive critique of attempts to defend *Hume's Dictum* on analytic and on synthetic *a priori* grounds.

[40] Sober (1982).

[41] But see Jackson (1998: 125–7) for a response to Sober's argument.

[42] Shafer-Landau (2003: 91) and Majors (2005: 488) use this strategy and appeal to Sober's example to respond to Jackson (1998). See Streumer (2013a) for counter-responses and see Suikkanen (2010) for a nice overview of the debate.

[43] See Parfit (2011: 296–7) for a similar example.

is complex while the former is simple. But defenders of *Hume's Dictum* will respond that the complexity is in the predicate 'being the square root of 4' and that complexity in properties cannot be inferred from complexity in predicates.[44] However, there is an intuitive case to be made for the view that the property of being the number 2 and the property of being the positive square root of 4 are not identical. Being the positive square root of 4 is an *interesting* property of the number 2, whereas being the number 2 is not. Similarly, consider the property of being *Hume's Dictum* and the property of being the correct dictum about whether there are relations of necessary co-extension between distinct properties. If *Hume's Dictum* is correct, *Hume's Dictum* has both properties necessarily. But *Hume's Dictum* has the first property trivially, simply by virtue of being identical to itself. The second property, by contrast, is an interesting property that *Hume's Dictum* has non-trivially and, it seems, not simply by virtue of being identical to itself.[45] Hence, if *Hume's Dictum* is correct, this is intuitively a counterexample to the thesis, since it then follows, counterintuitively, that being *Hume's Dictum* and being the correct dictum about whether there are relations of necessary co-extension between distinct properties, are identical properties. This somewhat paradoxical result is likely to reduce the appeal of *Hume's Dictum*, although it is not likely to suffice to establish the falsity of *Hume's Dictum*. I doubt that there is an example that achieves this.

The more general, and for our purposes more important, lesson is that the force of the first queerness argument is held hostage to more general issues in metaphysics. In particular, its force depends on whether the suggested counterexamples to *Hume's Dictum* are valid. If they are, non-naturalists can straightforwardly reject (P3). If they are not, non-naturalists can point out more cautiously that *Hume's Dictum* strikes widely and that, consequently, it is not clear that no valid counterexample is forthcoming, or that *Hume's Dictum* does not overgeneralize. It would therefore be premature to accept (C1) and (C2) on the basis of (P3).[46]

[44] Streumer 2008.

[45] Thanks to Jens Johansson and Bart Streumer for discussions of examples of this kind.

[46] Campbell Brown (2011) has formulated what he claims to be a 'new and improved' supervenience argument against non-natural moral properties that builds on Jackson's original argument. The key premise in Brown's argument is that there are no *redundant* properties, where a property is redundant if and only if it is not needed to distinguish possibilities. The rationale for the ban on redundant properties is ontological parsimony (Brown, 2011: 212). However, as Erik J. Wielenberg (2011) has argued, this argument overgeneralizes implausibly since it rules out some theistic views and some views about qualia in the philosophy of

It is notable that Mackie made no explicit appeal to *Hume's Dictum* in arguing that non-naturalists are committed to a metaphysically queer supervenience relation. One can only speculate about why this is. Perhaps he wanted to point to something distinctively queer about this very relation, and not to something as general as *Hume's Dictum*. For all we have said here, *Hume's Dictum* may or may not be correct. But the point is that insofar as *Hume's Dictum* is a premise in the first queerness argument, this argument becomes less interesting as an argument against moral properties; *Hume's Dictum* strikes too widely.[47]

Brute Connections

However, Tristram McPherson has recently formulated a challenge to non-naturalism that does not rely on the controversial *Hume's Dictum*. Instead, his argument is based on a thesis he calls *Brute Connection*, i.e., that 'the non-naturalist must take the supervenience of the [moral] properties on the base properties to involve a brute necessary connection between [distinct] properties' and a thesis he calls *Modest Humean*, i.e., that 'commitment to brute necessary connections between [distinct] properties counts significantly against a view'.[48] *Modest Humean*, says

mind. Moreover, it is not clear that non-natural moral properties are in the end redundant in Brown's sense. For the non-naturalist can respond that non-natural moral properties are needed to distinguish moral possibilities from moral impossibilities.

[47] However, one might wonder whether Mackie would accept this verdict. After presenting the epistemological queerness argument he says that appeals to companions in guilt are an 'important counter' and that 'the only adequate reply [...] would be to show how, on empiricist foundations, we can construct an account of the ideas and beliefs and knowledge that we have of [the alleged companions in guilt]' (1977: 39). (Thanks to Ruth Chang for reminding me about this passage.) Would Mackie have given a similar response to purported counterexamples to *Hume's Dictum*? This is far from obvious. Mackie takes the epistemological queerness to rest on a kind of empiricist epistemology (but see the next subsection for a discussion of how Mackie came later to undermine the argument), but there is no obvious connection between empiricist metaphysics and *Hume's Dictum*. For example, empiricists could well accept Sober's argument that the property of being an equiangular triangle and the property of being an equilateral triangle are distinct but necessarily connected (see the main text above). Mackie did, however, endorse a methodological principle he called 'the elimination of unexplained coincidence' (1976: 66). He viewed this principle as an appeal to a 'sort of simplicity [that] is of the greatest importance as a guide to the choice between alternative [...] hypotheses' (1976: 66–7). But the elimination of unexplained coincidence principle is clearly different from *Hume's Dictum*. In fact, it is highly similar to a principle called *Modest Humean*, to which we turn next

[48] McPherson 2012: 217. McPherson sometimes speaks about 'discontinuous' rather than 'distinct' properties.

McPherson, is a 'methodological cousin' of *Hume's Dictum* and it is modest in that it rules out neither necessary connections between distinct properties nor brute necessary connections.[49] From *Brute Connection* and *Modest Humean* we can derive the conclusion that moral non-naturalism's commitment to brute necessary connections between moral and natural* properties counts significantly against the view. But *Brute Connection* can be questioned.

By 'brute' McPherson means 'inexplicable'.[50] But in the light of what we said above, is it really correct that non-naturalists are committed to the view that the connection between moral properties and natural* properties is inexplicable? This brings us back to the urge that non-naturalists explain supervenience. To recap, we need to be careful to distinguish two explanatory projects. The first is to explain why the moral supervenes on the natural*. As we saw, theses S_1 and S_2 are plausibly viewed as conceptual truths. It is often difficult to offer explanations of conceptual truths (for example, *why* is it conceptually true that a circle is a closed plane figure with all points equidistant from a fixed point? *why* is it conceptually true that *ought* implies *can*?) but as we also saw, we can come to realize that S_1 and S_2 are indeed conceptual truths by reflecting on our moral concepts and by imagining a speaker who flouts one or both of S_1 and S_2. Our claim was that such a speaker manifests failure to grasp our moral concepts. Again, the point is that since S_1 and S_2 are supposedly conceptual truths, the best we can do to explain them is to engage in this kind of conceptual reflection. Beyond that it is not clear that further explanations are available.

The second explanatory project is to explain why certain moral properties supervene on certain natural* properties, e.g., why rightness supervenes on maximizing happiness, as the hedonistic utilitarian thinks. It is presumably here that McPherson thinks the non-naturalist is committed to a brute, i.e., inexplicable, necessary connection between distinct properties. But the hedonistic utilitarian explains the necessary connection between rightness and the property of maximizing happiness by appeal to the fundamental moral principle that says that it is necessary that the property of maximizing happiness is the one and only property that makes actions right. To defend this principle, in turn, one has to engage in

[49] McPherson 2012: 217. Like *Hume's Dictum*, however, *Modest Humean* generalizes beyond the moral and the normative.

[50] McPherson 2012: 206.

argumentation in normative ethics. In what sense, then, is it inexplicable that rightness supervenes on certain natural* properties, such as the property of maximizing happiness? This reasoning generalizes, of course. The only possible kind of response to the second explanatory project, i.e., that of explaining why certain moral properties supervene on certain natural* properties, consists in appeals to substantive moral principles about which kinds of properties have the further property of making objects have certain moral properties.

McPherson considers a rejoinder like this one and finds it 'a puzzling suggestion [that] facts about the existence and distribution of [...] metaphysically robust [moral] properties [are] explained by appeal to ethical truths'.[51] I take it that what McPherson finds puzzling is the suggestion that there can be ethical explanations of metaphysical facts. But why is this so puzzling? Suppose again for the sake of illustration that first-order moral enquiry establishes that hedonistic utilitarianism is true, i.e., that an action is right if and only if it maximizes happiness. We can then go on to ask what the relation is between the property of being happiness-maximizing and the property of being right; in particular, is it one of identity or is it a necessary relation between distinct properties? Suppose first that the property of being right is identical to the property of being happiness-maximizing, i.e., that a version of moral naturalism is true. Establishing that moral properties are identical to natural properties requires metaphysical arguments.[52] But the metaphysical fact that a specific moral property, e.g., rightness, is identical to a specific natural property, e.g., the property of being happiness-maximizing and not to some other natural property, is explained by our findings in first-order moral theory. On this view, then, there can be ethical explanations of metaphysical facts. Note also that on this view the property of being right is metaphysically robust; it is a natural property, after all.

If we suppose instead that the properties of being right and being happiness-maximizing are distinct but necessarily connected, i.e., if we suppose that a version of moral non-naturalism is true, the case is parallel. Establishing that moral properties are not identical to natural properties requires metaphysical arguments.[53] But establishing which specific

[51] McPherson 2012: 220.

[52] See, e.g., Jackson (1998) and Sturgeon (2006b) for such arguments.

[53] See, e.g., Enoch (2011; 105–9); FitzPatrick (2008); Huemer (2005: 94f.); Parfit (2011: 324–36) for such arguments. See also the discussion in Sections 5.1 and 6.3.

moral properties supervene on which specific natural properties requires first-order ethical arguments. On this view too, there can be ethical explanations of metaphysical facts. Or suppose finally that rightness is realized by a variety of distinct natural properties, i.e., that a version of naturalistic moral pluralism is true. Establishing that moral properties are realized by natural properties requires metaphysical arguments.[54] But establishing which specific natural properties realize which specific moral properties requires first-order ethical arguments. On this view too, then, there can be ethical explanations of metaphysical facts. What this shows is that non-naturalists are not alone in being committed to ethical explanation of metaphysical facts, including facts about metaphysically robust properties. Naturalists may share the same commitment. Hence it does not seem especially problematic for non-naturalists to appeal to substantive moral principles in their explanations of why certain moral properties supervene on certain natural* properties.

Perhaps this does not get to the heart of the matter, however. McPherson and other critics of non-naturalism might object that fundamental moral principles simply *state* necessary connections between distinct properties; they do not *explain* them. Note, however, that the hedonistic utilitarian's fundamental principle that we have worked with says more than just that there is a necessary connection between rightness and maximization of happiness; it says that the property of maximizing happiness is the only property that *makes* actions right. It may now be objected that the account of supervenience I have offered on non-naturalism's behalf still involves a brute necessary connection between distinct properties, namely the making-relation between an action's having a certain base property, e.g., the property of maximizing happiness, and its having a certain moral property, e.g., the property of being right. According to *Modest Humean*, commitment to such a relation counts significantly against a view.

In response, non-naturalists can revert to the claim that some properties have the further *sui generis* and non-natural property of being right-making.[55] Indeed, non-naturalists are committed to this because

[54] See, e.g., Brink (1989) for such arguments.

[55] See one of Huemer's responses to Blackburn's superveniece challenge (Huemer, 2005: 207). For an early account of right- and wrong-making properties, see Broad 1946: 103–8. Since right- and wrong-making properties need not make actions all things considered right or wrong, Broad's terms 'right-tending' and 'wrong-tending' may be preferable.

of their commitment to some fundamental moral principle(s) like 'the property of maximizing happiness is the only property that makes actions right'. If this principle is true it is necessarily true, and hence it is necessarily true that the property of maximizing happiness has the further, relational, property of making actions right. McPherson and other critics of non-naturalism might object that a *sui generis* non-natural property of being a right-making property is mysterious. But this would deprive the supervenience argument of its dialectical force. For on this reading, the argument is just an instance of a highly general worry about *sui generis* non-natural properties, and facts. Such worries can be substantiated as worries about motivation or about irreducible normativity, or more particularly about irreducibly normative favouring relations. We will discuss these worries in Section 5.3 and Chapter 6. The point for now is that on the reading presently under consideration, the supervenience argument becomes dialectically otiose in that it does not add anything of interest to highly general worries about *sui generis* non-natural properties and facts.

The account of supervenience that we have offered on non-naturalism's behalf is not a quietist account, along the lines of, e.g., Kramer (2009). The account offered here is not ontologically uncostly, since it involves commitment to non-natural properties of being right-making, wrong-making, ought-making, etc. But that commitment is not an additional cost to what non-naturalists are committed to already. Non-naturalists can explain supervenience without incurring additional ontological costs.

Before closing the discussion of the first queerness argument, let us comment on another popular response, which also utilizes the companions-in-guilt strategy in that it parallels a popular view in philosophy of mind, according to which mental properties are functional properties realized by physical properties.[56] According to this response, moral properties are functional properties realized by natural properties. This view, which was briefly described above, takes every instance of a moral property to be an instance of a natural property. It is thus a version of moral naturalism. But as we now know, in arguing that supervenience is metaphysically queer, Mackie is not targeting naturalism. He is targeting the non-naturalist view that every instance of a moral property is an instance of a non-natural property that obtains in virtue of a distinct

[56] Brink 1984.

natural property. Moral naturalists are, according to Mackie, not committed to a metaphysically queer notion of supervenience. As we saw in the previous subsection and as we shall see again in Chapter 6, the fault with naturalism lies elsewhere, i.e., in its inadequate account of moral and normative discourse and difficulties in capturing the irreducible normativity of moral facts.

To sum up this section, our construal of the first queerness argument involved *Hume's Dictum* as a key premise. But *Hume's Dictum* is a controversial metaphysical principle that generalizes beyond the moral and the normative. The force of the first queerness argument is therefore held hostage to more general issues in metaphysics. We have also seen that the charge that moral non-naturalists must take supervenience relations between distinct properties to be brute relations reduces to a general worry about *sui generis* non-natural properties and facts. This worry will be substantiated and further examined in Section 5.3 and in Chapter 6.

5.2. The Second Queerness Argument: Knowledge

The second queerness argument has a different focus from the other three. The point of this argument is not to establish that there are no moral facts and properties, but that we do not (and perhaps cannot) gain knowledge about moral facts and properties. Hence the argument, if successful, does not establish error theory about moral judgement, but rather scepticism about moral knowledge.[57] We can therefore call it the epistemological queerness argument. As we shall see, however, the epistemological queerness argument rests ultimately on the claim that moral facts and properties are metaphysically queer.

Having asked what in the world is signified by the 'because' in statements like 'Eating meat is wrong because it promotes suffering', Mackie goes on to ask how we are supposed to know about the alleged non-natural relation between wrongness and promoting suffering.

> It is not even sufficient to postulate a faculty which 'sees' the wrongness: something must be postulated which can see at once the natural features [in virtue of which

[57] Mackie says that 'the argument from queerness [...] has two parts, one metaphysical, the other epistemological'(1977: 38).

eating meat is wrong], and the wrongness, and the mysterious consequential link between the two (1977: 41).

Here it sounds as if the mental faculty, or whatever we choose to call it, by which we come by knowledge of wrongness and other moral properties and the links to the natural properties on which they supervene, would have to be queer. But it is seldom noticed that Mackie himself implicitly retracts or undermines this argument in his later work. Here he says more modestly that intuitionist non-naturalism à la Price, Moore, and Ross requires 'some kind of intuition',[58] or 'a special faculty of moral intuition'.[59] In his attempt to construct a plausible version of intuitionist non-naturalism, he goes on to say that

> there is no need to think of this 'special faculty' as a separate organ of the mind. As Price says, all that is required is that the understanding, the aspect of our minds which can discover objective truths, *has the ability* to discover, among others, this particular sort of necessary truth of supervenience (1980: 147, Mackie's italics).

This sounds strikingly similar to what contemporary intuitionist non-naturalists say *in defence* of their position. Consider Philip Stratton-Lake:

> Mackie and others object to the intuitionists' epistemology on the ground that it assumes we have some strange faculty for perceiving moral properties But [...] no such faculty is assumed by intuitionists. They claim that certain moral propositions can be known by intuition, not because they think we have such a sixth sense, but because they think these propositions are self-evident. Intuition is [...] a way of grasping the truth of certain (*a priori*) propositions. [...] [There is] no reason why we should think that [synthetic] *a priori* knowledge requires such a mysterious faculty. All it requires is the ability to understand and think (Stratton-Lake 2002a: 22).[60]

It is tempting, then, to think that what Mackie finds queer about moral knowledge is not a supposed faculty of moral intuition but the very idea of synthetic *a priori* knowledge. Schematically, we can put the argument as follows:

(P5) Moral knowledge requires synthetic *a priori* knowledge.
(P6) Synthetic *a priori* knowledge is queer.

[58] Mackie 1982: 117.
[59] Mackie 1980: 147.
[60] Eighteenth-century moral rationalists often made similar points in response to their sentimentalist critics. For instance, in criticizing sentimentalist Francis Hutcheson's notion

(C3) Hence, moral knowledge requires knowledge that is queer.
(P7) If moral knowledge requires knowledge that is queer, moral knowledge is queer.
(C2') Hence, moral knowledge is queer.

Some naturalist moral realists will want to question (P5), but since we know that Mackie had already rejected naturalism by the time he presented his argument from queerness, I will set such objections aside. Most non-naturalist moral realists accept (P5). But even granted (P5), it is plain that the second queerness argument, like the first, generalizes beyond the moral and the normative. The reason is that (P6) applies not only to moral knowledge.

Much philosophical knowledge seems to be synthetic *a priori*. Consider, for example, the question of whether there are abstract entities or whether everything that exists is ontologically continuous with a naturalistic view of the world. Knowledge of such matters would seem to be synthetic and a *priori*.

Standard examples of synthetic truths thought to be knowable by *a priori* intuition include 'Nothing can be red and green all over at the same time' and the laws and inference rules of logic, such as the law of non-contradiction and *modus ponens*.[61] To apprehend the necessary truth of such propositions is, according to defenders of intuition as a way of knowing about the external world, to apprehend *a priori* ways reality *must* be.[62] Defenders of intuition as a way of acquiring moral knowledge say the same about apprehending the necessary truth of fundamental moral propositions. Hence it is far from clear that the way in which we come by moral knowledge would be 'utterly different from our ordinary ways of

of a special *moral sense* by which we perceive moral relations, rationalist John Balguy asked whether Hutcheson would say that we perceive arithmetical and geometrical relations by 'an *intellectual sense* superadded to our understanding' (Balguy 1991 [1734]: 399). Since Balguy believed that the answer is no, he went on to ask why Hutcheson 'ascribe[s] [moral] perceptions to a *moral* [sense]' (Balguy 1991 [1734]: 400, all italics Balguy's).

[61] Both examples appear in BonJour (1997) and Huemer (2005) and the latter in Ewing (1947). Ewing argued that the thesis that all *a priori* knowable propositions are analytic can be refuted by applying the thesis to itself. The thesis itself certainly seems *a priori* but it does not seem to be analytically true since its denial is not self-contradictory. If the analytic and the synthetic are mutually exclusive and exhaustive it follows that the thesis is synthetic *a priori*, in which case its truth, if knowable, implies its falsity (Ewing 1970: 86).

[62] BonJour 1997: 107.

knowing everything else'.[63] Once again the companions-in-guilt strategy proves useful to critics of the argument from queerness.

Mackie gives no clear support of (P6), that is, he is not specific about exactly how and why synthetic *a priori* knowledge would be queer. But his discussion of moral properties as non-natural properties that somehow depend on natural properties and that we perceive by intuition concludes with the following reflection:

> How much simpler and more comprehensible the situation would be if we could replace the moral quality with some sort of subjective response which could be causally related to the detection of the natural features on which the supposed quality is said to be consequential (1977: 41).

But if moral knowledge is or requires synthetic *a priori* knowledge and if there are other examples of synthetic *a priori* knowledge, it is not clear that the moral non-naturalists' account of moral epistemology is *epistemologically* less simple or less comprehensible than alternative accounts. Mackie is right that accounts, such as his own, that omit non-natural properties and facts are *metaphysically* simpler and perhaps more comprehensible metaphysically. But then the epistemological queerness argument boils down to a worry about the metaphysical queerness of moral properties and facts. To substantiate this worry, Mackie must rely on the other three queerness arguments that directly target metaphysical queerness. Hence the epistemological queerness argument does not stand on its own feet.

The first two queerness arguments thus generalize beyond the moral and the normative in problematic ways. They fail to isolate uniquely queer features of moral and normative properties and facts. Next we turn to an argument that is more successful in this particular respect, although unsuccessful all things considered.

5.3. The Third Queerness Argument: Motivation

Consider the following oft-cited passage from Mackie's 1977 book:

> Plato's Forms give a dramatic picture of what objective values would have to be. The Form of the Good is such that knowledge of it provides the knower with both

[63] Mackie 1977: 38.

a *direction and* an overriding *motive*; something's being good both *tells* the person who knows this to pursue it and *makes* him pursue it. An objective good *would be sought* by anyone who was acquainted with it, not because of any contingent fact that this person, or every person, is so constituted that he desires this end, but just because the end has *to-be-pursuedness* somehow built into it. Similarly, if there were objective principles of right and wrong, any wrong (possible) course of action would have not-to-be-doneness somehow built into it. Or we should have something like [Samuel] Clarke's necessary relations of fitness between situations and actions, so that a situation would have a *demand* for such-and-such an action somehow built into it (1977: 40, all emphases added).

This passage contains at least two possible grounds for the claim that moral facts (what Mackie in this passage calls 'objective values' and 'objective principles of right and wrong') are queer, which pave the way for two different queerness arguments. Unfortunately, Mackie does not clearly distinguish them. Let us try to do so.

Notice first that *telling* a person to perform some action, or *giving her a direction*, or *demanding* that she perform some action, is different from *motivating* her to do so or *making* her do so. One could do either of these things without doing the other. This, along with Mackie's formulation that moral facts would provide both direction *and* motive, indicate that Mackie means to capture two different relations in the quoted passage.[64] On the one hand, moral facts are or entail demands that agents act in certain ways. This is a *normative* relation. On the other hand, moral facts motivate anyone who knows about them, or is acquainted with them, to act in accordance with them. This is a *psychological* relation. It is notable that Mackie speaks both about *knowledge of* and *acquaintance with* moral facts. I shall take him to mean that it is necessary that anyone who has knowledge by acquaintance, i.e., first-hand knowledge, of some moral fact, is motivated to act in accordance with this fact. For example, it is necessary that anyone who has knowledge by acquaintance that torture is morally wrong is thereby motivated to refrain from torturing. This is in line with Mackie's formulations and, as we shall see presently, it fits well into the reconstruction of the motivational queerness argument to be offered below.

The normative and the psychological relations seem clearly distinct but Mackie claimed that objective moral facts have both features. Here he may once again have been influenced by the eighteenth-century moral

[64] On this point, see also Kirchin (2010).

rationalist Richard Price, whose work Mackie cites approvingly at various places and who maintained that '[t]o perceive or to be informed how it is *right* to act, is the very notion of a *direction* to act. And it must be added that it is such a direction as implies *authority*, and which we cannot disregard without remorse and pain.'[65] To perceive an objective moral fact is thus to perceive an authoritative demand for action and insofar as one realizes that one cannot disregard such a demand without remorse and pain, perception of such a demand entails motivation to act in accordance with it.

Talk of objective facts *telling* people to act so and so, and of facts *demanding* certain courses of action, is obviously metaphorical. But such talk is akin to what is nowadays a widely accepted explication of the notion of a normative reason. According to this explication, a normative reason for an action is a fact that *counts in favour of* that action.[66] The *favouring relation* is normative, as are the *telling*-relation and the *demanding*-relation.[67] On most views, whether some fact counts in favour of some course of action is independent of whether agents are or would be motivated by these facts, or by their counting in favour of some course of action. In other words, most philosophers nowadays distinguish sharply between *normative reasons* and *motivating reasons* and take them to be logically independent.[68] But Mackie did not distinguish so sharply. This is unfortunate, since it conceals the fact that there are at least two queerness arguments to make here: one focusing on the normative force of moral facts—their being facts about what counts in favour of certain courses of action, or about what courses of action are demanded—and one focusing on the motivating force of moral facts—their being such as to motivate anyone acquainted with them to act in certain ways.[69] The latter is the topic of this section, while the former will be discussed in Chapter 6.

[65] Price 1991 [1787]: §713, Price's emphases.

[66] See, e.g., Scanlon (1998) and Parfit (2001, 2011) for influential discussions.

[67] Perhaps the telling and demanding relations differ merely in degree or strength and not in kind.

[68] Of course, some contemporary philosophers hold that normative reasons in some way or other reduce to motivating reasons, but that does not affect the point that there are two queerness arguments to be extracted from the passage from Mackie quoted above.

[69] On Parfit's interpretation, Mackie's argument is all about motivation (Parfit 2011: 448–52). While it is clear that Mackie sometimes conflates normativity and motivation, Parfit's interpretation is overly uncharitable.

Mackie's alleged mistake of mislocation and two interpretations

On a common interpretation, Mackie's claim that moral facts would make anyone acquainted with them motivated to act, indicates commitment to a version of *motivational internalism*, i.e., the thesis that there is a necessary connection between making a moral judgement and being to some extent motivated to act in accordance with it.[70] Jamie Dreier calls this thesis 'the practicality requirement' and attributes it to Mackie.[71] But we shall see that whether Mackie in fact accepted motivational internalism is highly questionable.

Remember that his claim is that anyone who knows or is acquainted with a moral fact is motivated to act in accordance with this fact and that this would be queer. Mackie did not spell out clearly *why* this would be queer. One possible interpretation is that he presupposed a version of the Humean theory of motivation, according to which desires are motivationally efficacious and beliefs are motivationally inert mental states: no belief can motivate without the aid of an independent desire or produce desire without the aid of a more fundamental desire, and being motivated to act requires a desire and a means-end belief, where any desire and belief can be modally pulled apart.[72] Someone who was acquainted with a moral fact, i.e., someone who knew first-hand that, say, some course of action is right, would simply in virtue of this fact, i.e., irrespectively of his or her desires, be motivated to take this course of action. This would *not* be queer, it seems, if belief on its own could motivate or produce desire, without the aid of an independent desire. In other words, this would not

[70] See, e.g., Brink 1989, chap. 3; Sinnott-Armstrong 2010: 57, 59; West 2010: 183–4; cf. Shepski 2008: 372–3.Two clarifications: First, Mackie says that 'the Form of the Good is such that knowledge of it provides the knower with [...] an *overriding* motive' (1977: 40, emphasis added), but motivational internalism need not be formulated in such a strong manner. According to a weaker and less implausible formulation, it is necessarily the case that anyone who makes a moral judgement is *to some extent* motivated to act in accordance with it. Second, by 'making a moral judgement' I mean the mental act of accepting a moral judgement and not the linguistic act of uttering a moral sentence.

[71] Dreier 2010: 74, 76, cf. 81–2. 'The practicality requirement' is Michael Smith's term, see Smith 1994, esp. chapters 1 and 3.

[72] For a statement and defence of the Humean theory of motivation, see, e.g., Smith 1994: Ch. 4. As we saw in Chapter 2, there is rather strong textual evidence that Hume himself did not endorse the Humean theory of motivation.

be queer unless some version of the Humean theory of motivation was true.[73]

In support of this reading it is worth noting what Mackie goes on to say right after the famous passage, quoted in the opening of this section. Mackie considers Hume's claim that 'reason alone can never be a motive to any action of the will'[74] and suggests that

> [s]omeone might object that Hume has argued unfairly from the lack of influencing power (*not contingent upon desires*) in ordinary objects of knowledge and ordinary reasoning, and might maintain that values differ from natural objects precisely in their power, *when known*, automatically to influence the will. To this Hume could, and would need to, reply that this objection involves the postulating of value-entities or value-features of quite a different order from anything else with which we are acquainted [. . .] (1977: 40, emphases added).

Note that for value-entities or moral facts automatically to influence the will would be for them to be such that when they are known they influence the will without the aid of independent desires, that is, their influencing power is not contingent upon desires. But if belief, and hence knowledge, could motivate action or produce desires in ways that are not contingent upon independent desires, why would the objection to Hume involve postulating entities 'of quite a different order from anything else with which we are acquainted'? Indeed, if belief could motivate action or produce desires in ways that are not contingent upon other desires, it would seem that any (supposed) fact that is the object of such belief would have the power to influence the will and this would be *explained by* the fact that belief can motivate action or produce desires, without the aid of independent desires. But if no belief on its own has this power, just as the Humean theory of motivation says, the power to influence the will must be located in the value-entities or moral facts, just as Mackie says.

Given this interpretation of the argument, it seems fair to ask whether the proper *locus* of the queer motivational force is not the moral *belief* or *judgement* rather than the moral *fact*. In a recent article, Jamie Dreier claims that Mackie 'mislocated the queerness' in that he located it in the subject matter of moral beliefs, i.e., moral facts, rather than in moral beliefs themselves, i.e., in the mental states.[75] Mackie's argument points to a

[73] This seems to be Brink's interpretation of Mackie (Brink 1989: 43).
[74] T 2.3.3.1; SBN 413.
[75] Dreier 2010: 82.

queer feature of moral belief, the natural conclusion of which is that moral judgements are motivationally efficacious desire-like attitudes rather than motivationally inert beliefs. To Dreier, Mackie's mistake 'seems very strange'.[76] But the conclusion that moral judgements are desire-like attitudes rather than beliefs is so obviously in tension with Mackie's other views that we should hesitate strongly to attribute to him an argument premised on a standard version of motivational internalism. But then how is the argument to be understood?

Before answering that question we should take notice of a problem with the interpretation that the argument in *Ethics: Inventing Right and Wrong* (1977) involves as a premise the Humean theory of motivation. The problem is that in *Hume's Moral Theory* (1980), Mackie rejected the Humean theory of motivation. Here is what he said, in criticizing Hume's arguments against moral rationalism:

> There might be some non-ordinary sort of what was still factual information, some special sort of belief or even knowledge supplied by a moral sense as the objectivist interpretation understands it, which does make moral distinctions that can in and of themselves influence action (1980: 54).
>
> [The] psychological thesis [that] motivation always involves a desire as well as belief [is overstated]. The belief in objective moral requirements, made explicit by such writers as Clarke and Price and Reid, but implicit in much ordinary thinking, can in this curious way act as a motive on its own, even if [...] that belief is false (1980: 141f.).

And perhaps most unequivocally, '[i]t is evident that there can be sets of moral and factual beliefs which are, by themselves, motives to action'.[77]

One interpretive possibility is that Mackie in 1980 abandoned the Humean theory of motivation and along with it the motivational queerness argument. In support of the interpretation that Mackie changed his mind in this way, it is notable that in the later book he emphasizes the queerness worries concerning supervenience and knowledge and—as we shall see below—that he conflates motivation and normativity.[78]

However, another interpretive possibility is that what Mackie finds queer all along is not that moral belief *can* give rise to motivation, either directly or indirectly. Perhaps what he finds queer is rather that moral

[76] Dreier 2010: 82; cf. Copp 2010: 146; Sinnott-Armstrong 2010: 60–1.

[77] Mackie 1980: 53.

[78] Mackie 1980: 54–5, 150.

facts would be such as to *guarantee* motivation in anyone acquainted with them.[79] In support of this interpretation it is worth repeating Mackie's claim that '[a]n objective good would be sought by *anyone* who was acquainted with it [. . .] just because the end has to-be-pursuedness somehow built into it'[80] and that 'values [have a] power, when known, *automatically* to influence the will'.[81] This would be queer, given that no belief is such as to *guarantee* motivation, although some beliefs *can* give rise to motivation.

A considerable merit of this interpretation is that it avoids attributing to Mackie a change of heart about the Humean theory of motivation. It should be acknowledged, however, that a demerit of this interpretation is that it may leave the motivational queerness argument without a clear target. As we shall see in the next section, however, Richard Price may have endorsed the view that acquaintance with moral facts guarantees motivation.[82] But as we shall also see, it is clear that moral realists are not committed to this view.

The motivational queerness argument reconstructed and rejected

Here then is a suggestion of how to understand the argument: Mackie thought that according to the ordinary concept of moral facts, such facts exert motivational pull on anyone acquainted with them. Admittedly, it is not obvious what is meant by 'motivational pull' and the phrase is not Mackie's, but I use it in an attempt to provide a plausible reconstruction of the argument. Perhaps motivational pull can be likened to a kind of *magnetic* force of attraction and repellingness exerted on the human psyche. In one of his arguments for emotivism, C. L. Stevenson appealed to what he called 'the magnetism of the good'. This is the alleged phenomenon that '[a] person who recognizes X to be "good" must *ipso facto* acquire a stronger tendency to act in its favour than he otherwise would have had'.[83] Stevenson of course took this to support an account according to which moral judgements are (primarily)

[79] A conversation with Uri Leibowitz helped me realize this second interpretive possibility.

[80] Mackie 1977: 40, emphasis added.

[81] Mackie 1977: 40, emphasis added.

[82] As we saw in the previous chapter, Wittgenstein seems to have shared Mackie's conception of moral facts, at least in this particular respect. Mackie may also have been right that Plato adhered to this view, see, e.g., *Protagoras* 358c-d.

[83] Stevenson 1937: 16.

non-cognitive attitudes rather than beliefs. Hence, Stevenson drew roughly the conclusion Dreier thinks should also have been Mackie's.

But we know that by the time Mackie presented his argument from queerness he had already rejected non-cognitivist accounts. As we have seen, he thought that first-hand knowledge of moral facts entails that the knower is motivated to act and he seems to have held that no belief can in this way guarantee motivation. So he needed to hold on to the thesis that moral facts would exert a motivational pull, perhaps comparable to magnetic force, on the human psyche. Perhaps this motivational pull would work by way of generating desires in whoever is acquainted with moral facts. The sketchiness of the details here is of course a weakness in the argument. We will get back to this presently. Note in the meantime that what supposedly guarantees that anyone acquainted with a moral fact is motivated to act is the motivational pull of such facts, so the proper locus of the queer motivational force is moral facts rather than moral belief. No mistake of mislocation is committed.

We can now begin to see why it makes sense to interpret Mackie as claiming that it is knowledge by acquaintance of moral facts that entail motivation. The reason is that in order to be affected by the motivational pull of a moral fact one has to be in some sort of direct causal contact with this fact.[84] It is not enough to have mere second-hand knowledge about it, such as knowledge by testimony. Moreover, we can now see why it is highly doubtful that Mackie accepted standard motivational internalism, according to which there is a necessary connection between making a moral judgement and being motivated to act accordingly. Mackie endorsed the cognitivist view that moral judgements are beliefs and in order for the motivational queerness argument to get off the ground he must have held that no belief guarantees motivation, and in particular that moral belief is not necessarily linked to motivation. Had he also endorsed a standard version of motivational internalism, he would have been forced

[84] One might wonder whether one can be in any sort of causal contact with facts about mere possibilities, or facts about the future, e.g., the fact that telling a lie would be wrong or that telling a lie tomorrow will be wrong. But such facts can be inferred from more fundamental moral facts, for example, that lying is (*pro tanto*) wrong. As we saw in Chapter 1, on many versions of moral realism, fundamental moral facts are necessary facts. According to Price, for example, fundamental moral truths are 'immutable' and 'necessary' (1991 [1787]: §684). On my interpretation, Mackie thought that moral realists must hold that one can be in causal contact with fundamental moral facts from which one can infer moral facts about mere possibilities and moral facts about the future.

to the view that moral judgements are queer and consequently that there are no moral judgements, since no belief is necessarily linked to motivation.[85] But this most certainly was not Mackie's view; he thought that there are moral judgements and that they are uniformly and necessarily false. Alternatively, he would have been forced to the non-cognitivist view that moral judgements are not beliefs, as Dreier suggests. But we have already seen that Mackie rejected non-cognitivism on independent grounds.

It is notable that in *Ethics: Inventing Right and Wrong*, Mackie does not say that there is a necessary connection between moral judgements or moral beliefs and being motivated to act. The necessary connection is claimed to hold between *knowledge by acquaintance* with moral facts and being motivated to act. *Knowing*—and *a fortiori knowing by acquaintance*—are factive relations, so this view allows that there is no necessary connection between making false moral judgements or having false moral beliefs and being motivated to act. What Mackie appeals to, then, is not motivational internalism in its standard version, but a version of the Socratic doctrine that knowing the good entails motivation to do the good.[86] According to Mackie's version of this doctrine, when one judges first-hand that an action has a moral property one judges or presupposes that it has a property that exerts motivational pull on anyone acquainted with it. This allows for the possibility of judging that an action has a moral property without being motivated to act (since the judgement might be mistaken, as indeed it necessarily is, according to moral error theory), though it would be incoherent to judge first-hand that an action has a moral property and to judge simultaneously that one is not motivated to act.

Thus Mackie's motivational queerness argument presupposes neither the Humean theory of motivation, nor a standard version of motivational internalism, according to which there is a necessary connection between making a moral judgement and being motivated to act accordingly. Rather, the argument presupposes a necessary connection between first-hand

[85] Had Mackie endorsed a non-standard version of motivational internalism, such as *de dicto* internalism, he need not have been forced to this view. On *de dicto* internalism, see Tresan (2006).

[86] Richard Price also endorsed a version of the Socratic doctrine. According to Price, 'I cannot *perceive* an action to be right without *approving* it' (1991 [1787]: §687, first emphasis added). Price thinks everyone will agree that 'the perception of right and wrong does *excite* to action and is alone a sufficient *principle* of action' (§757, Price's emphases). Note that Price too seems to have in mind first-hand knowledge, as he talks about *perceiving* an action to be right.

knowledge of moral facts and motivation to act accordingly. Mackie held that moral facts would be such as to attract or repel the human psyche, to the effect that when we come to know first-hand of a moral fact we are moved to act, not because of antecedent desires but because we are under the influence of these forces. But such motivational forces of attraction and repellingness are queer and since these forces are essential features of moral facts, moral facts are queer. Schematically, we can present the argument like this:

(P8) First-hand knowledge of moral facts guarantees moral motivation (i.e., motivation to act in accordance with the moral facts).
(P9) False moral belief does not guarantee motivation to act in accordance with the believed moral facts.
(P10) If first-hand knowledge of moral facts guarantees moral motivation and false moral belief does not, then moral motivation stems from the motivational pull of moral facts exerted on the human psyche.
(C4) Hence, moral motivation stems from the motivational pull of moral facts exerted on the human psyche.
(P11) Any fact that exerts motivational pull on the human psyche (i.e., any fact such that knowledge by acquaintance of that fact guarantees that the knower is motivated) is queer.
(C2") Hence, moral facts are queer.

Note two things about this argument. First, in contrast to the first two queerness arguments, this third one promises not to overgeneralize since it explicitly mentions moral facts and moral belief in (P8)–(P10). Second, this reconstruction attributes to Mackie a coherent argument and avoids attributing to him a mistake of mislocation. But whether this queerness argument is also *plausible* is another matter. In fact, each premise of the argument looks shaky. In order to support (P9) and to enable us to assess (P11), proponents of the argument must give a more detailed description of what the motivational pull of moral facts is supposed to be and how it is supposed to work. Proponents must also establish that it is a feature of the commonsense moral concepts that moral facts do exert the alleged queer motivational forces on the human psyche. And this will not be an easy task. Some philosophers claim that some version of the internalist view that there is a necessary link between moral judgement and motivation to act, is rooted in our commonsense moral concepts. Michael Smith, for example, claims that his version of motivational internalism is a platitude.[87] While I find this highly doubtful, it is arguably even more doubtful that Mackie's version of the Socratic doctrine—viz. that there is a necessary connection between knowing first-hand that some action is, e.g., wrong, and motivation to act—is platitudinous.

In any case, both standard versions of motivational internalism and Mackie's version of the Socratic doctrine face the challenge that our commonsense concept of, e.g., wrongness, seems to allow for the possibility that people sometimes judge, and even know, first-hand that some action is wrong without being at all motivated not to do it, either because they are on the particular occasion too weak-willed to muster any motivation to act on their judgement or knowledge, or because they do not care about morality quite generally. People of the latter sort are known as *amoralists* and are familiar from fiction and, some would say, from real life. Weakness of will is a phenomenon that most people are all too familiar with. Both amoralism and weakness of will are phenomena that moral realists have appealed to in their responses to Mackie.[88]

Non-naturalists and other moral realists can thus concede that the kind of motivational pull Mackie has in mind would be a queer feature of moral facts. But they can plausibly reject (P8) and maintain that moral beliefs and moral knowledge motivate only accompanied by some independent desire, e.g., a standing desire to act rightly. The latter is a version of *motivational externalism*, i.e., the view that there is no necessary connection between making a moral judgement and being motivated to act.[89] Mackie did not consider externalist views in *Ethics: Inventing Right and Wrong* but he did in his *Hume's Moral Theory*, in the context of discussing Jonathan Harrison's treatment of Hume's claim that 'morals [. . .] have an influence on the actions and affections'.[90] Harrison suggests that realists can accommodate this by holding that the influence of moral beliefs on actions and affections is contingent on an independent desire to do what is right.[91]

87 Smith, 1994: Ch. 3.

88 For example Brink (1989: 49–50, 59–62) and Shafer-Landau (2003: 145–7).

89 According to Graham Oddie's non-naturalistic theory of value, desires are 'value seemings' on the basis of which evaluative judgements are made (Oddie, 2005). If moral non-naturalists incorporate a version of this view they might be able to respond successfully to the motivational queerness argument without committing to motivational externalism.

90 T 3.1.1.6; SBN 457.

91 Harrison 1976: 13–14. As Harrison notes (1976: 14), Hume himself says at one point '[t]is one thing to know virtue and another to conform the will to it' (T 3.1.1.22; SBN 465).

Mackie responds that at least for non-naturalists this would be a 'big concession' they would be reluctant to make.[92] In Mackie's view, non-naturalists 'are concerned to defend the metaphysical view which is represented by the way in which [...] moral terms [such as "right" and "wrong"] combine a descriptive logic with a prescriptive force, namely that there are objective requirements or categorical imperatives in the nature of things'.[93] But, Mackie goes on to claim, 'Harrison's suggestion would abandon this claim; it would save the objectivity of moral distinctions from Hume's attack only by giving up their prescriptivity'.[94]

It is obvious that Mackie conflates normativity and motivation here. That there are objective requirements or categorical imperatives in the nature of things is plausibly taken to mean that there are moral facts that obtain independently of such things as people's desires and human conventions—i.e., that there are mind-independent moral facts—and these facts are normative in the sense that they entail that there are facts that favour certain courses of behaviour, where the favouring relation is irreducibly normative. So for instance, the fact that murder is wrong entails that there is irreducibly normative reason not to murder, or a (*pro tanto*) requirement not to murder. But non-naturalists who are also externalists about moral motivation maintain that just as we can fail to be motivated by true or false judgements about subjective and conventional reasons and requirements, we can fail to be motivated by true or false judgements about objective and non-conventional, or irreducibly normative, reasons and requirements. Hence Harrison's suggestion, commonly endorsed by moral realists, does not at all have the implications Mackie claims it has.[95]

To sum up this section: The motivational queerness argument looks initially to be better suited for its purpose than the first two since it does not generalize beyond the moral and the normative. But secondly, in order to

However, Hume's claim is not inconsistent with the view that there is a necessary connection between accepting a moral judgement and being *to some extent* motivated to act in accordance with it. One can fail to conform one's will to one's moral judgement if moral motivation is not overriding. Hence Hume's claim is not inconsistent with motivational internalism.

[92] Mackie 1980: 54.

[93] Mackie 1980: 55.

[94] Mackie 1980: 55.

[95] Harrison is understandably perplexed by Mackie's criticism in his review of *Hume's Moral Theory*, see Harrison (1982: 71–5). In fairness to Mackie, it should be noted that he is far from the only twentieth-century moral philosopher to conflate normativity and motivation; see Parfit (2006) for discussions of a number of examples.

avoid attributing to Mackie a mistake of mislocation and to avoid forcing on him a conclusion he rejects, we had to impute to ordinary speakers a concept of moral facts that is unlikely to square with their actual moral concepts. Thirdly, there is a promising externalist response to the argument and Mackie's critique of the externalist response misses its mark completely. I conclude that when reconstructed and deconstructed, the motivational queerness argument is not compelling.

6

How to Understand Mackie's Argument from Queerness (II)

We saw in the preceding chapter that the first three queerness arguments are unsuccessful. The argument concerning supervenience overgeneralizes or reduces to an instance of a general worry about *sui generis* non-natural properties and relations. The argument concerning knowledge is really an argument for moral scepticism rather than moral error theory. This argument too overgeneralizes and in the end it does not stand on its own feet. The third argument, concerning motivation, rests on the premise that it is a feature of the ordinary conception of moral facts that first-hand knowledge of moral facts guarantees motivation to act. Not only is this view highly problematic in itself, it is also implausible to claim that it is a feature of the ordinary conception of moral facts. The fourth queerness argument remains to be examined. This is the topic of this chapter.

Although poorly presented by Mackie, this argument has considerable force. As we shall see, it generalizes beyond the moral to the normative, but unlike the first two queerness arguments, it does not generalize beyond the normative. It will be argued that the upshot of this is that error theory cannot plausibly be restricted to the moral domain. A plausible error theory must take the form of an error theory about irreducibly normative favouring relations, or more generally about irreducible normativity. What this amounts to will be explained and explored in the next section. Objections and further implications will be considered in Section 6.3 and in Part III.

6.1. The Fourth Queerness Argument: Irreducible Normativity

We have seen that Mackie failed to distinguish clearly between motivation and normativity and in particular between the claim that moral facts are *intrinsically motivating* and the claim that they are *objectively prescriptive*. The best understanding of the former claim, it was argued in Section 5.3, is that moral facts exert motivational pull on anyone who is acquainted with them; the best understanding of the latter claim, it will be argued here, is that they entail irreducibly normative reasons. We discarded the motivational queerness argument in Section 5.3. But several commentators have noted that the most acute of Mackie's queerness worries does not target the alleged motivating pull of moral facts, but the irreducible normativity of moral facts.[1] Error theorists have sought to articulate this kind of queerness, using a variety of phrases. Mackie thought that moral facts are queer in that they are objectively prescriptive, and we have seen that he also says that they are queer in that they *tell* agents to behave in certain ways[2] and in that they are *intrinsically action-guiding.*[3] According to Joyce, morality's queerness can be articulated in terms of *strong categorical imperatives*[4] that have *inescapable authority*;[5] or in terms of *non-institutional* oughts and reasons[6] that *really bind* agents;[7] or in terms of *practical clout*[8] or *practical oomph*[9].

These phrases may all be meant to capture the same kind of allegedly queer feature, but it is not evident what the phrases mean and it is consequently not clear what the alleged queerness consists in.[10] In previous work I maintained that moral facts are queer because they are or entail *categorical reasons.*[11] I now believe that the best articulation is that moral facts

[1] Garner (1990); Joyce (2001); Finlay (2008); Robertson (2008); Olson (2010). Not all of these authors use the same terms to identify the target, however.

[2] Mackie 1977: 40.

[3] Mackie 1977: 32.

[4] Joyce 2001: 37–42.

[5] Joyce 2006: 60–2, 192–9.

[6] Joyce 2011a: 523.

[7] Joyce 2011a: 524.

[8] Joyce 2006: 57–64.

[9] Joyce 2006: 63; 2011a: 525

[10] At one point Joyce speculates that 'morality may be imbued with a deeply mysterious kind of force—a kind of primitive feeling of "being bound by rules and ends" that resists explication' (2011a: 525).

[11] Olson, 2011a.

are queer in that they are or entail facts that count in favour of or require certain courses of behaviour, where the favouring relation is irreducibly normative.[12] Remember that for a fact to be an irreducibly normative reason is for that fact to count in favour of some course of behaviour, where the favouring relation is irreducibly normative. The fact that is the reason need not be irreducibly normative. Strictly speaking, then, it is the irreducibly normative favouring *relation*, or reason relation, that is queer. For brevity and ease of exposition I shall sometimes say that irreducibly normative reasons are queer (they are queer in that they have the irreducibly normative property of counting in favour of some course of behaviour).

In order to get a better grip on this, let us begin by noting the commonplace that many reasons depend crucially on agents' desires, in the sense that if the agent loses the desire, she loses the reason. For example, there is a reason for me to visit the local bar this evening because they are showing a football match I desire not to miss. So the fact that the local bar is showing the match is reason for me to go there. But it is obvious that this fact's being a reason for me to go there is contingent on my desire not to miss the match. Were I somehow to lose my desire not to miss the match, the fact that it is shown at the local bar would, *ceteris paribus*, no longer be a reason for me to go there. In other words, I could escape the reason to visit the local bar this evening by dropping my desire not to miss the match. It is tempting to say that this indicates that my reason to visit the bar is hypothetical and that hypothetical reasons are unproblematic for moral error theorists. But as we shall see in Chapter 8, error theorists like Mackie have been too cavalier about hypothetical reasons. Here I shall not attempt to answer the question in what sense error theorists can recognize a reason for me to visit the bar (we get back to this in Chapter 8). My aim here is only to illustrate an intuitive contrast between moral reasons and many other reasons.

Now consider moral facts. Suppose for instance that it is morally wrong to eat meat and that one ought morally to donate 10% of one's income to Oxfam. The fact that it is morally wrong to eat meat entails that there is a reason not to eat meat. The reason—the fact that counts in favour of not eating meat, that is—might be that eating meat is detrimental to human and non-human well-being. Likewise, the fact that one ought morally to

[12] Some moral facts are or entail facts that make actions permissible, where the 'permissibility-making' relation is irreducibly normative.

donate 10% of one's income to Oxfam entails that there is a reason to do so. The reason might be the fact that donating to Oxfam promotes human well-being.

In these cases the reasons are not contingent on the agents' desires. Whether or not agents desire to promote human and non-human well-being, they have moral reasons not to eat meat and to donate 10% of their income to Oxfam. That they have such reasons is entailed by the facts that it is morally wrong to eat meat and that one ought morally to donate 10% of one's income to Oxfam. One cannot escape moral reasons by adverting to one's desires in the way I can escape my reason to visit the local bar this evening by jettisoning my desire to watch the match.[13]

It is important to see that this point is not about motivation. As we saw in the previous chapter, it does not seem impossible to recognize moral facts, e.g., that it is morally wrong to eat meat and that one ought morally to donate 10% of one's income to Oxfam, and yet not be motivated to abstain from eating meat and to donate to Oxfam. One may simply not care, or care very little, about morality. But the point we are now making is about normativity, not psychology.

In order further to clarify the notion of irreducible normativity it is useful to relate to John Broome's recent work on reasons and normativity. Here is how Broome explains how he understands normativity:

> [I]n one sense 'normative' simply means to do with norms, rules, or correctness. Any source of requirements is normative in this sense. For example, Catholicism is. Catholicism requires you to abstain from meat on Fridays. This is a rule and it is incorrect according to Catholicism to eat meat on Fridays. So Catholicism is normative in this sense. But I do not use 'normative' in that sense. In my sense, it means to do with ought or reasons. Given a rule or a requirement we can ask whether you ought to follow it, or whether you have reason to do so (2007: 162).

Broome is right that given any norm—or rule, or requirement—we can always ask whether we ought to comply with it or whether there are reasons to comply with it. But a problem with his claim that normativity is to do with ought or reasons is that 'ought' and 'reason' are both polysemous

[13] Cf. Bernard Williams on the inescapability of moral obligation: 'the fact that an agent would prefer not to be [...] bound by [moral] rules will not excuse him' (Williams 2006: 177; *cf.* 178). Cf. also Wittgenstein's distinction between 'absolute' and 'relative' judgements of value and the example he uses to illustrate it, quoted in Section 4.2. The example clearly indicates that Wittgenstein took moral judgements to be absolute judgements of value.

terms. Let us focus on 'reason' (the points I make can be made about 'ought' too). There are many uses of 'reason' in which it means nothing normative in Broome's sense. For example, it seems perfectly fine to say that according to Catholicism there is *reason* to abstain from eating meat on Fridays and to mean by this simply that it is incorrect according to the rules of Catholicism to eat meat on Fridays.

Other examples of the same kind are not difficult to find. Consider grammar or etiquette. The claim that there are reasons for writers in English not to split the infinitive might simply mean that splitting the infinitive is inappropriate according to (some) rules of grammar; the claim that there are reasons for male guests to wear a tie at formal dinners might simply mean that this is required by the rules of etiquette. Or consider chess or football. The claim that chess players have reasons not to move the rook diagonally might simply mean that this is incorrect according to the rules of chess; the claim that football players have reasons not to play the ball to their own goalkeeper while under pressure might simply mean that doing so is likely to provide the opponent team with opportunities to score. To give a final example, the claim that soldiers have reasons to comply with the orders of a general might simply mean that doing so is to comply with the orders of someone superior in military rank, which is part of the role of being a soldier.

Someone might protest that all of these examples are in fact normative claims because they all invoke standards of correctness in the respective areas or disciplines, be it Catholic rules of conduct, or grammar, etiquette, chess, football, or military rules. But as Broome will agree, 'correct' is in these contexts not a normative term.[14] To say that some behaviour is correct or incorrect according to some norm, N, is not to say anything normative. It is merely to say something about what kind of behaviour is required, recommended, or forbidden by N. *The normative question*, as Broome calls it,[15] concerns whether there are irreducibly normative reasons to comply with N. Alternatively, one could suggest that to say that some behaviour is correct or incorrect according to some norm is to say something *reducibly* normative, since, as Broome notes, 'normativity' in one sense simply means to do with norms, rules, or correctness. But when

[14] Anandi Hattiangadi makes this point in the context of semantic normativity. See Hattiangadi 2007: 59.

[15] Broome 2007: *passim*.

I talk about normativity in what follows I shall mean irreducible normativity, unless otherwise indicated.[16]

This shows two things relevant to our discussion. First, error theorists can recognize that there are reasons that do not depend on agents' desires. There is nothing metaphysically queer about conventional norms, rules, or standards of correctness that require or recommend various courses of behaviour.[17] For example, there need be nothing metaphysically queer about there being a reason for writers in English not to split the infinitive since, in one sense of 'reason', this is just for there to be a rule of grammar according to which splitting the infinitive is inappropriate; there need be nothing metaphysically queer about there being a reason for male guests at formal dinners to wear a tie, since, in one sense of 'reason', this is just for there to be a standard of etiquette according to which male guests at formal dinners are required to wear a tie. A soldier might not *desire* to comply with the general's order and he might have no other desires whose satisfaction would be promoted by his compliance, but he can still be said to have reasons to comply with the general's order since complying with the orders of those of superior military rank is part of the role of being a soldier.

The same goes for chess players and football players; they might not desire to play by the rules and they need not even desire to win. Agents can occupy roles they have no desire to fulfil and engage in activities they have no desire to succeed in. Hence error theorists can recognize reasons that reduce to facts about agents' *roles* and rule-governed *activities*. This should not be surprising. Mackie did not deny that there are rules and standards according to which certain agents in certain situations ought to, or have reason to, behave in certain ways, and Richard Joyce does not deny that there are what he calls 'institutional reasons'.[18] The kinds of reasons error theorists can recognize I shall call *reducible* reasons. Reducible reasons are reducible to facts about what promotes desire satisfaction, or to correctness norms that may or may not be conventional.[19]

[16] My distinction between reducible and irreducible normativity corresponds to Hattiangadi's distinction between norm-relativity and normativity (2007: 51–64) and to Parfit's distinction between normativity in the rule-implying sense and normativity in the reason-implying sense (2011: 308–10).

[17] For an account of conventional norms on which they are not ontologically fundamental additions to naturalistic worldviews, see Searle (2010).

[18] Mackie 1977: 25–7; Joyce 2001: 39–42.

[19] See the discussion in Section 6.3.

The second thing relevant to our discussion that this shows is that we cannot simply say that normativity is to do with reasons, because sometimes the claim that there is reason to ϕ might just mean that ϕing is correct according to some norm. For example, the fact that there is according to Catholicism a norm according to which it is incorrect to eat meat on Fridays can be expressed as the claim that there are according to Catholicism reasons not to eat meat on Fridays. As we saw, given any norm, N, we can always ask the normative question whether there are reasons to comply with N. We are then not just asking whether it is correct according to some other norm, N', to comply with N. That of course only invites the question whether there are reasons to comply with N'. When we ask the normative question we ask about irreducibly normative reasons. To take another example, since there is a law against speeding in traffic, we might say that I have a legal reason to stay within the speed limit. But I can also ask whether I have reason to act in accordance with this legal reason. I am not then asking whether there is some further law or rule that requires me to act in accordance with the legal reason; I am asking whether there is irreducibly normative reason to act in accordance with the legal reason.

To say that some fact, F, is an irreducibly normative reason for an agent, A, to behave in a certain way, e.g., to comply with N, is to say that F counts in favour of A's complying with N where the favouring relation is irreducibly normative. It is not reducible, for example, to facts about what would promote satisfaction of A's desires, or to facts about A's roles or engagement in rule-governed activities. Broome's use of 'normativity' according to which normativity means to do with reasons thus needs qualification. We could say that normativity is to do with irreducibly normative reasons, and more exactly with irreducibly normative favouring relations.[20] This is admittedly not very illuminating. But on the other hand it is very doubtful that we can get much further in attempting to throw light on the notion of normativity, which I and many other philosophers take to be a primitive notion.[21]

[20] As mentioned in the main text above we could also say—no more illuminatingly—that irreducible normativity is to do with irreducibly normative favouring relations and reducible normativity with reducible favouring relations. But again, when I talk about normativity in what follows I shall mean irreducible normativity, unless otherwise indicated.

[21] We could of course use other terms than 'reasons' and 'favouring relations' but we would then only be going around within the normative circle (cf. Blackburn 1998: 107).

The question that interests Broome is whether the requirements of rationality are normative. He says about moral requirements that they are surely normative, i.e., that it is necessarily true that if morality requires you to ϕ, then there are reasons for you to ϕ. Broome does not distinguish between reducible reasons and irreducibly normative reasons, but I shall take him to mean the latter. In fact, Broome claims that it is necessarily true that if morality requires you to ϕ, then *that fact* is a reason for you to ϕ.[22] This may sometimes be so. Suppose, for example, that morality requires you to maximize happiness. There is then reason for you to maximize happiness, and one might suggest that the reason is the fact that morality requires you to maximize happiness. This is not obviously so, however. An alternative view is that if morality requires you to maximize happiness, then for any action, A, the fact that A maximizes happiness is the reason to perform A. To take another example, suppose that morality requires you to keep a promise to a friend. It might be thought that in such a case the reason to keep the promise is the fact that your friend will be hurt if you break it, and not the fact that morality requires you to keep it. So one might question Broome's claim that is necessarily true that if morality requires you to ϕ, then that fact is a reason for you to ϕ. However, it does seem highly plausible that it is necessarily true that if morality requires you to ϕ, then there are irreducibly normative reasons for you to ϕ. Error theorists of the kind I am interested in agree with everything said so far.[23]

Unlike Broome, however, error theorists maintain that there are no irreducibly normative reasons. Error theorists thus accept error theory not only about morality but about normativity more generally. Since morality is normative in the sense of entailing irreducibly normative favouring relations, there are no moral facts and moral claims are uniformly false. Schematically, we can put the argument as follows:

(P12) Moral facts entail that there are facts that favour certain courses of behaviour, where the favouring relation is irreducibly normative.

[22] Broome 2007: 165.

[23] Some error theorists may deny that moral facts entail that there are facts that are irreducibly normative reasons. They might hold instead that moral facts entail that the desires of all fully rational beings converge. For example, the fact that I morally ought not to eat meat entails that all fully rational beings desire that I do not eat meat. But since the desires of fully rational beings do not converge, there are no moral facts. See Joyce (2011b).

(P13) Irreducibly normative favouring relations are queer.
(C5) Hence, moral facts entail queer relations.
(P4') If moral facts entail queer relations, moral facts are queer.
(C2") Hence, moral facts are queer.

An error theory based on this argument takes the form of an error theory about irreducibly normative favouring relations, or irreducible normativity for short. An important question is whether the argument generalizes objectionably beyond the moral, as did the first and the second queerness arguments. If there are other kinds of reason relations, besides moral reason relations, that are irreducibly normative, the argument does generalize to these as well. However, unlike the first and the second queerness arguments, this one does not generalize beyond the normative so it is more restricted than the first two, which, as we saw, have general ramifications for issues in metaphysics and epistemology that do not concern normativity. Whether the fourth queerness argument does generalize objectionably will be considered briefly in Sections 6.3 and 7.1 and at greater length in Chapter 8.

In the meantime, let us scrutinize the premises of the argument. Let us first consider whether (P12) is true. Following others,[24] we can call the claim that moral facts are or entail irreducibly normative reasons (and correspondingly that moral claims are or entail claims about irreducibly normative reasons) *the conceptual claim*. We have already seen that non-naturalists and error theorists unite in accepting the conceptual claim.[25] But while non-naturalists also accept the *ontological claim* that there are irreducibly normative reasons in reality,[26] moral error theorists reject it.

[24] E.g. Smith (1994) and Miller (2003). Smith and Miller may not understand the conceptual claim in exactly the way I do, however.

[25] Not all moral error theorists need accept the conceptual claim that moral facts entail irreducibly normative reasons, however. Some moral error theorists may hold with Smith (1994) that moral facts entail that the desires of fully rational agents converge. But since no such convergence is forthcoming, there are no moral facts. See n. 23.

[26] Among them are Nagel (1986); Scanlon (1998); Shafer-Landau (2003; 2009). Dworkin (1996) spends a fair bit of time criticizing Mackie's argument about motivation. As I note above, this queerness worry is not particularly forceful. Dworkin is much swifter about the worry that moral facts are queer because they would be or entail irreducibly normative reasons. Dworkin says: 'There is nothing bizarre in the idea that a moral duty necessarily supplies a moral reason for action, however. That can be true only in virtue of what "duty" and "reason" mean' (1996). It is easy to see that Dworkin simply restates the conceptual claim. He

Some moral naturalists aim to demystify moral facts by rejecting the conceptual claim in one way or other. They agree with Mackie that the concepts he targets are defective. But they deny that ordinary moral discourse is committed to these concepts in the first place. For example, in his response to Mackie, David Brink argues that whether there are reasons for an agent to act in accordance with moral facts 'will depend upon contingent (even if deep) facts about the agent's desires and interests'.[27] But as I have already argued, this is a deeply counterintuitive move. It is this counterintuitiveness that Mackie wanted to capture when he claimed that naturalistic analyses of moral judgement leave out 'the categorical quality of moral requirements.'[28]

As we argued above, one cannot escape a moral reason to donate to Oxfam simply by adverting to one's lack of a relevant desire. Moreover, even if most or all people do have desires whose satisfaction would be promoted by their donating to Oxfam, or more generally by their compliance with moral norms, it is difficult to accept Brink's view that whether there are reasons for people to donate to Oxfam, or more generally to comply with moral norms, depends on whether doing so would promote fulfilment of their desires and interests. This would simply be the wrong explanation of why there are reasons to donate to Oxfam, or more generally to comply with moral norms.[29]

The most elaborate attack on the conceptual claim is developed in Stephen Finlay's recent work.[30] Seeing where it goes wrong will serve to

does not attempt to answer the question how there can be facts that in themselves favour certain courses of behaviour, where the favouring relation is irreducibly normative. See also Sinnott-Armstrong (2010: 58f.).

[27] Brink 1984: 114. See also Schroeder 2007: chap. 6.

[28] Mackie 1977: 33. Similarly, Joyce argues that moral naturalism fails to capture the 'inescapable authority' or 'practical clout' of moral facts, see Joyce 2006: 190–8.

[29] An anonymous reviewer asked whether this commits error theorists to holding that Brink, along with Foot (1972) and Williams (1981), who all deny (P12) lack a proper grasp of morality. I believe that anyone who holds that moral facts are irreducibly normative, e.g., Broome and error theorists, are committed to holding that Brink, Foot, and Williams endorsed mistaken theories about morality. Here I believe common sense is on the side of Broome and the error theorists. Needless to say, ordinary speakers are unlikely to use the phrase 'irreducibly normative' when expressing the thought that (P12) expressed. That is because the phrase is not part of ordinary discourse. But the thought expressed in (P12) is not alien to ordinary moral thinking.

[30] See Finlay (2008), (2009), and (2010). Foot (1972) delivered an early attack on the conceptual claim that invigorated a long-standing debate. Joyce (2001) responds to Foot; Finlay's 2008 article is largely a critique of Joyce. Joyce (2011a) responds to Finlay (2008) and Finlay (2011) is a counter response to Joyce.

illustrate the costs associated with rejecting the conceptual claim and hence to support (P12) in the fourth queerness argument. This is the task in the following section.

6.2. In Defence of the Conceptual Claim

In his recent article 'The Error in the Error Theory' (2008), Finlay argues that moral claims—and indeed all normative claims—are, or should be understood as, relativized to some (contextually implicit) end or system of ends. By 'end' Finlay means 'a possible aim for action or object of desire'.[31] He also makes clear that his view amounts to 'a naturalistic reduction of the relation of "counting in favour of" to a relation specifiable in only non-normative terms'.[32] According to this view, for a fact, F, to be a reason to ϕ, relative to an end, *e*, is for F to explain why ϕing would be conducive to *e*.[33] Finlay adds that whether a reason *matters* to an agent depends on her attitudes, in particular her cares or concerns.[34] For example, there might be moral reasons for an agent to donate 10% of her income to Oxfam, irrespective of her attitudes. One such reason, let's assume, is that Oxfam works to relieve world hunger and relies as an organization on donations. This fact explains why donating to Oxfam is conducive to the end of stopping world hunger. But this reason matters to the agent just in case her donating 10% of her income to charity would conduce to satisfaction of her cares and concerns. As Finlay sometimes puts it, moral claims lack 'absolute authority'.[35]

According to Finlay, then, the error in the error theory is that it attributes to ordinary moral discourse an error that simply is not there; ordinary moral claims are not and do not entail claims about irreducibly normative reasons, so the conceptual claim is false. I shall argue that the view that all moral claims are relativized to some end has some very implausible implications and that it does not avoid commitment to various forms of error theory. This becomes especially clear when we focus on fundamental moral claims.

[31] Finlay 2006: 8. [32] Finlay 2006: 8. [33] Finlay 2006: 8.
[34] Finlay 2006: 17. [35] Finlay 2008: 351–2.

Finlay on disputation evidence for the conceptual claim

Finlay seeks to undermine various sources of evidence for the conceptual claim.[36] I shall comment on one such source, since this ties in with my arguments against Finlay's relativistic view to be offered below. We tend to pursue moral arguments even with people whom we take not to share our fundamental moral views, and we do so with the objective of convincing them that we are right and they are wrong. This suggests that we do take moral judgements to be absolutist rather than relativistic. Following Finlay, we can call this 'disputation evidence' for the conceptual claim.[37]

Finlay makes two points in response. First, he claims that 'most moral discourse takes place between people who share their fundamental moral values, and assume that they share these values'.[38] Second, Finlay claims that to the extent that disputation between speakers who do not share fundamental moral values does occur, withholding relativizations of moral judgements is to be seen as a pragmatic device to win the opponent over. Withholding the moral standards or system of ends to which one's moral judgements are relativized 'is a rhetorical way of expressing the *expectation* (demand) that the audience subscribes to the speaker's ends or standards'.[39]

Finlay's first point underestimates the prevalence of fundamental moral disagreement in many current societies. Even a cursory glance at

[36] Finlay 2008: 352–60.

[37] Finlay 2008: 355

[38] Finaly 2008: 356.

[39] Finlay 2008: 357 (Finlay's emphasis). It is a familiar fact that we sometimes withhold relativizations to standards or ends for rhetorical purposes and in cases where the relativizations are obvious to the involved parties. Finlay points out that it would be strange for a rugby captain to prefix his advices about rugby tactics with an 'in order to win', or 'in order to score a try' (2008: 353). But a crucial disanalogy is that it *would not* be strange for a moralizer to make moral claims like 'Irrespective of your desires, aims, roles, or activities, you ought not to torture animals for fun'. By contrast, it *would* be strange for a rugby captain to express his advices about tactics by saying something like 'Irrespective of the aim to win or score, and irrespective of your role as teammate, you ought to play so and so'. Were the moralizer to prefix his claim that one ought not to torture animals for fun with an 'in order to fulfil your desires', or 'in order to fulfil a certain role or comply with the rules of certain activities', the claim would likely change its character or lose a good deal of its rhetorical force (as I argue in the main text below). Were the rugby captain to prefix his advices about rugby tactics with an 'in order to win the game', or 'in order to score a try', he would merely be unnecessarily explicit. *Cf.* Joyce (2011a).

public political debate in many countries will reveal fundamental moral disagreements between conservatives and feminists; socialists and neo-liberals; cosmopolitans and nationalists; etc. Moreover, fundamental moral disagreement between, e.g., ethical vegetarians (who believe that animal suffering is on a par morally with human suffering) and speciesists (who believe that humans are especially valuable *qua* being humans) and between pro-choice and pro-life activists regarding abortion, are not uncommon in everyday conversations.[40] We need not step outside the confines of academic moral philosophy to find many cases of fundamental moral disagreement between utilitarians and deontologists; Rawlsians and Nozickians; anarchists and communitarians; etc. Finlay asks us to 'survey the moral judgements made on television or radio talk shows and news broadcasts, and try to recall the last time [we] engaged in moral discourse with someone like Charles Manson or a neo-Nazi'.[41] But why assume that the person with whom you have a fundamental moral disagreement is such a depraved character? She might rather be a utilitarian, a Nozickian, a liberal, a conservative, a socialist, a nationalist, a speciesist, or a pro-life activist.[42]

Finlay's second point backfires. The idea that moral judgements are partly rhetorical devices used to put pressure on people to behave in certain ways is congenial both to moral error theory and to Finlay's relativist theory, but it fits better with the former. First, it fits well with a hypothesis congenial to moral error theory, namely that part of the reason why moral thought and talk evolved is their coordinating and regulative functions that are highly useful from an evolutionary perspective. In Mackie's words, morality evolved partly as 'a device for counteracting limited

[40] It is a familiar fact that seemingly fundamental moral disagreement sometimes stems from non-moral disagreement, e.g., empirical or theological (Finlay 2008: 356–8). But it would be implausible and uncharitable to consider all, or even most, cases of seemingly fundamental moral disagreement as stemming from non-moral disagreement. Furthermore, people sometimes doubt or wonder whether the fundamental moral standard they accept is correct. When people ask such questions they are not merely doubting or wondering whether some courses of behaviour conduce to some end. (I get back to this in the main text below.)

[41] Finlay 2008: 356.

[42] Finlay argues that it is not enough merely to locate fundamental moral disagreement between speakers. In order to count as evidence it must also be established that speakers recognize that they are involved in fundamental moral disagreement (2008: 356f.). But it is not uncommon for people to recognize that they are involved in fundamental moral disagreements. This often happens in ideological debates, for example.

sympathies'.[43] It is a plausible conjecture that moral discourse fulfils these functions better if moral claims entail claims about irreducibly normative reasons, than if they are reduced to claims about what would conduce to some end.[44]

Second, the most straightforward explanation of why moral claims have the kind of rhetorical force that demand certain behaviour is that the conceptual claim is true: moral claims have rhetorical force *because* they are or entail claims about irreducibly normative reasons. Compare the following two claims:

Spoon 'It is bad manners to eat peas with a spoon.'
Tax 'It is morally wrong to cheat on your tax declaration.'

In both *Spoon* and *Tax* the standard or end to which the claims are supposedly relativized are withheld. But *Spoon* and *Tax* differ in that *Tax* has a lot more rhetorical force than *Spoon*. Finlay's proffered explanation is that '[m]oral standards or ends are of pressing concern to [us], [and this explains] why we are much more serious and intransigent about our moral appraisals than we are about our appraisals of manners'.[45] But one would expect the difference in seriousness and intransigence between moral claims and etiquette claims to be reflected in the concepts we use to make them. The conceptual claim makes good on this expectation: the fact that moral standards or ends are of especially pressing concern to us explains why moral claims entail claims about irreducibly normative reasons.

Furthermore, if moral claims and etiquette claims were of the same status, insofar as both kinds of claims reduce to claims about what would conduce to some end or accord with some standard, it is hard to see how moral claims could *maintain* their greater rhetorical force—someone who does not care about the relevant standard or end could waive *Tax* with the same ease as someone who does not care about table manners could

[43] Mackie 1977: 107–15. Here Mackie draws on Warnock (1971). In the words of Philip Kitcher, one of the original and primary functions of morality is to 'remedy altruism failures' (Kitcher 2011: 8–9). We return to this point in the next chapter.

[44] Cf. Joyce (2006); Olson (2010). There is the possibility that ordinary speakers believe falsely that moral claims do entail claims about irreducibly normative reasons when in fact they reduce to claims about what would conduce to some end. In other words, there is the possibility that ordinary speakers are systematically mistaken about the meaning of moral terms. But this view seems considerably more far-fetched than the view that ordinary speakers are systematically mistaken about moral metaphysics. See the main text below.

[45] Finlay 2008: 354.

waive *Spoon*. The conceptual claim provides a straightforward explanation of why moral claims maintain greater rhetorical force than etiquette claims. It also explains straightforwardly why *Tax* cannot be waived with the same ease as *Spoon*.[46] This is simply because unlike etiquette claims, moral claims entail claims about irreducibly normative reasons.

Against Finlay's relativist theory

Finlay holds that the *essential application conditions* for moral terms, i.e., 'the criteria on which a [moral] concept or term is applied', are relational, even in the use of speakers who avowedly accept the conceptual claim: 'An action is judged to be *morally wrong* if and only if it is supposed that it frustrates certain ends or violates certain standards'.[47]

Taken in one sense, Finlay's claim about essential application conditions for *moral wrongness* is entirely innocuous. Any ordinary moralizer who judges, e.g., a particular action wrong will agree that that particular action violates the moral standard she endorses at the time of her utterance.[48] To cut any ice, then, Finlay's contention must be that *all* moral claims, and not just moral claims about particular actions, are relativized to standards.

It is a plain fact that we make moral judgements not only about particular actions but also about other things, including persons, institutions, societies, and *moral standards*. For instance, one might judge that some utilitarian moral standard is correct and that deontological moral standards are incorrect, or that some utilitarian moral standard is more likely to be correct than deontological moral standards. But on Finlay's relativist theory such claims become problematic.

Consider the following claim, which many utilitarians endorse:

(UC) Utilitarian standard U—according to which an action is right if and only if it would bring about at least as great a balance of happiness over unhappiness as any other available alternative, and wrong otherwise—is the correct moral standard.

[46] Cf. Joyce's response to C. L. Stevenson's claim that moral claims are imperatives disguised as assertions (Joyce 2001: 14–15).

[47] Finlay 2008: 365 (Finlay's emphasis).

[48] Even moral particularists will agree. They will add only that that the standard in question is irreducibly situation specific.

It should be uncontentious that (UC) is a moral claim.[49] But utilitarians who utter (UC) certainly do not mean to say that U is correct relative to some distinct moral standard or ends; they mean to say that U is the correct fundamental moral standard.

At this point there are two main options for relativists like Finlay. One is to take fundamental moral claims like (UC) to deviate from the general pattern of analysis in that they are not to be relativized to ends. Perhaps fundamental moral claims could be given an expressivist analysis, or perhaps they could be analyzed along the lines of error theory or fictionalism.[50] The drawback of this kind of option is that it leads to an unhappily *disunified* metaethical theory. If expressivism, error theory, fictionalism, or some other non-relativist account, gives a plausible analysis of fundamental moral claims, one expects that account to give an equally plausible analysis of non-fundamental moral claims, such as claims about the moral status of particular actions.

Moreover, disunified theories are unattractive in that they invite a double load of critique. For example, a disunified theory that gives an expressivist analysis of fundamental moral claims and a relativist analysis of non-fundamental moral claims is vulnerable both to standard objections to expressivism and to relativism. To mention just one example of such a standard objection, consider the fact that embedding fundamental moral claims in complex contexts gives rise to the notorious problems that expressivists face concerning embedded moral claims.[51] These considerations place a heavy burden of proof on defenders of disunified metaethical theories.

The second main option is to hold that fundamental moral claims do not deviate from the general pattern of analysis and maintain that they be relativized to themselves. An advantage of this option is that it

[49] Might Finlay avoid the problem by denying that (UC) is a moral claim? In addition to being blatantly ad hoc, this move would allow deriving moral conclusions from non-moral premises. For instance, it follows from (UC) that if some possible action, ϕ, would bring about a greater balance of happiness over unhappiness than some alternative, ψ, then ψ is wrong. The claim that ψ is wrong, and that it is wrong because it would be suboptimal in this way seems a clear example of a moral claim. But then Finlay's theory would violate Hume's Law in that it would entail that some moral claims—e.g. the claim that ψ is wrong—are entailed by some non-moral claims—e.g. (UC) in conjunction with some further non-moral premises.

[50] See Finlay 2009: 334–5 for these tentative suggestions.

[51] This problem is known as the 'Frege-Geach problem'. See Schroeder (2010) for a recent discussion. See also Section 9.2.

leads to a unified metaethical theory. Finlay has recently made a suggestion along these lines.[52] The thought is that fundamental moral claims express tautologies. More specifically, any normative claim is implicitly or explicitly prefixed by an 'In order that *e*' clause, where *e* is some end. 'In order that *e*, it ought to be the case that one perform ϕ' expresses the claim that if one performs ϕ, the likelihood that *e* be realized is greater than it would be if some alternative to ϕ were performed. The utilitarian fundamental moral claim that one ought not to perform actions that fail to maximize happiness is thus to be understood as the following tautological claim: 'In order that one does not perform actions that fail to maximize happiness, it ought to be the case that one not perform actions that fail to maximize happiness.' It is of course trivially true that if one does not perform actions that fail to maximize happiness, the likelihood that one does not perform actions that fail to maximize happiness is greater than it would be if actions of some other kind were performed instead. Let us call this suggested analysis of fundamental moral claims the 'tautology approach'.

The tautology approach has many troublesome implications. Here I shall briefly highlight four interrelated problems.[53]

(i) *No absolutely correct fundamental moral standard.* I said above that utilitarians who endorse (UC) do not mean to say that U is correct relative to some *distinct* moral standard. Neither do they mean to say that U is correct relative to itself. It is trivially true that any fundamental moral standard is correct relative to itself, but utilitarians who endorse (UC) mean to say something that is not trivially true, namely that U is correct in a non-relativized way, i.e. that U is the *absolutely* correct fundamental moral standard.[54] But according to the tautology approach, there is no absolutely correct fundamental moral standard. Hence the tautology approach vindicates error theory about absolutely correct fundamental moral standards.

[52] Finlay 2009: 334. It should be noted, however, that Finlay describes this analysis of fundamental moral claims as 'preliminary' and 'speculative' (2009: 334).

[53] Finlay himself considers some of them (2009: 334).

[54] Similarly, as Matt Bedke pointed out, those who reject (UC) do not mean to deny a trivial truth. They normally mean to deny that U is the absolutely correct fundamental moral standard.

(ii) *No incorrect fundamental moral standard.* Ordinary speakers normally assume that it is possible to be mistaken about which fundamental moral standard is correct. They normally deem incorrect any fundamental moral standard that appears incompatible with the ones they endorse. For instance, an ethical vegetarian might believe that any fundamental moral standard that sanctions eating meat is incorrect; a pro-life activist might believe that any fundamental moral standard that sanctions abortion is incorrect. But according to the tautology approach, these beliefs are false.[55] As we saw in *(i)*, any claim to the effect that some fundamental moral standard is correct is trivially true, so there is no such thing as an incorrect fundamental moral standard. Hence the tautology approach implies an error theory according to which claims to the effect that some fundamental moral standard is incorrect are uniformly false.

(iii) *No disagreement in asserted content.* What has been said in *(ii)* illustrates that speakers who apparently disagree about fundamental moral standards, e.g. utilitarians and deontologists or ethical vegetarians and speciesists, disagree at most 'in attitude' but not in what is asserted. This means that the common belief that when such speakers make different fundamental moral claims they disagree in what they assert, is false.[56]

(iv) *No informative fundamental moral claims.* Many moral philosophers as well as many ordinary speakers believe that their fundamental moral claims are informative, often unobviously true, and perhaps even highly controversial. But the tautology approach implies that these beliefs too are false.

Finlay might retort that attributing false beliefs about fundamental moral standards to ordinary speakers is not a big cost since fundamental moral claims appear rarely in ordinary moral discourse. When they do they

[55] A speciesist moral standard, S, is of course incorrect relative to a non-speciesist moral standard, NS. But the claim that S is incorrect relative to NS is not a claim to the effect that S is an incorrect *fundamental* moral standard. To maintain that S is an incorrect fundamental moral standard, the ethical vegetarian must make the false claim that S is incorrect relative to itself.

[56] The tautology approach shares this problem with expressivism. Unlike the former, however, expressivism is not committed to the implausible view that any fundamental moral claim is trivially true.

function as conversation stoppers whose point it is to demand motivation and action, rather than to convey semantic content.[57]

But this is unconvincing. First, as has already been indicated, it is not uncommon for ordinary speakers to appeal to fundamental moral standards in, e.g., debates about ideology, vegetarianism, or abortion. It is of course debatable how frequently cases of fundamental moral disagreements occur. (Finlay suspects that they occur a lot less frequently than I suspect that they do.) But irrespective of this empirical issue, it is clear that fundamental moral beliefs and disagreements are of crucial importance to many people. Many people take very seriously their doubts about whether the fundamental moral standard they accept is really correct. In asking such questions they do not doubt or ponder trivial truths. The tautology approach, then, implies error theory about possibly large, and definitely crucial, parts of ordinary moral thought and discourse.

Secondly and relatedly, I agree that fundamental moral claims often function to demand motivation and action, but it is implausible that they do not normally also function to convey semantic content. After all, many ordinary speakers, and not just moral philosophers, are willing to engage in debates about fundamental moral standards. It is implausible that fundamental moral claims function merely as conversation stoppers in such debates. Open-minded participants typically hold their views about fundamental moral standards open to scrutiny and revision. As points *(i)*–*(iv)* have already indicated, they do not normally take them to be trivially true.[58]

Let us sum up. The tautology approach agrees with moral error theory in taking claims to the effect that some fundamental moral standard is absolutely correct to be uniformly false, and even goes beyond it in taking

[57] Finlay 2009: 334. According to Finlay, this conversational function of fundamental moral claims is 'quite compatible with their being tautologous' (2009: 334). Cf. Finlay 2009: 334, n. 41.

[58] Finlay acknowledges in a footnote that it is a 'serious objection' that 'since people don't ordinarily take themselves to be asserting end-relational propositions when they utter ought-sentences, it is most unlikely that they are' (2009: 335, n. 41). The serious objection I press above is that since people do not ordinarily take themselves to be asserting tautologies when they make fundamental moral claims, it is highly unlikely that they are. Finlay postpones a full response to these objections to a future occasion, but advertises that his response will rely on 'distinguishing sharply between what we mean by our words and what we think we mean' (2009; 335, n. 41). This amounts to an error theory according to which ordinary speakers are systematically mistaken about what they mean by (some of) their words.

claims to the effect that some fundamental moral standard is incorrect also to be uniformly false. Furthermore, it attributes to most moral philosophers and users of ordinary moral discourse false beliefs about disagreement about fundamental moral standards and about the logical and epistemic status of fundamental moral claims—while such claims are normally taken to be informative, often unobvious, sometimes highly controversial and mutually inconsistent, they are all trivially true. I submit that attributing all these errors to ordinary moral discourse is more far-fetched than attributing error about moral ontology.

Relativists like Finlay might of course attempt to develop alternatives to the tautology approach. But it seems that any such alternative view leads to a disunified metaethical theory. And as suggested above, defenders of disunified theories must accept a heavy burden of proof. Until relativists like Finlay have elaborated a plausible analysis of fundamental moral claims, their case against the conceptual claim remains unconvincing. I conclude that Mackie's theory fits better than Finlay's with ordinary moral thought and talk. Hence, I conclude that Finlay's challenge fails and that (P12) of the fourth queerness argument remains plausible.

6.3. Queerness and Companions in Guilt

One might attempt to resist the conclusion that moral facts are queer by denying premise (P4') of the fourth queerness argument, i.e., the premise that if moral facts entail queer relations, moral facts are queer. But remember that we have said that moral facts are facts about what other facts (for example, the fact that performing some action would be conducive to the general happiness) favour certain courses of behaviour (for example, performing the action that would be conducive to the general happiness), where the favouring relation is irreducibly normative. It seems difficult to deny that if the irreducibly normative favouring relation, or instances of it, is queer, then the fact that it obtains is also queer,

Let us therefore consider the premise that irreducibly normative favouring relations are queer (P13). In what way are they queer? Well, recall that irreducibly normative reasons are facts that require, or count in favour of, certain ways of behaviour, where the requiring or favouring relation is irreducibly normative. For example, it is not reducible to facts about agents' desires, roles, or engagement in rule-governed activities. As we have seen, it is no metaphysical mystery how there can be a fact that counts in favour of not splitting the infinitive. The fact that an act is a splitting of an infinitive counts in favour of not performing that act, and on a reductive understanding of 'counting in favour', for that fact to count in favour of not performing that act simply is for it to be the case that not performing that act accords with a grammatical rule according to which splitting the infinitive is inappropriate. It is likewise no metaphysical mystery how there can be a fact that counts in favour of male guests wearing a tie at formal dinners. The fact that an action is the wearing of a tie by a male guest at a formal dinner counts in favour of performing that action, and on a reductive understanding of 'counting in favour', for that fact to count in favour of performing that action simply is for that action to accord with the rule of etiquette that requires male guests at formal dinners to wear a tie.

Irreducibly normative reasons are very different. The irreducibly normative favouring relation is not reducible to an action's property of being a means to the satisfaction of some desire, or an action's property of being in accord with some rule or norm. When the irreducibly normative favouring relation obtains between some fact and some course of behaviour, that fact is an irreducibly normative reason to take this course of behaviour. Such irreducibly normative favouring relations appear metaphysically mysterious. How can there be such relations?

Non-naturalists can retort that it is not clear what kind of explanation we ask for here. They could maintain that it is a fundamental fact about reality that there are irreducibly normative reason relations, and they could refuse head-on to admit that there is anything *queer* about such relations.

This illustrates that the issue here is at a bedrock metaphysical level. It is difficult for error theorists to convince those who find nothing queer about irreducible normativity. And vice versa, of course. So the stubborn response from the non-naturalist seems to leave her and the error theorist in a stalemate, staring incredulously at each other.

One way out of the stalemate might be for moral non-naturalists to appeal to companions in guilt. We saw in Chapter 5 that such appeals are effective as responses to the first and second queerness arguments. A prominent companions-in-guilt response to the argument against irreducible reasons is that rules of logic are irreducibly normative. One way of understanding this claim is to take rules of logic to be norms of correct reasoning. For example, it might be argued that the *modus ponens* rule entails that if an agent believes *p* and believes *if p then q*, there is reason for that agent to believe *q* or give up at least one of the prior beliefs. The standards of correctness in the examples considered above, e.g., in grammar, etiquette, chess, football, etc., are conventional and hence *mind-dependent*. As moral non-naturalists are quick to point out, however, it is much less plausible, that the rules of logic are conventional and mind-dependent.[59]

Error theorists can respond that even if rules of logic are mind-independent, the reason to believe *q* or give up at least one of the prior beliefs in the aforementioned example is reducible. Here is how they can do that: the claim that if one believes *p* and believes *if p then q*, there is reason to believe *q*, or give up at least one of the prior beliefs, simply amounts to the claim that according to the *modus ponens* rule, if one believes *p* and believes *if p then q*, it is correct to believe *q*, or give up at least one of the prior beliefs. But as we noted in Section 6.1, 'correct' is in contexts like this one not a normative term. The *modus ponens* rule is an example of a rule that tells agents what there is reason to do *qua* (occupying the role of) reasoners, or *qua* engaging in the activity of reasoning. To say that there is reason *qua* engaging in the activity of reasoning to comply with the *modus ponens* rule is simply to say that complying with the rule is in accordance with standards of correct reasoning. This leaves open the normative question whether there are irreducibly normative reasons to comply with these rules or standards of correctness. Error theorists are of course committed to answering this latter question negatively. This means that while error theorists can maintain that *modus ponens* is a correct rule of inference and that, say, *affirming the consequent* is not, they cannot maintain that there are irreducibly normative reasons to reason in accordance with *modus ponens* rather than in accordance with *affirming the consequent*.

In other words, rules of logic and standards of correctness in reasoning—whether conventional or non-conventional, or mind-dependent or mind-independent—do not entail irreducibly normative reasons to comply with them. There obtains no irreducibly normative favouring relation between on the one hand an agent believing *p* and believing *if p then q*, and on the other hand the agent believing *q* or giving up at least one of

[59] Huemer 2005: 113–15.

the prior beliefs. One might of course hold the *substantive* view that there are *epistemic* reasons for anyone who believes p and believes *if p then q*, to believe q or give up at least one of the prior beliefs. If epistemic reasons are irreducibly normative, moral error theorists are committed to the view that such claims are systematically false.[60] But the point here is that moral error theorists need not deny that there are standards of correctness in logic and reasoning. Rules of logic and other kinds of facts about abstracta, e.g., mathematical facts, may be metaphysically problematic in a number of ways but they do not display the feature that moral error theorists find especially queer about moral facts—they do not entail irreducibly normative reasons.

At this point non-naturalists are likely to look for other companions in guilt. In Chapter 8 we shall consider arguments that appeal to the irreducible normativity of hypothetical reasons and epistemic reasons. We shall also consider the view that irreducibly normative reasons are ontologically respectable because they are indispensable for purposes of deliberation.

If no such argument succeeds, one remaining option for non-naturalists is to turn to a more stubborn strategy. Such a strategy appeals to Moorean arguments (see Chapter 7) in order to establish that some moral judgements are true and that we know them to be true, or that we are highly confident that they are true. We can therefore justifiably infer that there are irreducibly normative properties and facts. As one contemporary non-naturalist says about irreducible normativity, '[i]f this is obscurantist, [...] we have no choice but to embrace the mysteries'.[61]

But if we give up on moral realism we need not accept the mysteries. We can try to explain why we tend to talk and think as if there are moral facts and irreducibly normative reasons although there are none. This is the topic of Chapter 7.

[60] Epistemic reasons will be further discussed in Chapter 8.
[61] Shafer-Landau 2003: 205.

7

Debunking Moral Belief

Critics of moral error theory may feel that the conclusions reached in Chapters 5 and 6 provide very weak support for moral error theory. After all, we have argued that only one of Mackie's four queerness arguments has force and we conceded in Section 6.3 that it is extremely difficult to give a compelling argument for why irreducibly normative favouring relations are intolerably queer since the issue here is metaphysically bedrock.

In Section 7.1 below we shall consider an argument to the effect that moral facts are ontologically respectable because they are indispensable to the project of vindicating moral thought and talk. According to this Moorean argument, the beliefs that there are moral facts and that some moral judgements are true are more credible than the view that there are no moral facts and that no moral judgement is true. The Moorean argument is *prima facie* forceful, but it can be undermined by appeal to debunking explanations of moral belief. The kind of debunking explanation on offer here is one according to which moral belief is evolutionarily advantageous.

7.1. A Moorean Argument

An early proponent of Moorean arguments in moral philosophy was A. C. Ewing. When Ewing considered the view that no moral judgement is true, his response was to ask rhetorically: 'Do I not know that it would be wrong of me to go into the street and torture the first person I meet even if I happen to be so constituted that I should enjoy watching his sufferings?'[1] Ewing claimed that no one 'can seriously believe for an hour in the emergencies of daily life' that no moral judgement is true, and he went on to

[1] Ewing (1947: 30).

state his 'demand of a philosophy that it should be in accord with what we cannot possibly help believing in ordinary life.'[2]

Most philosophers will agree that this is too quick a refutation of moral error theory and that Ewing's general demand on philosophical theories suggests too easy a solution of many pressing philosophical problems. For example, it is plausible that in the emergencies of daily life we cannot help believe that we have free will, but this does not suffice to show that there is such a thing as free will. Neither does the fact that we rely routinely on inductive reasoning in ordinary life suffice to show that inductive reasoning is epistemically justified.

Ewing was certainly aware of such objections, but he held that the claim that there are no true moral judgements is simply less credible than many claims that entail its falsity, e.g., that torturing children for fun is morally wrong. This line of reasoning is the ethical analogue of G. E. Moore's defence of common sense against idealism and scepticism about the external world. Moore's strategy was to list a number of propositions that seemed to him comparatively more credible than the propositions idealists and sceptics offer in support of their views.[3] Now consider the following quick Moorean argument:

MP It is a fact that torturing children for fun is morally wrong.
MC Hence, there is at least one moral fact.

The Moorean premise (MP) and the Moorean conclusion (MC) are both inconsistent with standard moral error theory. (MC) clearly follows from (MP), so moral error theorists cannot dispute the argument's validity. Everything hangs on the credibility of (MP). As critics of error theory are quick to point out, (MP) and other propositions like it—e.g., that it is a fact that stealing is *pro tanto* morally wrong; that it is a fact that breaking promises is *pro tanto* morally wrong; that it is a fact that donating to charity is *pro tanto* morally right; etc.—seem highly credible. In particular, they seem comparatively more credible than the key premise in the moral error theorist's argument.[4]

[2] Ewing (1947: 32). Recall also Ross's claim that we apprehend that conscientiousness or benevolence is good with as complete certainty, directness and self-evidence as we ever apprehend anything (see Section 4.3).

[3] Moore (1959).

[4] Another kind of Moorean argument would go directly from (MP), via (MC), to the rejection of standard moral error theory, without appeal to the confidence with which we endorse (MP). But (MP) is too blatantly question-begging for that argument to have dialectical force.

Moral non-naturalists may argue that given (MP), we have to accept that moral facts are not queer. Alternatively, they can argue that moral facts are *prima facie* queer but that on reflection they no longer appear queer. When we consider premises like (MP), we realize that there are moral facts. In this respect, moral facts are like aardvarks, neutrinos, and impressionist paintings, which, as we saw in Chapter 5, may appear *prima facie* queer but no longer appear queer—or at any rate not queer enough to be judged unreal—when we reflect on how our beliefs about them fit in with the rest of our beliefs about the world.

In parallel with Moore's commonsensical challenge to idealism and scepticism about the external world, then, one might suggest that for someone who is undecided concerning the truth and falsity of moral error theory, it is rationally justifiable to believe the premise in which one's initial credence is comparatively higher.[5] So if one finds (MP) initially more credible than (P13), one can reject the fourth queerness argument. Moreover, if one finds (MP) comparatively more plausible than its negation, one is entitled to conclude that at least some premise in any valid argument for standard moral error theory is false, and one can therefore reject standard moral error theory wholesale.

7.2. A Debunking Response

It is not clear that the Moorean line of argument is equally forceful against moral error theory as against idealism and scepticism about the external world.[6] The obvious way for moral error theorists to respond to the Moorean argument is to offer debunking explanations of our moral beliefs, such as the one expressed in (MP). While Mackie did not consider Moorean arguments explicitly he did offer debunking explanations of why belief in moral facts 'has become established and is so resistant to criticisms.'[7] As we saw in Chapter 5, such explanations are profitably seen as the second step of the argument from queerness. Mackie's explanations

The Moorean argument considered in the main text is supposed to have dialectical force precisely because most people endorse (MP) and suchlike propositions with strong confidence.

[5] Huemer 2005: 116–17; Enoch 2011: 118–21. Cf. Nagel 1996: 115.

[6] See McPherson (2009) for a helpful discussion. As McPherson notes, Moore himself did not employ the Moorean arguments in ethics.

[7] Mackie 1977: 42.

appeal to a large extent on the social and evolutionary advantages of moral belief.[8]

Some critics of error theory have sought to explain morality in similar ways. For example, non-cognitivist Simon Blackburn agrees with cognitivist Mackie that part of the explanation of why moral thought and talk evolved and persist is their social usefulness as devices for solving coordination problems.[9] The thought is in brief that natural selection has tended to favour certain patterns of human behaviour, such as reciprocating favours; sticking to agreements; punishing perpetrators; parents looking out for their kin; and so on.[10] These natural selection processes have played a part in shaping our current systems of norms; they account for why we tend to believe, e.g., that there are reasons to return favours, keep promises, hold perpetrators responsible for their misdeeds, and for parents to look after their kin. Human beings will of course sometimes be tempted to violate some of these norms. Breaking promises and omitting to return favours often make sense from a narrowly egoistic perspective. Moral thought and talk enter the picture as social devices that serve to enforce compliance with these norms. We judge that those who fail to return favours and keep their promises act *morally wrongly*; they are liable to *moral blame*, i.e., to attitudes of resentment and dislike.

The thoughts that get expressed in moral discourse provide the 'pressures [that] need to exist if human beings are to meet their competing needs in a social, cooperative setting.'[11]

One of the great benefits of moral thought and discourse is that they enable some of these pressures to come from within individuals themselves, via internalizations of norms. Most people recognize a kind of authority in moral norms, which makes them feel *bound* to act in accordance with them. In Richard Joyce's words, moral thought and talk function both 'as a bulwark against weakness of will [and] as an interpersonal commitment device.'[12] In short, there is such a thing as moral thought and talk partly because '[w]e need [it] to regulate interpersonal relations, to

[8] Mackie 1977: 42–4, 107–15; 189–95; 232–5; 1985b.

[9] Blackburn 1993c: 168–70. See also Allan Gibbard (1990). Gibbard agrees with Blackburn that evolutionary considerations support non-cognitivism.

[10] The *locus classicus* here is Darwin's discussion in *The Descent of Man*, especially chapters 3 and 5.

[11] Blackburn 1993c: 168.

[12] Joyce 2006: 208.

control some of the ways in which people behave towards one another, often in opposition to contrary inclinations.'[13]

In fact, we should be a bit more careful here. Shaun Nichols has argued that claims like Blackburn's and Mackie's provide plausible explanations of why and how morality persists in human life. But the question of why and how people come to believe in the authority of moral norms in the first place calls in part for a different answer. Nichols suggests that a plausible answer is that fundamental moral norms originate in affective responses, such as the intense distress most people feel when witnessing suffering in others.[14]

Witnessing suffering in others tends to give rise to intense distress in most human beings and this is at least part of the explanation why most people are strongly motivated to enforce and comply with norms against harming innocents, such as animals and children. Reactive distress causally explains beliefs to the effect that violations of norms against harming are generalizably wrong.[15] This point is familiar from the psychological thesis in the characterization of moral projectivism in Chapter 1, according to which affective attitudes such as disapproval and approval causally explain experiences of moral wrongness and rightness as mind-independent features.

Debunking theories à la Mackie, Joyce, and Nichols have the advantage of predicting that certain moral beliefs will be held with a high degree of confidence, and they also explain why this is so. The explanation is that the regulative and coordinating functions they facilitate are of such vital importance to us, and that belief in some moral propositions, such as (MP), have a direct origin in affective attitudes. The hypothesis that moral belief stems partly from affective attitudes also explains why moral error theory is *emotionally* difficult to accept. When one considers the numerous atrocities committed in the past century it may feel sickening to maintain that none of them were in fact morally wrong, even to proponents of moral error theory.[16] Error theory about other matters, such as colour, numbers, causation, and so on, may be *intellectually* difficult to accept but

[13] Mackie 1977: 43.

[14] Nichols 2004, esp. 178–89.

[15] Nichols 2004: 180.

[16] Like Charles Pigden, many proponents of moral error theory may think of themselves as 'reluctant nihilists'. See Pigden (2007).

they do not face the same kind of emotional resistance. This goes some way to explain why reactions to error theory about morality are sometimes rather fierce, while reactions to error theories in other domains are less so.

As I have already mentioned, however, not all advocates of evolutionary debunking accounts of moral belief are error theorists. Simon Blackburn holds that such accounts support non-cognitivism rather than error theory or any other view according to which moral attitudes are primarily cognitive. Here is Blackburn:

> [I]t is the direct consequences of pressure on action that matter. Evolutionary success may attend the animal that helps those that have helped it, but it would not attend any allegedly possible animal that thinks it ought to help but does not. In the competition for survival it is what the animal *does* that matters. This is important, for it shows that only if values are intrinsically motivating is a natural story of their emergence possible (1993c: 168-9, Blackburn's emphasis).

In other words, it is deeds that matter and beliefs about what ought morally to be done and about what is morally required, etc., would be from the evolutionary perspective superfluous add-ons to the deeds and the desire-like states of mind that motivate them.

Blackburn is of course right that from the evolutionary perspective it is deeds that matter, or at least deeds that matter most. But this is not to say that evolutionary explanations of morality prompt us to go as far as to accept the internalist view that there is a necessary connection between moral judgement and motivation to act. As we saw in Chapter 2, the Humean hypothesis that much of morality, such as norms against harming, stem from affective feelings, such as the reactive distress of witnessing suffering in others, suffices to establish a reliable but contingent connection between moral judgement and motivation. Such a reliable but contingent connection seems to be all that is needed to make moral judgement a useful device for regulating and coordinating behaviour. It is not clear what, from the evolutionary perspective, would be gained by a necessary connection between moral judgement and motivation, where the motivation to act could anyway be overridden by competing concerns. And versions of internalism that postulate a necessary connection between moral judgement and *overriding* motivation to act seem implausibly strong; they would rule out the possibility of deliberately doing what one takes to be morally wrong.

Note that the Humean hypothesis tells us something about the aetiology of moral judgements, not about their meaning. The distress we tend to feel when witnessing others suffer explains why we believe, via projection of these attitudes, that inflicting harm on innocent people is wrong. But it does not mean that to judge such behaviour wrong is primarily to have or express such feelings or non-cognitive attitudes. Affective feelings of e.g. empathy provide motivation to act but we need cognitivist moral thought and talk to keep us in check and exercise pressure on others and ourselves when these feelings are overshadowed by egoistic or parochial concerns. Such overshadowing is likely to be frequent when resources are scarce and competition fierce, which has presumably been the case during most stages of human history. That is part of the reason why belief in objective moral requirements is evolutionarily advantageous. Beliefs about what one ought morally to do are thus socially useful devices and not superfluous add-ons. In his early defence of moral error theory, Mackie gave the following example:

> Suppose we approve of hard work: then if as well as a feeling of approval in our own minds there were an objective fact like 'hard work is good', such that everyone could observe the fact and such that the mere observation would arouse in him a like feeling of approval, and even perhaps stimulate him to work, we should eventually get what we want done: people would work hard. And since what we want does not exist in fact, we naturally construct it in imagination: we objectify our feelings so thoroughly that we completely deceive ourselves. I imagine that this is the reason why our belief in moral objectivity is so firm (1946: 82-3).

It is worth stressing here that what seems especially useful is belief in irreducibly normative reasons. That gives moral belief 'the authority required' for regulating interpersonal and intrapersonal behaviour.[17] For as we noted in Chapter 6, the normative question cannot be adequately answered by pointing out that some course of behaviour has the naturalistic property of being in accordance with some set of conventional norms, or being such as to promote desire satisfaction. So this argument has force not only against non-cognitivism but also against many versions of moral naturalism.[18]

[17] Mackie 1977: 34. Mackie speaks of 'objective validity' as that which gives moral belief the required authority.

[18] For elaboration of this point, see Joyce 2006: 190–209.

I have given only extremely rough summaries of careful elaborations of evolutionary explanations of morality that others have offered.[19] Defenders of the Moorean argument might protest that irrespective of the causal genesis of our beliefs in propositions like (MP) and (MC), we still hold them with great confidence because they seem if not self-evident, at least immensely plausible in their own right. Suppose, then, that the moral non-naturalist accepts debunking explanations of the kind that have been sketched here. Suppose, that is, that she accepts that our moral beliefs are the upshot of evolutionary and social pressures, but still maintains that there are irreducibly normative properties and facts and that some of our moral beliefs are true. For example, evolution may have favoured the belief that well-being is good. Nevertheless, the moral non-naturalist may hold, it is an irreducibly normative fact that well-being is good, and the evolutionary forces acting on our beliefs explain the correlation between the belief that well-being is good and the irreducibly normative fact that well-being is good.[20]

There are several things that error theorists can say in response. First, they can agree that debunking explanations of some kind of belief, i.e., explanations in which the putative truth of the content of that kind of belief plays no explanatory role, need not on their own cast doubt on the credibility of the content of that kind of belief. In that respect 'debunking' may be a misleading term. Error theorists can maintain that what undermines the credibility of the content of moral beliefs is one or more of the queerness arguments. The primary point of debunking accounts is to explain why we tend to have moral beliefs although they involve systematic mistakes and are uniformly false, and thereby to respond to Moorean arguments against moral error theory.

Second, error theorists can argue more offensively that to the extent that evolutionary debunking explanations of the kind we have sketched briefly are plausible, it seems overly dogmatic or epistemologically self-confident to maintain that our strongly held moral beliefs license ontological conclusions about moral properties and facts. At least it seems so if the ontological conclusions are grounded in our own confidence that certain moral propositions are true.

[19] See, for example, Churchland (2010); Hauser (2006); Joyce (2006); Kitcher (2011); Nichols (2004).

[20] For a response of this kind, see Enoch 2011: 167–76.

Third, moral error theorists can apply Occam's razor. If our moral practices and beliefs can be explained without appeal to irreducibly normative properties and facts, a theory that dispenses with such properties and facts will have the advantage of being in this respect the more ontologically parsimonious theory. This is so whether or not we presuppose a naturalistic ontology. The moral non-naturalist could try to downplay the significance of ontological parsimony. But given that considerations of ontological parsimony are commonly invoked in theory assessments elsewhere in philosophy and in the natural and social sciences, such a response seems desperate.

Moral non-naturalists may instead object that appeals to considerations of parsimony seem to be appeals to *norms*. Consequently, the moral error theorist's argument against the existence of some norms, e.g. moral norms, seems to involve a hidden appeal to other norms, which makes it smack of self-defeat.[21]

In response, the moral error theorist should begin by distinguishing between two relevant kinds of parsimony considerations. One says that there *are* no entities that are explanatorily dispensable. This is clearly not an appeal to a norm of any kind. Another kind of parsimony consideration says that we *should* not assume that there are entities that are explanatorily dispensable. This is in line with Occam's razor as ordinarily formulated. The error theorist should concede that appeals to Occam's razor are indeed appeals to a norm. But this norm is conventional and hence metaphysically unproblematic. To say that a theory T offers a more parsimonious explanation of some phenomenon than a distinct theory T' is not to say that the comparative parsimony of T is an irreducibly normative reason to prefer T to T'. It is just to say that T is in one respect preferable to T' according to a standard of theory assessment commonly accepted by many philosophers, naturalists and non-naturalists alike, and commonly adopted in many natural and social sciences, to wit, that T is preferable to T' if T makes fewer problematic assumptions, e.g., about ontology, without loss in explanatory power. The reason why parsimony considerations are commonly invoked in philosophy and the sciences may well be that such considerations track the truth. That is, if we apply parsimony considerations

[21] Cf. Sayre-McCord, 1988: 277f.

we tend to be more successful in acquiring true beliefs than if we do not apply parsimony considerations.[22]

Appeals to norms of parsimony are thus unproblematic from the moral error theorist's perspective. Error theorists cannot consistently maintain, of course, that there are irreducibly normative reasons to abide by norms of parsimony and therefore irreducible normative reasons to prefer moral error theory to moral non-naturalism. All they can say is that according to methodological norms of parsimony, moral error theory is preferable to moral non-naturalism, and that such norms are truth-tracking in the sense that applying them tends to render us having true beliefs.[23]

Much more can certainly be said about debunking accounts of moral belief, and much more has been said by others. I submit that it is a fair verdict that what we have said so far undermines the Moorean argument against moral error theory. In conjunction with the queerness argument defended in Chapter 6 we now have what seems like a rather strong argument from queerness. The remaining part of the book deals with contemporary challenges to moral error theory and its implications for moral thought and discourse.

[22] There are quietist theories that make fewer problematic assumptions about ontology than both moral non-naturalism and moral error theory, simply because they make no claims at all about ontology. While such theories are more parsimonious, they are deficient in other respects, particularly in that they do not address pertinent questions about moral ontology.

[23] See the discussions in Sections 8.2 and 8.3.

PART III
Defence

8

Ramifications of Moral Error Theory

We saw in Chapter 5 that the first and second queerness arguments—focusing on supervenience and knowledge, respectively—generalize beyond the moral and the normative. They have controversial implications in metaphysics and epistemology. The fourth queerness argument does not overgeneralize in this way since it targets irreducible normativity. However, some critics have argued that generalizing beyond the moral to the normative is problematic enough. In this chapter we shall consider three versions of this challenge. According to the first, queerness arguments against moral facts and moral reasons apply equally to hypothetical reasons (Section 8.1) and according to the second they apply equally to epistemic reasons (Section 8.2). In the course of the discussion of the second challenge we shall consider and reject a recent argument to the effect that we cannot believe the error theory. According to the third challenge, the rejection of irreducible normativity has problematic implications for the possibility of practical deliberation (Section 8.3).

These challenges can all be viewed as companions-in-guilt responses to the fourth queerness argument, for the claim in each instance is of course that if arguments for moral error theory rule out hypothetical reasons, epistemic reasons, or deliberation, they prove too much. As Mackie noted, the companions-in-guilt line of response 'is an important counter to the argument from queerness'[1] but the versions to be considered in this chapter are ones that Mackie and other moral error theorists have overlooked or not taken seriously enough.

[1] Mackie 1977: 39.

8.1. Error Theory and Hypothetical Reasons

We have found that the most powerful queerness argument targets irreducibly normative reasons. It is easy to see that the argument generalizes: those who accept it are committed to error theory not just about moral discourse but about any discourse that involves commitment to irreducibly normative reasons. Some critics have argued that this is an embarrassment for moral error theory. It has been argued that the fourth queerness argument applies to *hypothetical reasons*, i.e., reasons to take the means to one's ends. This is a potential problem for many moral error theorists, who have wanted to accept hypothetical reasons and have held that claims about hypothetical reasons are sometimes true. Consider Mackie:

> 'If you want X, do Y' (or 'You ought to do Y') will be a hypothetical imperative if it is *based on* the supposed fact that Y is, in the circumstances, the only (or the best) available means to X, that is, on a causal relation between Y and X. The reason for doing Y *lies in* its causal connection with the desired end, X (1977: 27–8, emphases added).

Later on, Mackie says that 'the reason for doing Y is *contingent upon* the desire for X by way of Y's being a means to X' and later still that the desire for X '*creates* the reason for doing Y'.[2]

One might ask with Jean Hampton what it means exactly to say that hypothetical reasons are 'contingent upon' desires.[3] That is a fair question. And it is not answered by Mackie's claims that hypothetical reasons are 'based on' or 'created by', desires, or that they 'lie in' desires. Clearly, error theorists cannot hold that there are irreducibly normative reasons to take the means to one's end.

Richard Joyce responds to Hampton's challenge by distinguishing wide-scope from narrow-scope imperatives. According to Joyce, error theorists do not accept the truth of claims like 'You ought to (ϕ

[2] Mackie 1977: 29, 75 (both emphases added). Mackie thinks that once we have dispensed with categorical reasons it will be of no particular consequence whether Y actually is a means to X, or whether the agent knows or merely believes (truly or falsely) that it is: 'In each of these cases, the statement that [the agent] has a reason, and ought to [Y], is a thoroughly intelligible implementation of the general meanings of the terms' (1977: 77). Cf. Joyce 2001: 53–4.

[3] Hampton 1998.

if you want X and ϕing is the best means of achieving X)' but they do accept the truth of claims like 'If (you want X and ϕing is the best means of achieving X), then you ought to ϕ'.[4] In the second, narrow-scope claim, ϕing is prescribed 'hypothetically'.[5] The imperative 'depends for its legitimacy' on your wanting X; if you do not want X, the imperative 'evaporates'.[6] But what about the 'ought' in the consequent in the narrow-scope claim?

We have said that error theorists find it puzzling how there can be irreducibly normative favouring relations between some fact, *F*, and certain courses of behaviour, for example between the fact that eating meat is detrimental to human and non-human well-being and sticking to a vegetarian diet. But why would such an irreducibly normative favouring relation be any the less puzzling whenever and because *F* is a fact about the agent's desires and about what would bring about satisfaction of those desires, or because a desire of the agent is a necessary condition for *F*'s being one relatum of the irreducibly normative favouring relation? The imperative in hypothetical imperatives may evaporate if the agent changes her desires, but similarly, the imperative not to eat meat may evaporate if it turns out that eating meat is in fact not detrimental to human and non-human well-being. So why would hypothetical reasons and imperatives be any the less metaphysically puzzling than categorical reasons and imperatives?[7] This is yet another fair question.

In response to all these questions, error theorists should deny that hypothetical reasons are properly understood in terms of an irreducibly normative favouring relation. According to error theory, hypothetical reasons claims are true only if they reduce to empirical claims about agents' desires and (actual or believed) efficient means of bringing about the satisfaction of these desires.[8] So for instance, the claim that there is hypothetical reason for some agent to ϕ can be true if and only if it reduces to the claim that ϕing will or is likely to bring about the satisfaction of some of the agent's desires. Hence hypothetical reasons thus understood are instances of what I have called reducible reasons (see Chapter 6). Note, however, that error theorists need not claim that all claims about hypothetical reasons

[4] Joyce 2001: 122. [5] Joyce 2001: 122. [6] Joyce 2001: 35.

[7] This question is posed in Bedke (2010).

[8] Cf. Wittgenstein's view, as discussed in Section 4.2.

claims are reducible to empirical claims about means-ends relations. Sometimes we might want to say that the fact that a person desires X and that that person's ϕing is an efficient means for bringing X about is an irreducibly normative reason for that person to ϕ. Such claims, just like moral claims, are uniformly false.

It might be objected that reducing claims about hypothetical reasons to empirical claims about agents' desires and means to bringing about their satisfaction, removes the normativity of claims about hypothetical reasons since the reduction involves no mention of facts counting in favour of certain courses of behaviour. That is true but from the error theorists' perspective it is just as it should be; it is the counting-in-favour-relation that is being reduced, and reducing claims about hypothetical reasons to empirical claims is the only way of saving them from being uniformly false.

A related objection is that since claims to the effect that some action will or is likely to bring about the satisfaction of some desire are empirical, it is a violation of ordinary language to say that such claims are claims about *reasons* in any ordinary sense of the term. But this objection can be safely dismissed. 'Reason' is notoriously ambiguous and there is clearly a sense of the term that fits the proposed understanding of hypothetical reasons. For instance, we might say that there is reason for Sleepy to have an extra cup of black coffee this evening. On one reading of this claim that in some contexts will be the correct one, it means only that Sleepy has some desire (e.g., a desire to stay up late) that would be satisfied, or would likely be satisfied, were he to have an extra cup of black coffee. This reductive reading of hypothetical reason claims allows that such claims are sometimes used to give advice. Often we advise a person about how to act simply by pointing to some desire she has and to how she could go about satisfying it.[9] But in so doing we need not also be claiming that the person has an irreducibly normative reason to act in that way or drop her desire.

To make it even clearer that hypothetical reason claims need not be irreducibly normative, consider the fact that we might say that there was reason for Hitler to invade Britain during the Second World War. Typically, this will mean only that Hitler had some desire (e.g., a desire to win the war) that would have been satisfied, or would likely have been satisfied, had he invaded Britain. Thus there clearly is a usage of 'reason' in ordinary

[9] I am indebted to anonymous reviewer for raising this issue.

language according to which the term merely signifies connections between agents' desires and means to bringing about their satisfaction.

8.2. Error Theory and Reasons for Belief

Perhaps the most popular move among those who pursue the companions-in-guilt line of response to the argument from queerness is to appeal to epistemic reasons, or reasons for belief.[10] Just as moral reasons are facts that favour certain courses of behaviour, epistemic reasons are facts that favour certain courses of doxastic behaviour, such as forming or suspending certain beliefs. For example, the fact that I now have a visual experience of a computer in front of me is a reason for me to believe that there is now a computer in front of me; the fact that astronomers report observations of cosmological redshift is a reason to believe that the universe expands; and so on. This suggests that there are important structural similarities between moral and epistemic reasons. As Philip Stratton-Lake puts it:

> The difference between [moral] and epistemic reasons is [...] that they warrant different things. [Moral] reasons warrant pro-attitudes and actions whereas epistemic reasons warrant beliefs. If, therefore, one has doubts about the normative (warranting) relation itself, these doubts could not be localized in such a way as to avoid scepticism about epistemic as well as [moral] reasons (2002: xxvi).[11]

Similarly, Matt Bedke argues that moral and epistemic reasons are structurally isomorphic and concludes that '[i]f the favouring relation is metaphysically suspect [in the moral domain], it is suspect in the epistemic domain as well'.[12] Philosophers who—like Stratton-Lake and Bedke—appeal to epistemic reasons in the companions-in-guilt response to the argument from queerness thus maintain that the favouring relation in both the moral and the epistemic domains is irreducibly normative.

Other philosophers maintain that the epistemic favouring relation is reducible to some evidential relation. Against such views, however, one

[10] See, e.g., Bedke (2010); Cuneo (2007); Scanlon (1998); Stratton-Lake (2002).

[11] Stratton-Lake focuses widely on *practical* reasons rather than moral reasons more narrowly, but that is inessential in the present context. It is also inessential Stratton-Lake speaks of a relation of warrant rather than favouring. He would agree that the relation of warrant is irreducibly normative.

[12] Bedke 2010: 56.

might raise worries that parallel Mackie's and other's objections to naturalism in ethics, namely that such views leave out the crucial element of normativity. For example, when we say that the fact that there are plenty of very old fossils around is a reason to believe that life has existed on Earth for more than 6000 years, we typically do not just mean to say that the fact there are very old fossils around stands in some evidential relation to the fact that life has existed on Earth for more than 6000 years, we mean (also) to say that because there is this evidence, one *should* believe that life has existed on Earth for more than 6000 years.[13] The general thought here is that just as the normative question of what one ought or has reason to *do* cannot be satisfactorily answered by adverting to some purely natural property, the normative question of what one ought or has reason to *believe* cannot be answered by adverting to some purely natural property either (see Section 6.1).

Moral error theorists can of course question the alleged parallels between moral and epistemic reasons and take issue with the claim that the favouring relation in epistemology is after all irreducibly normative, but here I shall not pursue this line.[14] Instead I shall grant to opponents of error theory the premise that epistemic reasons are facts that count in favour of certain beliefs, where the favouring relation is irreducibly normative. It seems, then, that moral error theorists who hold that there are no irreducibly normative favouring relations are committed to accept *epistemic error theory*. This view is the analogue of moral error theory. Let us grant, then, that epistemic reasons are irreducibly normative, that an epistemic fact is a fact that entails that there are epistemic reasons for some agent or agents to have various beliefs, and that first-order epistemic claims are claims about what there are epistemic reasons to believe. Just as moral error theory holds that there are no moral facts and that no first-order moral claim is true, epistemic error theory holds that there are no epistemic facts and that no first-order epistemic claim is true. That moral error theorists are committed to epistemic error theory should be no surprise since we have already noted that the argument against irreducibly normative reasons generalizes beyond the moral to any area of thought and discourse that involves irreducibly normative reasons. The

[13] Bedke 2010: 56 and 2012: 122–3.

[14] See Heathwood (2009) for a defence of the view that epistemic reasons but not moral reasons are naturalistically reducible. See Rowland (2013, sect. 2) for criticism.

question now is how problematic the generalization to the epistemic domain is for moral error theorists.

Terence Cuneo has recently explored the parallelisms between moral and epistemic reasons in great detail.[15] He lists three allegedly undesirable results of epistemic error theory, each of which he takes to provide sufficient grounds for rejection. I shall discuss each of them and argue that they are in the end not as problematic as Cuneo maintains.

'Epistemic error theory is either self-defeating or polemically toothless'

The first objection comes in the form of a dilemma: either epistemic error theory is self-defeating or it is polemically toothless. To uncover the first horn, recall that according to epistemic error theory, there are no epistemic reasons. But insofar as the error theorist claims that her arguments, e.g., the queerness arguments, are epistemic reasons to believe that there are no epistemic reasons for belief, the theory becomes patently self-defeating. In short, if the queerness arguments are correct and if error theory is true, there are no epistemic reasons to believe the error theory.[16]

The error theorist avoids the first horn of the dilemma by distinguishing between arguments to the effect that *p* is true and arguments to the effect that there are reasons to believe that *p*.[17] In particular, the error theorist is offering arguments to the effect that the error theory is true. She is not offering arguments to the effect that there are epistemic reasons to believe that the error theory is true.[18] She is thus not committed to the patently self-defeating position that there are epistemic reasons to believe that there are no epistemic reasons.

[15] Cuneo 2007.

[16] Cuneo 2007: 117–18. Other writers have also put forward this argument against moral error theory. For instance, Stratton-Lake holds that '[epistemic error theory] seems to undermine itself, for it [says] that we have reason to be sceptical about reasons, and it implies that it is false that we have reason to be sceptical about reasons' (2002b: xxv). See also Parfit 2011: 293, 522, 619.

[17] On this point, see also Danielsson and Olson (2007); Fletcher (2009); Leite (2007); Olson (2009).

[18] Matt Bedke raised the worry that some will think that no series of propositions amounts to an argument unless some epistemic relation holds between them. I take it that the idea is that a set of propositions amounts to an argument only if the propositions expressed in the premises favour taking up certain doxastic attitudes to the proposition expressed in the conclusion. That is not how I think about arguments. I take an argument to be a series of propositions such that the propositions expressed in the premises indicate (or purport to indicate) that the proposition expressed in the conclusion is true. I thus take arguments to involve relations between propositions and not relations between propositions and doxastic

But now Cuneo claims that if error theorists hold that there are no epistemic reasons to believe their theory, they are impaled on the second horn of the dilemma: epistemic error theory becomes 'polemically toothless in the [...] sense [that] [n]o one would make a rational mistake in rejecting it'.[19] But since error theorists are not in the business of offering arguments about what would be rational to believe or about what there is epistemic reason to believe there is no harm in conceding that error theory is toothless in *those* debates. What is important is that error-theoretical arguments have bite in debates on where the truth lies in metaethics and metaepistemology; these are the debates with which error theory is concerned. And given that the aim of metaethical and metaepistemological inquiry is to get at the truth, error theory is not polemically toothless in these debates.

We have noted several times already that the term 'reason' is notoriously ambiguous, but the point bears repeating and it is now relevant anew. Although error theorists are committed to denying that there are epistemic—i.e., irreducibly normative—reasons for belief, they can maintain that there are *other* senses of 'reason' in which it might well be true that there are reasons for some agents to believe certain propositions.[20] These senses pick out reducible reasons for belief. I shall discuss briefly two kinds of reducible reasons, both of which we have encountered before (see Sections 6.1, 6.3, and 8.1): hypothetical reasons and reasons reducible to correctness norms.

First, *hypothetical* reasons for belief. For the error theorist, to say that there are hypothetical reasons for some agent to believe that p is simply to say that that agent has some desire or end that would be fulfilled, or is likely to be fulfilled, were she to believe that p. For instance, for agents who want to have true beliefs on matters of metaethics there are hypothetical reasons to believe the error theory, since believing in the error theory would

attitudes. An argument is of course typically offered as a reason for taking up a certain doxastic attitude, but that is not to say that the argument itself involves an epistemic relation. We shall have recourse to these points later in this chapter.

[19] Cuneo 2007: 117.

[20] To clarify, I do not claim that Cuneo and other critics of epistemic error theory are committed to denying that 'reason' is ambiguous in the ways I claim. Note also that I do not suggest anything in the way of conceptual revision or reform. My claim is that the term 'reason (for belief)' as used in ordinary discourse is ambiguous in that it can signify either epistemic reasons for belief (of which there are none, according to error theorists) or reducible reasons for belief (of which there are plenty, according to error theorists). Thanks to Bart Streumer for pressing me on this point.

satisfy that desire. This claim is tolerable for the error theorist since it is not irreducibly normative; it simply ascribes to an agent a desire and specifies how it would be satisfied.

Second, error theorists can recognize reasons for belief that apply to some agents in virtue of their roles or in virtue of their being engaged in some rule-governed or goal-oriented activities. In such cases, for there to be reasons for beliefs is for there to be correctness norms associated with the relevant roles and activities. For example, one might hold that it is correct for chaplains qua occupying the role of chaplains to believe the essentials of the Bible, in which case it is correct for chaplains to believe that God exists (irrespectively of whether it is actually true that God exists, and irrespectively of whether there are undefeated arguments to the effect that God exists). This may be expressed by saying that there are reasons for chaplains to believe that God exists. But this means only that it is correct for chaplains qua chaplains to believe that God exists. One might also hold that since the goal of many intellectual endeavours, e.g., metaethics and metaepistemology, is to get at the truth, it is correct for people engaged in such activities to have true beliefs on the subject matter, in which case there are reasons for metaethicists and metaepistemologists qua being engaged in these endeavours, to believe the error theory. For chaplains and metaethicists and metaepistemologists to fail to comply with those reasons is simply to fail to live up to standards of what it takes to be successful in their respective roles or activities. Such claims too are tolerable to error theorists since they are not irreducibly normative.

To sum up, the charge that epistemic error theory is self-defeating rests on the assumption that arguments to the effect that *p* amount to arguments to the effect that there are epistemic reasons to believe that *p*. But error theorists can distinguish between arguments to the effect that *p* and arguments to the effect that there are epistemic (irreducibly normative) reasons to believe that *p*. In particular, they can hold that their error-theoretical arguments are arguments to the effect that the error theory is true and not to the effect that there are epistemic reasons to believe the error theory. This also shows why there is no harm in conceding that epistemic error theory is polemically toothless in debates about what there are epistemic reasons to believe.[21]

[21] Richard Rowland (2013) has recently argued that if epistemic error theory is true, no one knows anything. This is because knowledge entails epistemic justification (Rowland 2013, sect. 2). But in order to pose a problem for epistemic error theory here, it must be established

'Epistemic error theory implies that there can be no arguments for anything'

Before coming to Cuneo's second 'undesirable result' I shall discuss the third since that can be dealt with in a way similar to the first. Cuneo claims that (A) '[a] statement's being offered as evidential support for a conclusion [. . .] is just a matter of its being offered as a *reason* for accepting that conclusion'.[22] By 'reason' Cuneo means epistemic (i.e., irreducibly normative) reason. From (A), Cuneo infers that (B) 'if [epistemic error theory] were true, it would be impossible that there were premises of an argument that provide evidential support for its conclusion'.[23] And from this—along with what he claims to have established as the first 'undesirable result'—he concludes that (C) '[e]ither epistemic [error theory] is self-defeating or it implies that there could be no arguments for anything'.[24]

We have seen in this chapter that epistemic error theory is not self-defeating. The tenability of (B) and of the second disjunct of (C) depend on the tenability of (A), i.e. that evidential support for *p* amounts to epistemic reasons to believe that *p*. Clearly, my response to the claim that epistemic error theory is self-defeating rests on a distinction between arguments to the effect that *p*, or evidential support for *p*, and epistemic reasons to believe that *p*. Cuneo may implicitly reject that distinction when he claims that evidential support for *p* just is a reason to accept that *p*, and he certainly seems to reject it when he notes that he uses 'the terms "evidence" and "(epistemic) reasons" more or less interchangeably'.[25] The basic disagreement, then, concerns whether the notion of evidence, or the evidential support relation, is itself irreducibly normative.

I concede that in colloquial contexts 'reason to believe that *p*' and 'evidence that *p*' are sometimes used interchangeably but there are plausible

the kind of epistemic justification that knowledge requires is irreducibly normative. But one might argue that for a subject to be epistemically justified in holding some belief, it suffices that the subject has some evidence that what she believes is true. Provided that evidence is not an irreducibly normative notion (see the next subsection), epistemic error theory does not imply that no one knows anything. Alternatively, one might hold that for a subject to be epistemically justified in holding some belief is simply for that belief to be reliably caused, where being reliably caused is a matter of meeting some non-normatively specified standard of reliability.

[22] Cuneo 2007: 121, Cuneo's emphasis.

[23] Cuneo 2007: 121.

[24] Cuneo 2007: 121.

[25] Cuneo 2007: 192, n. 12.

explanations of this that do not conflict with epistemic error theory.[26] First, in these contexts we might believe (mistakenly, according to error theory) that the fact that there is evidence that *p* is an irreducibly normative reason to believe that *p*.[27] But this does not establish that evidence is normative since—as we have seen already—facts that are reasons need not themselves be normative. Second, 'reason to believe that *p*' and 'evidence that *p*' might sometimes be used interchangeably because we believe that there are reducible reasons, of the kind discussed above, to believe in accordance with evidence with respect to whether *p*. That is, we believe that believing in accordance with evidence with respect to whether *p* in these contexts would satisfy some desire, or be correct according to the norms of a role we occupy or an activity we engage in. Clearly, this does not show that the notion of evidence is irreducibly normative.

Tom Kelly (2006; 2007) distinguishes between normative and non-normative notions of evidence and maintains that there is an everyday notion of evidence that is normative. Kelly writes:

> [O]n the view that evidence has no normative force of its own, it is mysterious why an explicit judgement to the effect that one's evidence strongly supports some proposition typically results in a belief that that proposition is true (2007: 468–9).

The alleged mystery dissolves as soon as we take into account a point just made: Explicit judgements to the effect that one's evidence strongly supports *p* typically result in belief that *p* because, typically, when we assess evidence for and against *p* we do so because we want to know whether *p*, we are interested in whether *p*, and we believe that were we to believe in accordance with evidence with respect to whether *p*, we would come to know whether *p*.[28] Note also that the idea that evidence has

[26] The term 'epistemic reason' is probably not frequent in colloquial contexts, but it is likely that the concept of epistemic reasons is present in ordinary thought and talk.

[27] Epistemic error theorists owe their opponents an explanation of why this mistaken belief has come about. I will not attempt to give such an explanation here, but given that beliefs based on evidence are in general evolutionarily advantageous, a debunking explanation that parallels the one about moral belief sketched in Section 7.1 does not seem far-fetched.

[28] Matt Bedke raised the question why there is no parity when we realise that certain beliefs would further other ends. Suppose you want to be free of stress from the thought of mortality and that you think that if you believe in an afterlife you will be free of it. Why does not this result in belief in an afterlife? Why does evidence play a role that these considerations do not? A plausible answer is that this is because it is so obvious that your thinking that believing in an afterlife will make you free of stress from the thought of mortality in no way indicates that the belief in an afterlife is true. Since believing that *p* involves the attitude of

'normative force' does not license the conclusion that evidence is normative. Compare: The idea that pain has normative force in the sense that the fact that an action would bring about pain is a reason against performing the action does not license the conclusion that pain is normative. We return to this point presently.

Kelly also asks us to consider

> a standard Bayesian explication of evidence, according to which to treat something as confirming evidence is to treat it as a reason to increase one's confidence that that hypothesis is true, while to treat something as disconfirming evidence is to treat it as a reason to decrease one's confidence. Given such an explication, there is an internal connection between recognizing something as evidence and recognizing it as a reason to change one's present view (2007: 467–8).

But this does not show that the concept of evidence is normative in any sense that would spell trouble for error theorists. That is, it does not show that the concept of evidence is irreducibly normative. In fact, Kelly's point serves to illustrate a point that has been made elsewhere in this book. Revising one's beliefs appropriately in the light of new evidence is correct according to the standards of Bayesianism, so there is in that sense reason to revise one's beliefs appropriately in the light of new evidence. Error theorists can thus grant an internal connection between recognizing something as evidence and recognizing it as a reducible reason to change one's present view. But according to error theory, there are no irreducibly normative reasons to revise one's beliefs in the light of new evidence. Error theorists who want to recommend compliance with standards of Bayesian belief revision can at most maintain that it tends to enhance cognitive success, i.e. that agents who revise their beliefs appropriately in the light of new evidence tend to have a higher proportion of true to false beliefs than they would otherwise have.

In distinguishing between on the one hand arguments to the effect that *p* or evidential support for *p* and on the other hand epistemic reasons to believe that *p*, I have relied on a non-normative notion of evidence that Kelly calls *indicator evidence*: *q* is evidence that *p* just in case *q* reliably indicates that *p*.[29] On my understanding of this notion—which may not overlap perfectly with Kelly's—indicator evidence can be logically

taking *p* to be true, it is normally difficult to base one's belief that *p* on something that one does not take to indicate that *p* is true.

[29] Kelly 2006: §3; 2007: 469–71.

conclusive, in which case the premises of a sound deductive argument are indicator evidence for its conclusion. It can also take the form of inductive or abductive arguments.

It is true that in order to determine whether some argument is a *strong* inductive or abductive argument one has to invoke norms of theory assessment, but as we saw in the preceding chapter, these norms are not irreducibly normative. They are conventional methodological norms typically adopted by scientists and philosophers in their professional activities. Hence error theorists can maintain that it is not in principle more difficult to determine whether some inductive or abductive argument is a *strong* argument than to determine whether some move in chess is a *good* move. But as noted previously, error theorists will have to concede that there is no irreducibly normative reason to accept the standards of theory assessment and inference rules typically adopted by scientists and philosophers, e.g., inference to the best explanation, rather than some other standard or inference rule, e.g., 'inference to the worst explanation'. Once again, error theorists can at most make the pragmatic claim that inference to the best explanation and other kinds of widely accepted inference rules and standards of theory assessment are better than the known alternatives at tracking the truth. This parallels the way in which moral error theory recognizes the wrongness of torture relative to UN declarations, but rejects irreducibly normative reasons to comply with such declarations. Error theorists can maintain that complying with UN declarations is more conducive to some desired end, such as the maintenance of respect for human life, than is non-compliance with UN declarations.

At this point one might worry that epistemic error theory has made itself otiose. If claims about evidence are naturalistically kosher, what is the error that permeates first-order epistemic discourse and why doesn't epistemic error theory collapse into epistemic naturalism?[30]

In response, it is worth pausing to recapitulate the dialectic. Critics of moral error theory argue that moral and epistemic reasons are alike in that the favouring relation in both ethics and epistemology is irreducibly

[30] Terence Cuneo, Hallvard Lillehammer, and Folke Tersman have all raised this worry. Matt Bedke raised the question why it matters to error theorists if claims about evidence are after all irreducibly normative. Could they not say simply that if they are, this just means that yet another area of thought and discourse is caught in the dragnet of error theory? If error theorists took this line they would be in the unfortunate position of subscribing to a theory according to which it is impossible to claim truly that there is evidence that the theory is true.

normative. For the sake of argument, I have granted the critics this view. Now, a common view in first-order epistemic discourse is that there are epistemic reasons to believe in accordance with evidence. As I have argued in this subsection, epistemic error theory holds that claims about evidence are not irreducibly normative, whereas claims to the effect that there are epistemic reasons to believe in accordance with evidence are.

The error in first-order epistemic discourse is precisely the supposition that there are epistemic, i.e., irreducibly normative, reasons to believe anything. Compare: Moral error theory holds that it is a non-normative claim that some act is an act of torture but that it is a normative claim that there are moral reasons not to torture. The latter kind of claim is never true. Epistemic error theory holds that it is a non-normative claim that a proposition, *q*, is evidence that a distinct proposition, *p*, is true but that it is a normative claim that *q* is an epistemic reason to believe *p*. The latter kind of claim is never true.

'Epistemic error theory rules out the possibility of epistemic merits and demerits'

Cuneo's second objection is that if epistemic error theory is true, none of our beliefs can be based on reasons and therefore none of our beliefs can display epistemic merits of being justified, warranted, rational, and the like. Once again, the first step of this argument equivocates on the slippery term 'reason'. Again, what error theorists deny is simply the existence of irreducibly normative favouring relations. Error theorists may well maintain that according to the standards of being a responsible believer, it is correct to believe that *p* only if one has sufficient evidence that *p*. Believing that *p* while lacking evidence that *p*, e.g., as an *idée fixe* or as a result of wishful thinking, is to fail to meet the standards of being a responsible believer (with respect to whether *p*).

It might be objected that to call someone a responsible (or irresponsible) believer is to commend (or criticize) that agent in a way that presupposes irreducibly normative reasons. Plausibly, when we charge a person with being epistemically or morally irresponsible we mean to say not only that the person fails to meet some standard of responsibility, but also that there are reasons for that person to change her ways and meet the standard in question. But it is far from clear that the only proper use of the term '(ir) responsible' is one that invokes irreducibly normative reasons. The error theorist can maintain that she uses 'responsible' (and 'irresponsible') in a purely descriptive fashion that indicates that the agent meets (or fails to meet) the standard for being a responsible believer, where the standard for being a responsible believer can be cashed out in purely descriptive terms. Such a standard might involve not consciously believing contradictions; believing the logical implications of one's beliefs if and when one contemplates these beliefs and the logical relations between them; believing only propositions one takes to be supported by evidence; and so on.[31] According to this purely descriptive use of the term 'responsibility', the norms associated with epistemic responsibility are comparable to those of etiquette and chess.

To give an analogy meant to show that such a purely descriptive use of the term 'responsible' is not an *ad hoc* stipulation, suppose that the standard for being a responsible mafioso involves not letting squealers go unpunished. Then to call someone a responsible mafioso is not necessarily to commend his behaviour but simply to make the descriptive claim that that agent does not fail to punish squealers and therefore meets the standard of being a responsible mafioso. Similarly, to call someone an irresponsible believer is not necessarily to reproach her for failing to comply with epistemic reasons but simply to make the descriptive claim that she fails to meet the standards of being a responsible believer. Error theory, then, does not rule out the possibility of standards of epistemic merit and demerit. It says that in order for claims about epistemic merit and demerit to be true, they must be understood as purely descriptive claims. Error theory does rule out, of course, irreducibly normative reasons to display these merits and avoid the demerits.

Cuneo also claims that epistemic error theory invites a Moorean-style paradox of the following sort:

(M) Epistemic error theory is true, but there is no (epistemic) reason to believe it.[32]

[31] One might object that to fail to meet such standards is to violate requirements of rationality and that such requirements entail irreducibly normative reason to comply with them. But it is in fact highly doubtful whether there are irreducibly normative reasons to comply with rational requirements. For an influential argument to the effect that rationality is not normative in this sense, see Kolodny (2005). Broome (2007) is officially agnostic on the matter; he concludes that he is unable to find an argument that establishes that rationality is normative.

[32] Cuneo 2007: 118.

But as long as the distinction between arguments to the effect that a proposition is true and arguments to the effect that there are epistemic reasons to believe that proposition is kept in mind there is from the point of view of error theory no paradoxical nature of (M) to be recognized. Again, if epistemic error theory is true there are no epistemic reasons to believe anything, including the theory itself.

Critics might insist that (M) is surrounded by an air of paradox that calls for explanation. Perhaps it is embarrassment enough for epistemic error theory that by the theory's own lights a claim such as (M) 'cannot even rise to the level of paradox.'[33] But provided that the aforementioned ambiguities of the term 'reason' are appreciated such an explanation is available to epistemic error theorists. They can hold that a speaker who acknowledges acceptance of the first conjunct of (M) conveys that there are, from the speaker's first-person perspective, grounds on the basis of which she accepts it. In other words, she conveys that there are arguments to the effect that epistemic error theory is true and on the basis of which she accepts the proposition that epistemic error theory is true. The speaker conveys this because if she failed to believe that there are such arguments she would believe a proposition she does not take to be supported by evidence and she would thus fail to meet the standard of being a responsible believer, as described above.

Thus, so as long as 'reason' in (M) means something like 'argument or evidence to the effect that the proposition expressed in the first conjunct is true', the air of paradox surrounding (M) is explained by the fact that anyone who accepts (M) fails to be a responsible believer (with respect to whether epistemic error theory is true). But again, whether a speaker does or does not meet the standards of being a responsible believer is, according to error theory, a purely descriptive, non-normative matter.

Epistemic error theory and the normativity of belief

We have seen that much of Cuneo's arguments against epistemic error theory rely on the claim that there is an intimate link between evidence that *p* and reasons to believe that *p*. This suggests that claims about evidence are themselves normative claims. In response, I have argued that it has yet to be shown that evidence is normative, and that even if there is a normative

[33] Cuneo 2007: 119.

notion of evidence there is also a non-normative notion to which the epistemic error theorist can appeal in order to distinguish between evidence or arguments to the effect that *p*, and reasons to believe that *p*. But perhaps there is an intimate tie between reasons for belief and the concept of belief, which makes the concept of belief itself—and belief ascriptions themselves—normative. This is a view that has become increasingly popular in recent literature and it is also one with which Cuneo expresses sympathy although he does not pursue it in detail.[34] To have a name for it we might call it *normativism* about belief.

Normativists might hold that belief ascriptions are constitutively normative, to the effect that ascribing to some agent A the belief that *p* is not only to ascribe to A the attitude of taking it to be the case that *p*, but also to claim that A is subject to certain norms to the effect that there is reason for A, for example, not to believe simultaneously that not-*p*; that there is reason for A not to disbelieve anything that she believes follows logically from *p*; that there is reason for A no longer to believe that *p* in the face of strong evidence that not-*p*; and so on. According to normativists, norms such as these serve to distinguish belief from other propositional attitudes that involve the attitude of *taking it to be the case that*, such as conjecture, imagining, supposition, wishful thinking, and the like.

According to normativism, then, belief ascriptions entail claims about what there is reason for agents to believe and not to believe. If these reasons are irreducibly normative, normativism implies that according to epistemic error theory no belief ascriptions are true. This would indeed be an undesirable result for epistemic error theorists.

The simplest and most plausible response on behalf of the epistemic error theorist is to agree with the normativists that norms of the kind mentioned above are distinctive of belief and belief ascriptions. But the error theorist should insist that these are correctness norms that do not entail irreducibly normative reasons. In order to distinguish belief from other attitudes such as conjecture, imagining, supposition, wishful thinking, and the like, it is not necessary to assume that the norms associated

[34] Cuneo 2007: 122. For recent defences of normativism about belief, see e.g. Shah and Velleman (2005); Wedgwood (2007); Karlander (2008); Shah and Evans (2012). For recent critiques, see, e.g., Bykvist and Hattiangadi (2007); Steglich-Petersen (2008); Gluer and Wikforss (*forthcoming*).

with belief ascriptions entail irreducibly normative reasons; it suffices to assume that they state what is required for an attitude to count as belief.

Above I suggested that someone who believes that *p* although she does not take *p* to be sufficiently supported by evidence, or even in the face of strong contrary evidence, might fail to meet the standards of being a responsible believer (with respect to *p*). We see now that an agent who clings to the belief that *p* in the face of strong evidence that not-*p* might not only fail to meet the standard of being a responsible believer (with respect to *p*), but also of believing that *p* in the first place. She might rather be engaged in wishfully thinking that *p*. If she repeatedly violates this norm, and others associated with the standard of belief, not only with respect to her belief that *p*, she might be considered to possess (very) few beliefs and possibly to possess no beliefs at all. But none of this suggests that ascribing to an agent the belief that *p* entails ascribing to that agent an irreducibly normative reason to give up the belief that *p* in the face of strong evidence that not-*p*.

By way of analogy, suppose a football player (who is not a goalkeeper) picks up the ball with her hands during play. Since she is violating a norm of football she is not in that instance playing football or perhaps she is playing outrageously poorly, relative to the rules and objectives of football. If she repeatedly violates this norm and others associated with the game of football she will be considered not to be playing football at all.[35] It is obvious that relative to the rules of football, there are reasons for players (who are not goalkeepers) not to pick up the ball with their hands during play. Similarly, relative to the norms of belief, there are reasons for agents not to cling to the belief that *p* in the face of strong evidence that not-*p*. But this only means that if an agent violates this norm she might not be counted as believing that *p* (rather than, e.g., wishfully thinking that *p*). There need be no suggestion that belief ascriptions entail irreducibly normative reasons. Epistemic error theorists are thus not committed to the arguably unpalatable result that no belief ascriptions are true.[36]

[35] Jamie Dreier gives a similar argument in response to the normativist challenge against metaethical expressivism. See Dreier 2002: 140–3.

[36] There is also another response to the objection. Suppose that normativists are right that the property of being a belief is irreducibly normative. If so, the property of being a belief supervenes on some other property, presumably some psychological property. Error theorists could then concede that while there is no property of being a belief, and consequently no true belief ascriptions, there are psychological properties on which the property of being a belief supervenes. That there are such psychological properties and consequently that there

Can we believe the error theory? Yes, we can!

Bart Streumer has recently argued that we cannot believe the error theory.[37] Somewhat surprisingly, he does not mean this as a criticism of error theory. Streumer holds both that the error theory is true and that the fact that we cannot believe it provides error theorists with undermining responses to many challenges against their view. However, his argument for the conclusion that we cannot believe the error theory is problematic in several ways.

Streumer holds, as I do, that a plausible error theory cannot be restricted to the moral domain; it must be an error theory about all normative judgements. His argument that we cannot believe such a theory is based on the following two premises:

(B1) We cannot fail to believe what we believe to be entailed by our own beliefs.

(B2) We cannot have a belief while believing that there is no reason for this belief.[38]

It is easy to see why, if (B1) and (B2) are true, we cannot believe the error theory. By (B1), if we believe the error theory, we cannot fail to believe that there is no reason to believe the error theory. By (B2), we cannot believe that the error theory is true and at the same time believe that there is no reason to believe the error theory.[39] Therefore, we cannot believe the error theory.

Let us note first that (B1) is highly dubious. Consider the preface paradox.[40] I believe about each sentence in this book that it contains no typographical error, since I have gone over the text many times and since colleagues and reviewers have read it carefully. I believe that if it is true about each sentence in the book that it contains no errors, there are no

can be true ascriptions of them, seem good enough. Alternatively, normativists could deny that the irreducibly normative property of being a belief supervenes on other properties. But then normativism about belief may be rejected by appeal to the principle that it is a conceptual truth that the normative supervenes on other properties. For an argument against normativism about the mental along these lines, see Steglich-Petersen (2008). Thanks to Jens Johansson for discussion here.

[37] Streumer (2013b: 195–6).

[38] Streumer (2013b: 196).

[39] By 'reasons for belief', Streumer means considerations that favour beliefs, where the favouring relation is irreducibly normative.

[40] Makinson (1965).

errors in the book. I do not believe the latter, however. Since books without typographical errors are extremely rare I believe that this one does contain them. I thus fail to believe what I believe is entailed by my own beliefs.

Streumer might respond that in this case I do not *fully* believe about every sentence in the book that it contains no error and/or that I do not fully believe that the book contains errors, and (B1) and (B2) should be read as claims about full belief.[41] It is not clear how and why this helps, however. Few defenders of error theory are as certain that the error theory is true as they are that 2+2=4 is true, or that *p or not-p* is true. Presumably, therefore, full belief should in this context not be understood as belief to degree 1, but belief to a high degree (whatever degree that is exactly). But then the preface paradox still stands. I can believe to a high degree about each sentence in this book that it contains no typographical errors and at the same time fail to believe that there are no typographical errors in the book.

Now consider (B2) and recall that my response to the objection that epistemic error theory is self-undermining was that while there are no reasons to believe the error theory, there are arguments to the effect that the theory is true. I thus hold that I can base my belief that the error theory is true on the argument from queerness, while maintaining that there are no reasons for belief.

According to Streumer,

> [...] reasons for belief are considerations that we *base* our beliefs on, and we cannot base a belief on a consideration without making at least an implicit normative judgement. Suppose that I base my belief that Socrates was mortal on evidence about human beings' mortality. In that case, I cannot see the evidence as merely causing me to have this belief, or as merely explaining why I have this belief. I must also make at least an implicit normative judgement about the relation between this evidence and this belief: I must take this evidence to support, or to justify, or to count in favour of this belief (2013b: 198, Streumer's emphasis).

However, Streumer offers little more than appeal to intuition and an example in support of the claim that whenever we base a belief on some consideration, this involves at least an implicit normative judgement. Note that even if we grant that this is true, it is presumably a highly unobvious truth. One could thus base one's belief that the error theory is true

[41] Streumer 2013b: 196

on some consideration, e.g., the argument from queerness, without realizing that in doing so one makes a normative judgement. Hence, this argument fails to show that we cannot believe the error theory. But of course, if we grant the truth of the claim that basing a belief on some consideration involves a normative judgement, we must conclude that belief in the error theory involves an inconsistency, albeit unobviously so.

But it seems to me that we should not grant it. First, consider the formation of belief on the basis of perception. Such processes of belief formation are typically spontaneous and involuntary, and it seems questionable that they involve normative judgements even implicitly. Small children and non-human animals form beliefs in the same way although they presumably lack the relevant normative thoughts.[42] Secondly, in the quoted passage, Streumer claims that if I base my belief that Socrates is mortal on evidence about human beings' mortality, I must take this evidence to support, justify, or count in favour of the belief. Insofar as there is an argument here, I believe it is based on an equivocation. 'Belief' sometimes refers to the *attitude* of belief and sometimes to the *thing (proposition) believed*. Reasons for beliefs are considerations that favour the attitude of belief. When we base a belief on some evidence, we need only judge that there is an evidential relation between the evidence and the proposition believed. We need not make any judgement at all about a relation between the evidence and the attitude of belief, other than a judgement about a relation that is entirely parasitic on the judgement about the relation between the evidence and the proposition believed. As Streumer agrees, the evidential relation between the evidence and the proposition believed is not irreducibly normative.[43] It is therefore difficult to see that I make an irreducibly normative judgement when I base a belief of mine on some evidence.

I can therefore base my belief that the error theory is true on the argument from queerness, without judging that this argument favours my attitude of believing that the error theory is true. I can thus maintain that while there are arguments on which I base my belief that the error theory is true, there are no irreducibly normative reasons for the attitude of

[42] I am indebted to Matt Bedke for this point.

[43] See Streumer 2013b: 205, n. 23. Streumer must agree that the evidential relation is not irreducibly normative since he holds that there is evidence that the error theory is true. If the judgement that there is evidence that the error theory is true were irreducibly normative, it would, by the theory's own lights, be false. It would then be difficult to see how Streumer could argue that the error theory is true.

believing that the error theory is true. Hence we can indeed believe the error theory.

8.3. Error Theory and Deliberation

Suppose I can spend the afternoon in one of the following two ways. I can either read a book on a topic that is relevant to my research project, or I can attend a seminar on a topic not relevant to my research but which I find interesting. Reading the book would be conducive to making progress on my current project. Attending the seminar would enlighten me on a topic with which I am not very familiar. I realize that I cannot with any seriousness both read the book and attend the seminar, so therefore I need to make up my mind about how to spend the afternoon. To that end I need to engage in deliberation.

David Enoch has argued that a serious problem for error theory resides in this everyday scenario. The problem is that deliberation presupposes irreducibly normative properties and facts. So if one rejects irreducibly normative properties and facts, one rejects deliberation. This seems to be a ramification of error theory that would make error theorists rather handicapped in many everyday situations. But is it really true that deliberation presupposes irreducibly normative properties and facts?

According to Enoch, deliberation involves *commitment* to there being irreducibly normative reasons.[44] Enoch is careful to point out that the commitment need not be understood as explicit belief, and it is even compatible with explicit rejection of irreducibly normative properties and facts, in which case the deliberator is being inconsistent. So what is meant by 'commitment' here? To give an example which is not Enoch's but which parallels his, we might say that in believing that the chair in my office will not give way to my bodily weight because it has never done so in the past, I am committed to an inductive inference rule that says that in reasoning about future events it is correct to rely on past experiences and assume that (*ceteris paribus*) the future will resemble the past, or something to that effect. Now, consider the statement 'I believe that the chair in my office will not give way to my bodily weight because it has never done so in the past, but I reject all inductive inference rules in reasoning about future events.'

[44] Enoch 2011: 74.

This sounds clearly inconsistent in that I claim to rely on an instance of a rule whose general application I go on to reject. Compare this to the following statement: 'I am deliberating whether to read a book or attend a seminar, but I do not believe there are any irreducibly normative reasons.' If deliberation really did somehow commit me to there being irreducibly normative reasons in the way my reasoning about the chair in my office commits me to inductive inference rules, the second statement should sound just as inconsistent as the first. But at least to my ear, the second does not sound inconsistent at all.

Enoch thinks the second statement is inconsistent because he holds that in deliberating one is trying to find out what it makes most sense to do.[45] And the question of what it makes most sense to do is an instance of the normative question; what it makes most sense to do is what there is most irreducibly normative reason to do. Enoch backs this up by appeal to phenomenological claims about what it feels like to deliberate. Deliberating, Enoch claims, is akin to trying to answer a factual question. In both cases the objective is to come up with the right answer.[46]

Enoch may be right that deliberation is akin to trying to answer a factual question and he may be right that deliberation sometimes aims at determining what it makes most sense to do. But it seems to me that the question one is trying to answer in deliberation is often what one most wants (to do), or most desires (to do). Given the complexities of many everyday situations, this can be a very challenging question. Consider again my choice of how to spend the afternoon. I desire to make progress on my current project and I also desire to be enlightened on a topic with which I am not very familiar. In deliberating I am trying to decide what I most desire. It is true that once I have taken into account all the complexities and decided that, say, my stronger desire is to make progress on my current project, it is still an open question what I *should* do, what there is most irreducibly normative reason for me to do. And the error theorist of course answers that there is nothing I should do in this sense, since there are no irreducibly normative reasons. But I cannot see that this somehow impugns or makes futile my deliberation about how to spend the afternoon, where my objective is to find out how I most desire to spend it. From my first person deliberative perspective, the need to arrive at a choice

[45] Enoch 2011: 72. [46] Enoch 2011: 73.

would seem no less pressing. So it seems to me that many everyday cases of deliberation require only reflection on one's desires and their comparative strengths, and do not involve commitment to irreducibly normative reasons.

But according to Enoch this would turn deliberation into an arbitrary affair. 'Deliberation—unlike mere picking—is an attempt to eliminate arbitrariness by discovering (normative) reasons and it is impossible in a believed absence of such reasons to be discovered.'[47] But once I have decided that my stronger desire is to make progress on my current project, it does not seem arbitrary to choose to spend the afternoon reading the book rather than attending the seminar. It might ultimately be an arbitrary matter that I have the desires I in fact have, but given that I do have these desires there need be nothing arbitrary about my choice. By way of analogy, consider (regulative) rules of football. It is in a sense arbitrary what these rules are, but it is not arbitrary for referees to make decisions based on them. For example, it is in a sense arbitrary that goalkeepers are not allowed to pick up the ball by hand when it has been played by a teammate. (After all, until fairly recently, this was not against the rules!) But given that this is now a rule it is not arbitrary for referees to award a free kick to the opponent team when this happens.

Critics of error theory might still demur, however. They might protest that taking deliberation to be a matter of finding out what one most wants or most strongly desires, makes deliberation an implausibly myopic and inward-looking project. But deliberation—or at least vital instances of deliberation, as for example when one tries to draw up life plans—is a markedly outward-looking project. To use Enoch's aforementioned phrase, one is trying to discover what makes most sense for one to do.

Let us note first that even if deliberation about what one desires most strongly is inward- rather than outward-looking, it need not be myopic since among the things one desires most strongly might be the weal and woe of others. But let us for the sake of argument assume that what has been said so far does not get the error theorist off the hook. Let us assume, that is, that Enoch is right that deliberation is essentially about discovering what there are irreducibly normative reasons for one to do. An obvious response from the error theorist that Enoch anticipates is that this only

[47] Enoch 2011: 74.

establishes that deliberation presupposes (tacit) *belief* in irreducibly normative reasons. In this way error theorists can hold that deliberation is indeed possible but based on an illusion. Similarly, nihilists about free will might argue that deliberation about what to do requires that we (tacitly) believe that we have free will but since we do not have free will, deliberation about what to do is based on illusion. In neither case, it might be argued, does the alleged indispensability if irreducibly normative reasons and free will license inferences about what there is, rather than merely inferences about what we have to believe (tacitly) in order to engage consistently and sincerely in deliberation.[48] In other words, these arguments from deliberative indispensability license no conclusions about ontology.[49]

But now consider the fact that arguments from *explanatory* indispensability are commonly taken to license conclusions about what there is, both in science and in everyday life. Consider the following familiar *inferences to the best explanation* (IBE): from observations of a vapour trail in a gas chamber physicists infer the presence of a proton[50]; from perturbations in the orbit of the planet Uranus mathematically able astronomers inferred the presence of another large celestial body, viz. the planet Neptune; from my observation that the streets are wet this morning I infer that it has been raining the night before; etc. Indeed moral error theorists rely on instances of IBE when they claim that moral belief is better explained by appeal to evolutionary considerations and psychological and sociological features of the human predicament, than by appeal to cognition of moral properties and facts. But now, Enoch argues at length for the following dialectical point:

> if you accept arguments from explanatory indispensability—inferences to the best explanation, that is—but you want to reject arguments from some other kind of

[48] None of this means that the error theorist or nihilist cannot engage in this kind of deliberation. True, the error theorist cannot sincerely engage in such deliberation while at the same time attending to her belief that error theory is true, or at least she cannot do so consistently. But as long as these beliefs are suppressed, deliberation seems much less problematic. Perhaps the options are of such deep concern to the deliberator that she forgets about the arguments for error theory she finds intellectually compelling and forms beliefs about what makes most sense to do. In so doing she would of course be inconsistent but her deliberation need not involve insincerity or related psychological difficulties. We return to similar issues in the next chapter.

[49] As Enoch notes (2011: 79, n. 71), this point is an instance of Barry Stroud's well-known critique of transcendental arguments. See Stroud 1968. See Shafer-Landau (ms) for a similar point.

[50] This is Harman's famous example in the opening chapter of his *The Nature of Morality* (1977).

indispensability (like deliberative indispensability), you have to present and defend a principled way of drawing the distinction between types of indispensability that can ground ontological commitments, and those that do not (2011: 66-7).

If, say, protons and planets are indispensable to the explanatory project, then we can infer, by IBE, that there are protons and planets. Why not say, analogously, that if irreducibly normative properties and facts are indispensable to the deliberative project, we can infer that there are irreducibly normative properties and facts? The response seems to me plain. The indispensability arguments that license ontological conclusions are exactly those that are truth-tracking, i.e., those that tend to render us having true beliefs. Employing IBE has rendered us having true beliefs about such things as protons and planets, and about mundane matters such as whether it has rained recently. This is because the world is explanation-friendly. Indeed, the explanation-friendliness of the world is the best explanation of the success of IBE. (Of course, IBE is not uncontroversial because it is not uncontroversial that the world is explanation-friendly. Some sceptics and scientific anti-realists hold that it isn't or adopt agnosticism about whether it is, and therefore do not accept IBE. But since Enoch and the error theorist both accept IBE I set these worries aside.)

By contrast, arguments from deliberative indispensability are not truth-tracking. For engaging in deliberation, if Enoch is right about what deliberation is essentially about, renders us having beliefs about what there are irreducibly normative reasons to do. And such beliefs are of course false, according to the error theorist. This is because the world is deliberation-*un*friendly: there are no irreducibly normative reasons. But what is the argument to the effect that the world is deliberation-unfriendly? Again the answer is plain. It is the argument from queerness that we scrutinized in Chapters 5 and 6. We saw that one version of this argument, namely the one that starts out from the queerness argument targeting irreducibly normative favouring relations, has considerable force.

Enoch holds that it would take a very strong argument to establish the conclusion that deliberation is illusory[51] and even after reading through Chapter 6 of this book, he and other critics of error theory are likely to hold that no version of the argument from queerness is up to the test. But this only takes us back to square one, namely to the controversy about the cogency of the argument from queerness. The debate about whether

[51] Enoch 2011: 78–9.

the world is in Enoch's sense deliberation-friendly is ultimately a debate about whether there are irreducibly normative reasons. The argument from deliberative indispensability establishes at most that error theorists are committed to holding that a certain kind of deliberation (deliberation about what there is most irreducibly normative reason to do) is illusory. But beyond this the argument offers no dialectical progress.[52]

[52] Enoch may well agree with this diagnosis of the dialectic. He claims that extant arguments to the effect that the world is not deliberation-friendly, e.g., the argument from queerness, are not successful and he devotes the second half of his book to establish this (2011: 79). In contrast, this chapter and Chapters 6 and 7 are devoted to establish that one version of the argument from queerness has considerable force and that error theorists can respond to many prominent objections.

9

Moral Error Theory, and Then What?

Suppose that we find the version of the argument from queerness defended in Chapter 6 convincing, or suppose that we are convinced by some other argument for moral error theory, such as the first three versions of the argument from queerness that were criticized in Chapter 5, or some of the other arguments for moral error theory that were mentioned in Chapter 1. Suppose, that is, that we become convinced that ordinary moral thought and discourse embody error that renders moral judgements systematically and uniformly false.[1] What is the upshot for ordinary moral thought and discourse?

In this chapter we consider three main responses; *moral abolitionism*, *moral fictionalism*, and *moral conservationism*. The first two views are familiar from recent metaethical debate. In Section 9.1 I consider and reject moral abolitionism. Moral fictionalism, which strikes me as more plausible, is considered and rejected in Section 9.2. In Section 9.3 I argue that moral error theorists are better advised to recommend what I call *conservationism*, i.e. preservation of ordinary (faulty) moral thought and discourse. We shall see that conservationism has affinities with ideas familiar from the writings of some historically prominent philosophers. Ultimately I suggest that assertions known to be false can be useful due to their pragmatic implicatures. I finish by considering the implications of moral error theory to normative ethics and the relevance of moral conservationism in this respect.

[1] Remember that the focus in Parts II and III of this book is standard and not moderate moral error theory.

9.1. Against Moral Abolitionism

It may seem that if one becomes convinced that moral error theory is true, the natural reaction is to recommend abolishing ordinary moral thought and discourse. This position has become known as moral *abolitionism*. It is fair to say that it is a minority view, but it has had some defenders. We may distinguish between *partial* and *complete* moral abolitionism. Proponents of the first kind of view claim that some subset of our moral concepts is erroneous and recommend abolishing this subset, but they need not recommend abolishing morality altogether. For example, G. E. M. Anscombe famously argued that our ordinary concepts of moral rightness and wrongness, ought, obligation, and so on, presuppose a legislative conception of ethics that is out of place in our secular age. She therefore recommended that we drop the deontic concepts and advocated a revival of Aristotelian virtue ethics.[2]

Complete moral abolitionists go farther and argue that morality in its entirety is infected by error or that it is in some other way problematic. Ian Hinckfuss is one representative of this view.[3] His attack on morality has two prongs. One is that moral thought and discourse carry untenable epistemological and metaphysical commitments and that moral properties and facts are not needed to explain anything, including our moral beliefs. Moral beliefs can be debunked. This is clearly very similar to Mackie's case for moral error theory.[4]

The second prong is Hinckfuss's claim that moral thought and discourse have all sorts of nasty consequences, such as elitism, authoritarianism, conflict, and war. One is tempted to say that this critique of what Hinckfuss calls 'the moral society' is *moral* in nature, but we can say more charitably that Hinckfuss claims to identify some consequences of moral thought and discourse that many people are opposed to, and that on this basis he recommends abolishing morality.[5]

[2] Anscombe 1958: esp. 8–9. Compare Bernard Williams' critique of the concept of moral obligation, see Williams 2006: Ch. 10. Like Anscombe, Williams favoured a revival of the virtues and it may be plausible to read him too as advocating partial moral abolitionism.

[3] Another is Richard Garner, see Garner (2007).

[4] Hinckfuss 1987: esp. sections 2.3–2.7.

[5] One may also wonder about the relevance of the first prong of Hinckfuss' attack on morality, if we assume that the second is successful. If moral thought and discourse really have the nasty consequences Hinckfuss insists on, why would it matter if there were after all non-natural moral properties and facts in reality? Would not a proponent of anti-elitism,

Are moral thought and discourse really guilty of all of Hinckfuss' charges? Consider elitism, for example. It may well be suggested that the general desire for various forms of praise and the disposition to admire the wealthy and powerful are at least as conducive to elitism in society as are moral thought and discourse. Adam Smith argued that such desires and dispositions tend to *corrupt* our moral sentiments; they are not the products of our moral thinking.[6] Moreover, elitism is often criticized on moral grounds, by means of moral vocabulary. The question whether moral thought and talk promote rather than demote all the consequences Hinckfuss discusses would be difficult to settle empirically. My suspicion, though, is that moral discourse is at least potentially more beneficial than detrimental to human and non-human well-being. In general, I agree with G. J. Warnock that a view like Hinckfuss'

> is scarcely more than an exaggeration of a point that is perfectly familiar and unsurprising—namely, that both individuals and groups are somewhat prone to consider, quite sincerely if self-deceivingly, as requirements of morality what suits themselves. To base on this a *general* indictment of morality is merely to insist, intelligibly though admittedly with the highest implausibility, that in fact this occurs not merely sometimes but always (1971: 156, Warnock's emphasis).[7]

Other error theorists have been more optimistic than Hinckfuss about the usefulness of morality. We have already seen that according to Mackie, '[w]e need morality to regulate interpersonal relations, to control some of the ways in which people behave towards one another, often in opposition to contrary inclinations.'[8] We have also seen that according to Joyce, '[m]oralized thinking and talking [function] as a bulwark against weakness of will [and] as an interpersonal commitment device.'[9] In a recent defence of moral fictionalism, Daniel Nolan, Greg Restall, and Caroline West point out that

> [m]oral discourse is extraordinarily useful. Morality plays an important social role in coordinating attitudes and in regulating interpersonal relations. Giving up

anti-authoritarianism, peace, etc., recommend that we in such a scenario simply ignore the moral properties and facts?

[6] TMS 1.3.2.

[7] Warnock's explicit target is a view he calls Marxist, which closely resembles Hinckfuss' view.

[8] Mackie 1977: 43.

[9] Joyce 2006: 208.

moral talk would force large-scale changes to the way we talk, think, and feel that would be extremely difficult to make (Nolan, Restall, and West 2005: 307).[10]

This last point is worth stressing. Given that moral thought and talk are to large extents based on emotions, and given the significant roles they play in social and personal human life, it would be exceedingly difficult to abolish moral thought and discourse.[11] We need to be able to trust agreements and to rely on other people's promises. The idea that it is morally wrong to violate agreements and break promises is an extraordinarily useful tool to ensure that agreements are respected and promises kept. For reasons of this kind, it seems likely that if morality were miraculously abolished, it would subsequently be reinvented.

9.2. Against Moral Fictionalism

Moral fictionalism has been the subject of considerable attention in recent metaethical debate. It is commonplace to distinguish between *revisionary* and *hermeneutic* moral fictionalism. The latter is put forward as an account of ordinary moral discourse, and it likens ordinary moral discourse to story-telling. Hermeneutic moral fictionalism does not address the central question of this chapter, which concerns the practical implications of moral error theory for ordinary moral thought and discourse. I shall therefore say no more about hermenutic moral fictionalism.[12] In the remainder of this book, 'moral fictionalism' will be used to denote revisionary moral fictionalism.

Moral error theorists who are also moral fictionalists maintain that in the wake of the realization that ordinary moral thought and discourse involve systematic errors, it would be useful to adopt a kind of thought in which moral propositions are not genuinely believed, and a kind of

[10] Nolan has informed me that although Nolan, Restall, and West defend moral fictionalism in their 2005, none of the three authors are card-carrying moral error theorists or moral fictionalists.

[11] I therefore disagree with Garner's claim that 'cutting back on moral pronouncements will be no more difficult than cutting back on swearing' (Garner 2007: 512).

[12] Hermenutic moral fictionalism is not a widely endorsed view. M. E. Kalderon is one of its few defenders (Kalderon 2005). Kalderon's hermeneutic moral fictionalism can be described as a combination of non-cognitivism about the psychology of moral judgement and cognitivism about moral semantics. For criticisms, see Eklund (2009) and Lenman (2008).

discourse in which moral utterances are not straightforward assertions about moral reality. In particular, it would be more useful to adopt moral fictionalism than to adopt abolitionism or to preserve ordinary, faulty, moral thought and discourse.

I shall focus on Richard Joyce's recent case for moral fictionalism.[13] Joyce advocates a version of what we might call *force moral fictionalism*. According to this view, the difference between ordinary moral discourse and moral fictionalist discourse lies not in the content of sentences uttered in the respective discourses, but in the illocutionary force with which moral sentences are uttered.[14] In ordinary moral discourse, utterances of moral sentences, like 'Torture is wrong', are genuine assertions, but in moral fictionalist discourse they are, according to force moral fictionalism, *pretence* assertions. Someone who utters the sentence 'Torture is wrong' merely pretends to assert the proposition that torture is wrong. Similarly, in ordinary moral thought, moral propositions are genuinely believed, but according to force moral fictionalism they are the content of mere pretence beliefs.

According to Joyce, moral fictionalism preserves important functions of ordinary moral thought and talk, particularly that of bolstering self-control and combating weakness of will. I shall argue that moral fictionalism has less going for it than Joyce suggests and that preservation of ordinary, faulty, moral thought and discourse seems in many ways a preferable alternative.

I shall raise three concerns about Joyce's defence of moral fictionalism. First, he claims that preserving ordinary moral discourse is not

[13] See Joyce (2001, 2005, 2006, 2007). Nolan, Restall, and West's case for moral fictionalism differs from Joyce's in that the former mainly catalogues alleged advantages of moral fictionalism over other anti-realist views, such as quasi-realism. I challenge some of Nolan, Restall, and West's claims in Olson (2011b).

[14] An alternative to force moral fictionalism is *content moral fictionalism*, according to which the difference between ordinary moral discourse and moral fictionalist discourse lies in the content of what is asserted. This view takes its inspiration from David Lewis's treatment of fictional discourse (Lewis 1983). An example of content moral fictionalism is the view that moral assertions are prefixed by a tacit 'according to the fiction operator'. On this view, 'Torture is wrong' means the same as 'According to the moral fiction, torture is wrong'. Joyce rejects content moral fictionalism in favour of force moral fictionalism on the ground that the former obscures the distinction between telling a story and describing a story, and he also argues that content moral fictionalism runs into trouble that force moral fictionalism avoids (see Joyce 2001: 199–204; 2005: 291). For a discussion of the general distinction between content fictionalism and force fictionalism, see Eklund (2007).

recommendable since false belief has detrimental effects. I argue that there are many counterexamples to this claim and that Joyce therefore has failed to give sufficient motivation for moral fictionalism. Second, it is not clear that engagement with fiction can bolster self-control in the way and to the extent Joyce suggests. Third, I argue that Joyce has overlooked significant costs associated with taking up and maintaining fictionalist attitudes to morality.

First of all, however, we need to clarify the supposed route from moral error theory to moral fictionalism. I argued in Chapter 6 that a plausible error theory takes the form of an error theory about irreducible normativity. What then of the moral error theorists' claim that we *ought* to adopt moral fictionalism? If the *ought* is moral or irreducibly normative, the claim is, by the error theorists' own lights, false, so the intended sense of 'ought' must be different. According to Joyce, the *ought* in question 'is just a straightforward, common-or-garden, *practical* "ought".'[15] The exact meaning of these phrases are not obvious, but the elaboration Joyce eventually offers suggests that the claim that we ought to adopt moral fictionalism is to be understood as a non-normative claim about a means-end relation. The thought is that a plausible cost-benefit analysis suggests that if we are persuaded by arguments for moral error theory, we ought to opt for moral fictionalism.[16] The costs involved are understood as preference frustration and the benefits as preference satisfaction. The *ought* is thus non-normative; the claim that we ought to adopt moral fictionalism should be taken to mean that moral fictionalism is a more efficient means to achieving desired ends (e.g. preference satisfaction) than its alternatives, abolitionism and conservationism.[17]

[15] Joyce 2001: 177, Joyce's emphasis.

[16] Joyce, 2001: 177; 2005: 288. I take it that something like this is also what Nolan, Restall, and West have in mind when they say that the intended sense of 'ought' is 'pragmatic, not moral' (2005: 310, cf. 322).

[17] One might suggest that the ought in question is fictional, but moral fictionalists would not want to say that it is, since they *assert* that it is *really true* that we would be better off adopting moral fictionalism. They do not merely *pretend* to assert this, or claim that it is only true *according to fiction*.

Joyce's case for moral fictionalism (i): the instrumental value of true beliefs

Joyce begins by identifying what he takes to be a crucial benefit of moral belief.

> The mere fact that I justifiably believe ϕing to be in my best interest simply does not ensure that I will ϕ. Humans are epistemically fallible creatures, and even when we are smart enough to see where lies the right answer, interfering factors like weakness of will, passion, accidie, etc., may provide obstacles to the right action being performed. [...] Moral thinking, I contend, is [...] an expedient [that] functions to bolster self-control against such practical irrationality. If a person believes ϕing to be required by an authority from which she cannot escape, if she imbues it with a 'must-be-doneness', if she believes that in not ϕing she will not merely frustrate herself, but will become reprehensible and deserving of disapprobation—then she is more likely to perform the action. In this manner, moral beliefs can help us to act in an instrumentally rational manner (2001: 184).

Abolitionism has the undesirable consequence of forgoing the expedient of moral thinking. Joyce's moral fictionalism, by contrast, promises to preserve it without commitment to false beliefs and assertions. His recommendation to a community of speakers persuaded by arguments for moral error theory is to keep using moral discourse, but without believing it.[18] As we have already seen, when it comes to moral utterances, the recommendation is that we pretend to express moral beliefs, i.e., that we pretend to assert moral propositions.

I believe that Joyce has not sufficiently motivated moral fictionalism over the conservationist policy that recommends sticking to ordinary moral thought and discourse, along with the false beliefs and assertions they involve. Joyce's case against conservationism is based on the claim that true belief is instrumentally valuable.[19] It is obvious that true belief is often of tremendous instrumental value and that false belief is often instrumentally disvaluable. (A person about to eat a poisonous fruit better believe that the fruit is poisonous, and attend to that belief!) This holds not only for empirical beliefs, but also for, e.g., mathematical beliefs (a person

[18] Joyce directs his recommendation to a community of moral error theorists, 'who share a variety of broad interests, projects, ends' (2001: 177). The promise is that replacing ordinary moral discourse with moral fictionalism will promote fulfilments of these interests, projects, and ends.

[19] Joyce 2001: 178. Joyce actually says that *truth* has instrumental value, but I shall take him to mean that *true belief* has instrumental value.

who is being chased by two predators and observes one of them retract better not conclude on that basis that no predator chases her!) Note that Joyce argues not merely that false belief is instrumentally disvaluable. He quotes William James, saying in effect that since we never know what true beliefs may become useful in various situations, it is instrumentally useful to acquire an expanding stock of true beliefs.[20]

But there are many counterexamples to the claim that true belief is instrumentally valuable and false belief instrumentally disvaluable. Philosophers have argued that most humans are under the illusion that we have libertarian free will and that this illusion is vital to many institutions and practices, which are in turn vital to individual and societal well-being.[21] It has also been argued that true beliefs on matters like personal identity, personal and temporal biases, and responsibility and desert, are detrimental to human well-being, and that there is consequently a choice to be made between true belief and leading a satisfactory human life.[22]

In a famous study, psychologists Shelley E. Taylor and Jonathon D. Brown argue that certain species of false belief, such as 'overly positive self-evaluations, exaggerated perceptions of controls and mastery, and unrealistic optimism are characteristic of normal human thought' and that 'these illusions appear to promote other criteria of mental health, including the ability to care about others, the ability to be happy or contented, and the ability to engage in productive and creative work'.[23] While these examples are of course controversial, they suggest that there are non-moral and empirical beliefs that—however false—are instrumentally valuable. If this is indeed correct, it is highly plausible that there are false, but instrumentally valuable, moral beliefs too.

Joyce is likely to respond that he does not defend the implausibly strong claims that true belief is always instrumentally valuable and false belief always instrumentally disvaluable; he is rather defending a general cognitive *policy* that recommends acquiring true beliefs and avoiding false ones.[24] Joyce identifies two rationales for such a truth-seeking policy. The

[20] Joyce 2001: 178.
[21] Smilansky 1998: esp. chapter 7.
[22] Persson 2005.
[23] Taylor and Brown 1988: 193.
[24] Joyce 2001: 179.

first is that a 'seemingly useful false belief [...] will require all manner of compensating false beliefs to make it fit with what else one knows'.[25]

It might well be true of some false non-moral and empirical beliefs that sticking to them requires implausible revisions of surrounding beliefs and ad hoc interpretations of available evidence. But it is far from clear that sticking to false moral beliefs requires anything, or objectionably much, of this kind. After all, many philosophers accept the thesis that the moral is autonomous from the non-moral or empirical, at least in the sense that no moral conclusions follow from purely non-moral or empirical premises.[26] If this thesis is correct, it is not clear why sticking to false moral beliefs would require implausible belief revisions.[27]

Joyce's second rationale for the truth-seeking policy is adapted from C. S. Peirce. He quotes Peirce saying that any alternative incompatible with the truth-seeking policy 'would lead to a rapid deterioration of intellectual vigor'.[28] The worry seems to be that adopting a policy that sometimes recommends sticking to false beliefs sets us off on a slippery slope, leading to cognitive disaster.

But this worry rests on an underestimation of our ability to discriminate in our cognitive policies. It is unclear why we should expect a pragmatic cognitive policy of sticking to what one at some level recognizes as false beliefs about some particular matter, to infect one's general commitment to a truth-seeking policy in any intellectual endeavour. For example, why expect someone who adopts a pragmatic policy regarding beliefs about libertarian free will to be less committed to a truth-seeking policy in mathematics? Why expect someone who adopts a pragmatic policy regarding beliefs about self-evaluations to be less committed to a truth-seeking policy regarding historical research? It is equally unclear why a pragmatic cognitive policy regarding morality would have any such negative repercussions. While I agree with Joyce that from the perspective of the error theorist, which cognitive policy is best to adopt is a complex

[25] Joyce 2001: 179.

[26] Joyce's rejection of 'evolutionary ethical naturalism' indicates that he accepts the autonomy of the moral. See Joyce 2001: 153–8.

[27] A related question is in what sense, if any, a convinced moral error theorist *can* stick to moral beliefs, such as the belief that torture is wrong. I will return to this question in Section 9.3.

[28] Joyce 2001: 179.

empirical question, my intermediate conclusion is that Joyce has not done enough to motivate moral fictionalism.[29]

Joyce's case for moral fictionalism (ii): moral fictionalism and the bolstering of self-control

Suppose you find yourself in a situation in which you are tempted to do something that is normally considered morally wrong, such as to shoplift or break a promise, because it serves your immediate egoistic purposes. Joyce holds that a fictionalist stance to moral wrongness bolsters self-control in such situations and thus helps you avoid actions that, by hypothesis, are not in your long-term best interest.

But if you are seriously tempted to shoplift or break a promise, why would a fictionalist attitude to the property of moral wrongness, which you believe are not instantiated, prevent you from doing so? In response to the worry that there is no causal link between engagement with fictions and motivation to act, Joyce points out that '[r]eading *Anna Karenina* may encourage a person to abandon a doomed love affair; watching *The Blair Witch Project* may lead one to cancel the planned camping trip in the woods'.[30] But these examples are not perfect analogies. Upon reading Anna Karenina I may come to *believe* that a love affair recently embarked on is hopeless; upon watching *The Blair Witch Project* I may come to *believe* that (there is at least a possibility that) a crazy serial killer roams the woods. And these *beliefs* about *reality* (the one more likely to be true than the other) may serve as partial explanations of subsequent behaviour. But the moral fictionalist's contention is that engagement with moral fiction can have a bearing on motivation and behaviour without prompting false moral belief about reality.[31]

[29] At one point Joyce says that sticking to a belief *p*, although one accepts that there is sufficient evidence that *p* is false, would be irrational (2001: 178). But error theorists need not agree that it follows from the fact that believing *p* would be irrational that there is irreducibly normative reason not to believe *p*. See p. 165, n. 31.

[30] Joyce 2005: 303.

[31] Karl Karlander suggested that engagement with fiction might prompt not only belief but also desire. I agree that this is so, but my claim above is that such desires are typically mediated by beliefs. I may come to desire to end a love affair because reading *Anna Karenina* prompted the belief that the love affair is hopeless; I may desire to emulate the behaviour of some fictional hero because I believe that that kind of behaviour is desirable.

Joyce is aware that the attempted analogies are imperfect and he goes on to describe the fictionalist attitude as a sort of precommitment.[32] Someone who has a precommitment not to break promises, for instance, is disposed not to break promises, but in detached critical contexts, she might well be disposed to answer 'no' to the question whether it really is morally wrong to break promises.[33] But if fictionalist attitudes are cashed out in terms of physical and psychological dispositions, the point of engaging with fictions becomes unclear. People may be committed to some cause without taking up fictionalist attitudes. A football fan may have and feel strong commitment to a certain team, manifested in dispositions to believe various things and to act and feel in various ways, without taking up fictionalist attitudes. Similarly, one may be committed to keep one's promises, not to steal, etc., without invoking fictions.

Joyce might respond by insisting that the point of engaging with moral fiction is that it enables us to have strong moral commitments without false belief. But it is not clear that this is a significant merit since, as we saw above, false belief need not be instrumentally disvaluable and might be instrumentally valuable. Moreover, we shall see presently that acquiring the physical and psychological dispositions moral fictionalism recommends, while avoiding (false) moral belief, requires costly mental efforts.

In this subsection I have made two points. First, the mechanism by which fictionalist attitudes to morality supposedly bolster self-control is unclear. Second, even if this mechanism were clarified, precommitment does not *require* fictionalist attitudes of any kind. So there is no automatic route to moral fictionalism from recognition that moral precommitments are instrumentally useful.

Moral precommitments and the costs of moral fictionalism

Joyce is clear that taking a fictional stance to morality is not a matter of

> an ongoing calculation that one makes over and over. It is not being suggested that someone enters a shop, is tempted to steal, decides to adopt morality as a fiction, and doing so bolsters her prudent though faltering decision not to steal. Rather,

[32] Joyce 2005: 303–8.
[33] Joyce 2005: 306.

the resolution to accept the moral point of view is something that occurred in the person's past, and is now an accustomed way of thinking (2001: 223-4; 2005: 306).

In other words, someone who takes up a fictionalist stance to morality adopts certain behavioural dispositions and backs them up by moralizing her thoughts, i.e. by thinking of certain actions as wrong, unfair, or undeserved, etc.[34] But given successful adoption of the relevant behavioural dispositions, it seems difficult in many cases to avoid *believing* the relevant moral propositions, as opposed to merely *accepting* them or *thinking* about them, or *pretending* to believe them. Imagine that a moral fictionalist has been trusted with some private information by a friend. Imagine also that the fictionalist realizes that were she to break the promise not to reveal this information to third parties, she can make personal gains. Still, she might not be at all inclined to break the promise. Given her moral precommitment and her concern for her friend it does not seem unrealistic that this is partly because she has slipped into *believing* that breaking the promise would be wrong. But by the lights of moral fictionalism, this would amount to a failure on her part, for moral beliefs are to be avoided.

To revert to Joyce's example, someone who enters a shop and finds herself with a temptation to steal accompanied by a belief that stealing is morally wrong should, by the lights of moral fictionalism, get rid of the belief and remind herself that morality is fiction. As is clear from the above quote, however, she should not try to rid herself of the belief on the spot; that would make it all the more likely that the temptation to steal wins out. One should rather constantly be on one's guard not to slip from moralized thought into moral belief. Such self-surveillance seems to involve occasionally reminding oneself that morality is fiction. But this reveals a deep practical tension in moral fictionalism, for it also seems that in order for moral precommitments to be effective in bolstering self-control, beliefs to the effect that morality is fiction need to be suppressed or silenced. But suppressing or silencing these beliefs while at the same time acquiring physical and psychological dispositions to behave in accordance with the fictional moral norms makes it all the more likely that one slips from moralized thought into moral belief.[35]

[34] Joyce 2005: 308–9.

[35] Note that my objection is not that there is no intelligible distinction between on the one hand genuine belief and on the other hand mere pretence belief or mere acceptance. For a response to this objection, see Joyce 2007: 70–2. Neither is my objection that merely accepting, or pretending to believe, a proposition without believing it is psychologically impossible.

The practical recommendations of moral fictionalism thus pull in opposite directions: One recommendation is to practice self-surveillance to make sure moral belief is avoided. This seems to involve occasionally attending to the belief that morality is fiction. A second recommendation is to suppress or silence belief to the effect that morality is fiction. This leads to instability in that while ways of thought and behaviour likely to prompt moral belief are recommended, moral belief is to be avoided. Occasional slips into moral belief are failures, even when they bolster self-control.

In sum, the kind of self-surveillance required to prevent fictionalist attitudes from transforming into beliefs is likely to make moral precommitments less effective in bolstering self-control. This is a cost of moral fictionalism that Joyce overlooks. The upshot is that in the cost-benefit analysis on which Joyce bases his case for moral fictionalism, the view does not come out well after all. In the following section I shall argue that conservationism is a better bet for moral error theorists.

9.3. The Case for Moral Conservationism

Conservationism unites with moral fictionalism in recommending that one adopt certain behavioural and reactive dispositions and think moralized thoughts, but it contrasts with moral fictionalism in denying that moral belief and genuine moral assertions are failures. According to moral conservationism, there is no need for self-surveillance to prevent slips from pretence moral belief and pretence moral assertion into genuine moral belief and genuine moral assertion, and there are consequently no associated costs of instability. Moral belief is to be embraced rather than resisted.

Conservationism is reminiscent of Hume's position in his brilliant essay 'The Sceptic', which contains several claims congenial to moral error theory:

> If we can depend upon any principle, which we learn from philosophy, this, I think, may be considered as certain and undoubted, that there is nothing, in

My objection is that acquiring pretence moral beliefs in a way that is effective in bolstering self-control without slipping into genuine moral belief is psychologically *very difficult*. And taking measures to avoid slipping into genuine moral belief is likely to make pretence moral belief *less effective* in bolstering self-control.

itself, valuable or despicable, desirable or hateful, beautiful or deformed; but that these attributes arise from the particular constitution and fabric of human sentiment and affection. [...] We may push the same observation further, and may conclude, that, even when the mind operates alone, and feeling the sentiment of blame or approbation, pronounces one object deformed or odious, another beautiful and amiable, I say, that, even in this case, those qualities are not really in the objects, but belong entirely to the sentiment of that mind which blames or praises (EMPL 162–3).

Anyone who shares Hume's sceptical outlook will have to face the question what attitude to take to morality, beauty, and what is commonly thought to be valuable elements in a worthwhile human life. It is clear that Hume himself rejected the abolitionist option, taking that to be a likely road to a miserable life. Instead he recommended that we 'bend our minds' and cultivate our characters in ways commonly thought to be characteristic of good human lives:

A man, who continues in a course of sobriety and temperance, will hate riot and disorder: If he engages in business or study, indolence will seem a punishment to him: If he constrain himself to practise beneficence and affability, he will soon abhor all instances of pride and violence. Where one is thoroughly convinced that the virtuous course of life is preferable; if he have but resolution enough, for some time, to impose a violence on himself; his reformation needs not be despaired of (EMPL 171).

Hume advocates habit as a 'powerful means of reforming the mind, and implanting in it good dispositions and inclinations'.[36] The message in 'The Sceptic' can be summarized as 'Try the virtuous life and you will (probably) like it!'[37] This is clearly congenial to moral conservationism.

But Hume's line, one might suggest, sits equally well with fictionalism. An even clearer parallel to conservationism is found in the attitude Blaise Pascal recommended that we take to God's existence. As is well known, Pascal argued on prudential grounds that we ought to believe in God, even though there is insufficient evidence that God exists.[38] He was well aware that we normally cannot believe at will, which was why he recommended that we act and think as if we believe in God (e.g. that we attend mass, take

[36] EMPL 170–1.

[37] Cf. Sobel 2009: Ch. 10.

[38] A difference between Pascal's case for Christian belief and the conservationist's case for moral belief is that while the latter takes moral belief to be false, Pascal did not take Christian belief to be false, but merely insufficiently supported by evidence.

holy water, etc.). The goal of these endeavours was belief in God, not mere pretence belief.[39]

There is also a parallel to draw between moral conservationism and the kind of two-level approach to moral thinking, advocated by utilitarians like J. S. Mill and R. M. Hare.[40] In brief, the idea is that we rely on non-utilitarian moral thinking and reasoning when we find ourselves in 'morally engaged' and everyday contexts and that we turn to utilitarian thinking and reasoning only in 'detached and critical' contexts. Similarly, conservationism recommends moral belief in morally engaged and everyday contexts and reserves attendance to the belief that moral error theory is true to detached and critical contexts, such as the philosophy seminar room.

An obvious worry is whether this kind of two-level thinking, or moral compartmentalization, is in fact feasible. Is it really feasible to be convinced—in the seminar room—that nothing is morally wrong and nothing morally right, and also to be convinced—out of the seminar room—that some acts are morally wrong and others morally right? One might suspect not, for even if an error theorist might be inclined to think and say that torture is wrong, she is still disposed—in detached and critical contexts—to hold that nothing is in fact morally wrong. Joyce stipulates that as long as one remains disposed to assent to the belief that moral error theory is true in detached and critical contexts, one does not believe that some acts are morally wrong and others morally right.[41]

This stipulation is questionable. In general, it does not seem impossible simultaneously to have an occurrent belief that *p* and a disposition to believe not-*p* in certain contexts. Indeed, we can go further and maintain that it is a psychologically familiar fact that we sometimes temporarily believe things we, in more reflective and detached contexts, are disposed to disbelieve. In such cases, the more reflective beliefs are suppressed or not attended to. This might be because of emotional engagement, affection, peer pressure, or a combination of these factors. For instance, someone might say truly the following about a cunning politician: 'I knew she was

[39] 'Endeavour, then, to convince yourself, not by increase of proofs of God, but by the abatement of your passions. [...] Follow the way by which they [the Christian believers] began; by acting as if they believed, taking the holy water, having masses said, etc. Even this will naturally make you believe, and deaden your acuteness' (Pascal No. 233).

[40] Mill 1998[1861]; Hare 1981.

[41] Joyce 2001: 193.

lying, but hearing her speech and the audience's reactions, I really believed what she said'. Or a deceived lover might say about his mistress, 'I knew she was lying, but when she told me that she cared about me I really believed her'. Hence we are sometimes *taken in* by what people say (be it cunning politicians, manipulative partners, etc.) in the sense that we believe what is said, even though we are disposed to believe, upon detached and critical reflection, that it is false.

Something similar might be going on with moral beliefs. The error theorist might say, 'I knew all along there is no such thing as moral wrongness, but hearing on the news about the massacre on civilians, I really believed that what the perpetrators did was wrong; I really believed that the UN ought morally to enforce a cease fire'. Or at a more personal level, 'I knew all along that there is no such thing as moral requirements, but when I realized that breaking the promise would badly hurt his feelings I came to believe I was morally required not to break it'.

Just as people might be seductive to the effect that it seems to us that what they say is true and that we virtually cannot help believing what they say, certain actions and events may engage our emotions of anger, empathy, etc., to the effect that it seems to us that the actions are morally wrong and that we virtually cannot help believing that they are morally wrong, no matter how intellectually compelling we find arguments in favour of moral error theory.[42] It appears realistic that in morally engaged and engaging contexts, affective attitudes like anger, admiration, empathy, and the like, tend to silence beliefs that moral error theory is true.[43]

We have seen that moral fictionalism takes moral belief in such contexts to amount to failure, as something to be resisted. One therefore needs to remind oneself more frequently and more forcefully that there is no

[42] Here is an analogy, for which I am indebted to David Enoch: Some optical illusions are such that it seems to us that one line is longer than another, even though we know that the lines are of equal length. It seems possible that in unreflective moments we believe, on the basis of how things seem, that one line is longer. Another analogy, for which I am indebted to Henrik Ahlenius, is this: Many utilitarians who are convinced that their theory is correct and that according to this theory, the bystander ought to push the fat man off the bridge in the famous trolley case (Thomson 1985), still feel an intuitive reluctance to make this judgement. This is presumably because moral judgements are often based on spontaneous and effortless reactions of like and dislike to real or imagined cases. It is no surprise that such judgements can conflict with the intellectual beliefs we form in the cool hour. For discussions, see Ahlenius (ms) and Greene and Haidt (2002).

[43] Hume at T 3.1.1.26; SBN 469.

such thing as moral wrongness, and as we saw in the previous section this recommendation in combination with other recommendations of moral fictionalism, invites instability. Moral conservationism, by contrast, sees no need for such reminders. One distinctive advantage of moral conservationism over moral fictionalism is thus that it does not give conflicting practical recommendations.

However, there is admittedly an amount of tension or potential instability in moral conservationism too, in that it recommends false belief. We have already seen that moral conservationism is not alone in this: The recommendation that we sometimes believe falsehoods and suppress true belief is a recurring phenomenon, both inside and outside philosophy,[44] and I have given examples meant to show that it is possible to have an occurrent belief that *p* and a disposition to believe not-*p* in reflective and detached contexts. Nevertheless, it is a fair question what would happen to moral discourse if speakers who are convinced that error theory is true do not succeed in their compartmentalizing endeavours, i.e. were they largely to fail to believe first-order moral claims. What would the moral conservationist's recommendation be in such a scenario?

In answering this question we need to distinguish interpersonal from intrapersonal cases. In interpersonal cases, a plausible recommendation is to keep making moral assertions, although they are known to be false, since their pragmatic implicatures make them useful. Plausibly, one pragmatic aspect of moral judgement is *imperatival*. Non-cognitivists at least since C. L. Stevenson (1937) have argued that the imperatival aspect constitutes the primary meaning of moral judgements. While error theorists and other cognitivists reject this they need not reject the thesis that moral claims pragmatically convey imperatives.[45] In a speaker community of moral error theorists, the claim that stealing is wrong could be generally recognized as literally false but as conversationally implicating the imperative 'Do not steal!' Note that this conservationist recommendation

[44] Garner concludes his defence of abolitionism by asking '[w]hat serious philosopher can long recommend that we promote a policy of expressing and supporting, for an uncertain future advantage, beliefs, or even thoughts, that we understand to be totally, completely, and unquestionably false?' (2007: 512). One answer extractable from what has been said here is that quite a few can and quite a few do.

[45] Joyce seems at one point to hold that it is part of the meaning of moral claims that they express conative attitudes. See Joyce 2006: 54–7, 70. In my view it is more plausible that moral claims conversationally implicate imperatives.

does not amount to a concession to moral fictionalism. The idea is not that an 'according to the fiction' operator prefixes moral claims or that moral utterances are made with non-assertoric force. Neither does it amount to a recommendation to adopt non-cognitivism as a replacement theory. The idea is still that moral claims express false propositions but that they conversationally implicate imperatives.[46]

In intrapersonal cases, a plausible recommendation is to go on thinking moralized thoughts and say to oneself, e.g., that stealing is wrong (although one believes it is false). For it is plausible that there is correlation between our motivationally efficacious attitudes of likes and dislikes and our moral judgements (we tend to judge morally wrong what we on reflection dislike and to judge morally right what we on reflection like), even if the correlation is not of the strong kind posited by some internalists about motivation. Hence thinking the thought—or saying to oneself—that stealing is morally wrong might function as a reminder that one normally, i.e. on reflection, dislikes stealing. In situations in which one finds oneself tempted to steal, such a reminder might bolster self-control since normally we want to avoid acting so as to become the objects of our own dislike.

It is fair to ask at this point why disliking stealing, or believing that one normally dislikes stealing, is not effective enough when it comes to bolstering self-control. In what way would self-control be bolstered further by moralized thoughts, such as the thought that stealing is wrong? The answer, I suggest, is that in situations in which one finds oneself tempted to steal, one's dislike of stealing and one's belief that one normally dislikes stealing are typically not cognitively and motivationally salient and perhaps even silenced. Thinking, or saying to oneself, that stealing is wrong (although one believes it is false) might serve to evoke and make cognitively and motivationally salient one's dislike of stealing or one's belief that one normally dislikes stealing.[47]

[46] Fictionalists too can appeal to the idea that moral claims conversationally implicate imperatives and that this phenomenon makes them useful in interpersonal cases. But then fictionalism will have made itself otiose.

[47] Thinking certain non-moralized thoughts might have the same kind of effects. For example, the thought that stealing would make one a thief might evoke the belief that one normally dislikes thieves, which, in conjunction with the desire not to become the object of one's own dislike, might bolster self-control. Thinking moralized thoughts, however, is likely to be especially effective in this regard, due to the strong correlation between moral judgements and motivationally efficacious attitudes of likes and dislikes.

How effective would such a stance to moral discourse be in bolstering self-control? Probably not as effective as it would be if belief in objective prescriptivity or irreducibly normative reasons were in place, but it might still be effective enough to render a moral conservationist policy worthwhile.[48]

Moral Error Theory and Normative Ethics

After having rejected objective values and moral properties and facts in the first part of his *Ethics: Inventing Right and Wrong*, Mackie proceeded in the second and third parts to discuss among other things substantive normative theories, the human good, and political morality. The normative theory Mackie ends up advocating is largely contractualist and right-based. It involves rights to liberty and self-determination, property rights, and equal opportunity rights. These rights are of course not self-evident normative truths. They are to be determined partly in terms of the extent to which they turn out conducive to the human good, and partly via political processes.[49] The good for an individual human being, according to Mackie, consists largely of pursuits of activities and ends that that individual finds worthwhile either intrinsically or because such activities benefit herself or people she cares about.[50] Because people's concerns and views about worthwhile activities are and will be irresolvably variant, a good and stable society must be some kind of liberal society in which toleration of different life plans is pervasive.[51]

To some readers it may seem a puzzling fact that Mackie engaged seriously in these kinds of first-order normative debate. If moral error theory is true, then any conclusions reached in normative and applied ethics are false. It may seem obvious, then, that moral error theory discredits these disciplines completely.

[48] I recently discovered that moral conservationism is rather similar to what Terence Cuneo and Sean Christy (2011) call 'moral propagandism' (cf. Joyce 2001: 214). Since the attitude to moral thought and discourse that Cuneo and Christy and I advocate on behalf of moral error theorists 'more or less leave[s] things as they are' (Cuneo and Christy 2011: 101), I believe that 'conservationism' is the more apt term. Some of the critical points Cuneo and Christy make against Joyce's moral fictionalism are similar to some of the points I have made in Chapter 9.

[49] Mackie 1977: 174.

[50] Mackie 1977: 170.

[51] Mackie 1977: 236.

But there is no deep puzzle here. We have seen that philosophers from Protagoras through Hobbes and Hume to Warnock have taught us that human beings need morality to coexist peacefully, to prevent conflicts, to regulate and coordinate behaviour, and to counteract limited sympathies. Since most social life presupposes something like a system of morality and since something like a moral system will or is likely to occur, intentionally or not, wherever there is social interaction, we need, according to Mackie, 'to find some set of principles which [are] themselves fairly acceptable to us and with which, along with their practical consequences and applications, our "intuitive" (but really subjective) detailed moral judgements are in "reflective equilibrium"'.[52]

To this end, we need to engage in normative theorizing. Typical adequacy constraints on normative theories are intuitive plausibility and acceptability, comprehensiveness, systematicity, simplicity, and applicability. Moral error theorists can without tongues-in-cheeks engage in the pursuit of theories that meet these criteria. The one criterion that cannot be met is of course that of truth. Mackie describes Rawls' project in *A Theory of Justice* as 'a legitimate kind of inquiry' and he contrasts it with Sidgwick's attempt to reveal objective moral truths.[53] The latter is not the way to think about normative theorizing and its goals, Mackie suggests.

However, given a conservationist view it is not clear where the harm lies in thinking about normative inquiry along Sidgwickian lines. To be sure, if we do this we run the risk of ending up with false moral beliefs, but as we have seen previously in this chapter, false beliefs need not be something to fear or shun. Since the Sidgwickian project is rather straightforward it may even facilitate first-order normative inquiry.

Mackie may have worried, however, that thinking about normative theorizing along Sidgwickian lines somehow reduces the chances of finding a satisfactory normative theory, i.e., of systematizing normative beliefs into interpersonal reflective equilibrium. He expressed a hope that 'concrete moral issues can be argued out without appeal to any mythical objective values or requirements or obligations or transcendental necessities'.[54]

[52] Mackie 1977: 105.

[53] Mackie 1977: 105–6. See Rawls (1999) and Sidgwick (1981).

[54] Mackie 1977: 199. He also hopes that we can do normative ethics 'without appeal to a fictitiously unitary and measurable happiness or to invalid arguments that attempt to establish the general happiness as a peculiarly authoritative end' (1977: 199). The target here is Mill's purported proof of the greatest happiness principle. See Mill 1998 [1861]: Ch. 4. For

I read this as a warning against justifying particular rules, rights, and policies by appeals to intuitions of irreducibly normative truths. Such appeals may invite dogmatism and either conservatism or extremism. Mackie speculated that

> [m]utual toleration may be easier to achieve if groups could realize that the ideals which determine their moralities in the broad sense are just that, the ideals of those who adhere to them, not objective values which impose requirements on all alike (1977: 235).[55]

This may be so. But it is not clear that thinking of first-order normative inquiry in terms of the Sidgwickian rather than the Rawlsian project would make participants less tolerant. What one needs to do in order to promote toleration is to keep one's mind open and recognize one's fallibility in reasoning and sensibility. This is by no means in tension with Sidgwick's project.

To conclude, moral error theory does not discredit normative ethics. The human predicament is such that we need to 'find principles of equity and ways of making and keeping agreements without which we cannot hold together.'[56] Our means of achieving this is to engage in first-order normative theorizing. This is not to discredit normative ethics, but to award it the highest importance.

Mackie's critique of Mill, see his 1977: 140–4, and for his general critique of utilitarianism, see 1977: Ch. 6.

[55] Similarly, we saw in Chapter 3 that Hägerström thought that the realization that our moral thoughts and judgements do not succeed in identifying and reporting objective moral truths would promote toleration and contravene fanaticism in moral and political debates.

[56] Mackie 1977: 239.

References

Ahlenius, H. ms. 'The Appeal to Intuitions in Ethics'. Unpublished manuscript.

Anscombe, G. E. M. 1958. 'Modern Moral Philosophy', *Philosophy* 33: 1–19.

Ayer, A. J. 1946 [1936]. *Language, Truth, and Logic*. New York: Dover.

Ayer, A. J. 1984. 'Are There Objective Values?' In his *Freedom and Morality and Other Essays*. Oxford: Clarendon Press.

Baillie, J. 2000. *Hume on Morality*. London: Routledge.

Balguy, J. 1991 [1734]. 'The Foundation of Moral Goodness'. In *British Moralists 1650–1800: I. Hobbes–Gay*, edited by D. D. Raphael. Indianapolis: Hackett. Originally published by Oxford University Press 1969, 387–408.

Bedke, M. 2010. 'Might All Normativity be Queer?' *Australasian Journal of Philosophy* 88: 41–58.

Bedke, M. 2012. 'Against Normative Naturalism', *Australasian Journal of Philosophy* 90: 111–29.

Blackburn, S. 1984. *Spreading the Word*. Oxford: Oxford University Press.

Blackburn, S. 1993a. 'Errors and the Phenomenology of Value'. In his *Essays in Quasi-Realism*. New York: Oxford University Press, 149–65.

Blackburn, S. 1993b. 'Supervenience Revisited'. In his *Essays in Quasi-Realism*. New York: Oxford University Press, 130–48.

Blackburn, S. 1993c. 'How to be an Ethical Anti-realist'. In his *Essays in Quasi-Realism*. New York: Oxford University Press, 166–81.

Blackburn, S. 1993d. *Essays in Quasi-Realism*. New York: Oxford University Press.

Blackburn, S. 1998. *Ruling Passions*. Oxford: Clarendon Press.

Boghossian, P. and D. Velleman 1989. 'Colour as a Secondary Quality', *Mind* 98: 81–103.

BonJour, L. 1997. *In Defence of Pure Reason*. Cambridge: Cambridge University Press.

Brink, D. O. 1984. 'Moral Realism and the Sceptical Arguments from Disagreement and Queerness', *Australasian Journal of Philosophy* 62: 112–25.

Brink, D. O. 1989. *Moral Realism and the Foundations of Ethics*. Cambridge: Cambridge University Press.

Broad, C. D. 1946. 'Some of the Main Problems of Ethics', *Philosophy* 21: 99–117.

Broad, C. D. 1951. 'Hägerström's Account of Sense of Duty and Certain Allied Experiences', *Philosophy* 26: 99–113.

Broome, J. 2007. 'Is Rationality Normative?' *Disputatio* 23: 161–78.

Brown, C. 2011. 'A New and Improved Supervenience Argument for Ethical Descriptivism'. In *Oxford Studies in Metaethics* 6, edited by R. Shafer-Landau. Oxford: Oxford University Press, 205–18.

Bykvist, K. and A. Hattiangadi. 2007. 'Does Thought Imply Ought?' *Analysis* 67: 277–85.

Bykvist, K. and J. Olson. 2009. 'Expressivism and Moral Certitude', *Philosophical Quarterly* 59: 202–15.

Bykvist, K. and J. Olson. 2012. 'Against the *Being For* Account of Normative Certitude', *Journal of Ethics and Social Philosophy*, www.jesp.org, vol. 6, no. 2.

Carritt, E. F. 1938. 'Moral Positivism and Moral Aestheticism', *Philosophy* 13: 131–47.

Churchland, P. M. 2010. *Braintrust*. Cambridge, MA: Harvard University Press.

Cohon, R. 2008. *Hume's Morality: Feeling and Fabrication*. Oxford: Oxford University Press.

Coons, C. 2011. 'How to prove that some acts are wrong (without using substantive moral premises)', *Philosophical Studies* 155: 83–98.

Copp, D. 2010. 'Normativity, Deliberation, and Queerness'. In *A World Without Values*, edited by R. Joyce and S. Kirchin. Dordrecht: Springer, 141–66.

Craig, E. 2007. 'Hume on Causality: Projectivist *and* Realist?' In *The New Hume Debate*, revised edition, edited by R. Read and K. Richman. London: Routledge, 113–21.

Cuneo, T. 2006. 'Saying What We Mean: An Argument against Expressivism'. In *Oxford Studies in Metaethics* 1, edited by R. Shafer-Landau. Oxford: Oxford University Press, 35–72.

Cuneo, T. 2007. *The Normative Web*. Oxford: Oxford University Press.

Cuneo, T. and S. Christy. 2011. 'The Myth of Moral Fictionalism'. In *New Waves in Metaethics*, edited by M. Brady. Basingstoke: Palgrave, Macmillan, 85–102.

Daly, C. and D. Liggins 2010. 'In Defence of Error Theory', *Philosophical Studies* 149: 209–30.

Dancy, J. 2006. 'Non-Naturalism'. In *The Oxford Handbook of Ethical Theory*, edited by D. Copp. Oxford: Oxford University Press, 122–45.

Danielsson, S. and J. Olson 2007. 'Brentano and the Buck-Passers'. *Mind* 116: 511–22.

Darwall, S. 2000. 'Normativity and Projection in Hobbes's *Leviathan*', *Philosophical Review* 109: 313–47.

Darwin C. 2010 [1871]. *The Descent of Man*, edited by M. T. Ghiselin. Mineola, NY: Dover.

DePaul, M. R. 1987. 'Supervenience and Moral Dependence', *Philosophical Studies* 51: 425–39.

Dreier, J. 1992. 'The Supervenience Argument Against Moral Realism', *Southern Journal of Philosophy* 30: 13–38.

Dreier, J. 2002. 'The Expressivist Circle: Invoking Norms in the Explanation of Normative Judgement', *Philosophy and Phenomenological Research* 65: 136–43.

Dreier, J. 2010. 'Mackie's Realism: Queer Pigs and the Web of Belief'. In *A World Without Values*, edited by R. Joyce and S. Kirchin. Dordrecht: Springer, 71–86.

Dworkin, R. 1996. 'Objectivity and Truth: You'd Better Believe it', *Philosophy and Public Affairs* 25: 87–139.

Eklund, M. 2007. 'Fictionalism'. *Stanford Encyclopedia of Philosophy*, edited by E. N. Zalta. At http://plato.stanford.edu/entries/fictionalism/

Eklund, M. 2009. 'The Frege-Geach Problem and Kalderon's Moral Fictionalism', *Philosophical Quarterly* 59: 705–12.

Enoch, D. 2011. *Taking Morality Seriously: A Defense of Robust Realism*. Oxford: Oxford University Press.

Evans, M. and N. Shah. 2012. 'Mental Agency and Metaethics'. In *Oxford Studies in Metaethics* 7, edited by R. Shafer-Landau. Oxford: Oxford University Press, 80–109.

Ewing, A. C. 1944. 'Subjectivism and Naturalism in Ethics', *Mind* 53: 120–41.

Ewing, A. C. 1947. *The Definition of Good*. London: Routledge & Kegan Paul.

Ewing, A. C. 1959. *Second Thoughts in Moral Philosophy*. London: Routledge and Kegan Paul.

Ewing, A. C. 1962. 'G. E. Moore', *Mind* 71: 251.

Ewing, A. C. 1970. 'Are All A Priori Propositions and Inferences Analytic?' *International Logic Review* 1: 77–87.

Field, H. 1989. *Realism, Mathematics, and Modality*. New York: Basil Blackwell.

Fine, K. 2005. 'The Varieties of Necessity'. In his *Modality and Tense*. Oxford: Oxford University Press.

Finlay, S. 2006. 'The Reasons that Matter', *Australasian Journal of Philosophy* 84: 1–20.

Finlay, S. 2008. 'The Error in the Error Theory', *Australasian Journal of Philosophy* 86: 347–69.

Finlay, S. 2009. 'Oughts and Ends', *Philosophical Studies* 143: 315–40.

Finlay, S. 2011. 'Errors upon Errors: A Reply to Joyce', *Australasian Journal of Philosophy* 89: 535–47.

FitzPatrick, W. 2008. 'Robust Ethical Realism, Non-Naturalism, and Normativity'. In *Oxford Studies in Metaethics* 3, edited by R. Shafer-Landau. Oxford: Oxford University Press, 159–206.

Fletcher, G. 2009. 'Uneasy Companions', *Ratio* 22: 359–68.

Foot, P. 1972. 'Morality as a System of Hypothetical Imperatives?' *Philosophical Review* 81: 305–16.

Garner, R. 1990. 'On the Genuine Queerness of Moral Properties and Facts', *Australasian Journal of Philosophy* 68: 137–46.

Garner, R. 2007. 'Abolishing Morality', *Ethical Theory and Moral Practice* 10: 499–513.

Garrett, D. 1997. *Cognition and Commitment in Hume's Philosophy*. New York: Oxford University Press.

Geach, P. T. 1956. 'Good and Evil', *Analysis* 17: 33–42.

Gibbard, A. 1990. *Wise Choices, Apt Feelings*. Oxford: Clarendon Press.

Gibbard, A. 2003. *Thinking How to Live*. Cambridge, MA: Harvard University Press.

Glüer, K. and Å. Wikforss. Forthcoming. 'Against Belief Normativity'. In *The Aim of Belief*, edited by T. Chan. Oxford: Oxford University Press.

Greene, J. and J. Haidt. 2002. 'How (and where) does moral judgment work?' *Trends in Cognitive Science* 6: 517–23.

Grice, P. 1989. *Studies in the Way of Words*. Cambridge, MA: Harvard University Press.

Hägerström, A. 1952. *Moralpsykologi*, edited by M. Fries. Stockholm: Natur och Kultur.

Hägerström, A. 1953. *Inquiries into the Nature of Law and Morals*, edited by K. Olivecrona, translated by C. D. Broad. Stockholm: Almqvist & Wiksell.

Hägerström, A. 1989. *Moralfilosofins grundläggning*, edited by T. Mautner. Uppsala: Kungliga Humanistiska Vetenskapssamfundet i Uppsala.

Hampton, J. 1998. *The Authority of Reason*. Cambridge: Cambridge University Press.

Hare, R. M. 1952. *The Language of Morals*. Oxford: Clarendon Press.

Hare, R. M. 1981. *Moral Thinking: Its Levels, Method, and Point*. Oxford: Clarendon Press.

Harman, G. 1977. *The Nature of Morality*. New York: Oxford University Press.

Harrison, J. 1976. *Hume's Moral Epistemology*. Oxford: Oxford University Press.

Harrison, J. 1982. 'Review of J. L. Mackie, *Hume's Moral Theory*', *Hume Studies* 8: 70–85.

Hattiangadi, A. 2007. *Oughts and Thoughts*. Oxford: Oxford University Press.

Hauser, M. D. 2006. *Moral Minds: How Nature Designed Our Universal Sense of Right and Wrong*. New York: Harper Collins Publishers.

Heathwood, C. 2009. 'Moral and Epistemic Open Question Arguments', *Philosophical Books* 50: 83–98.

Hinckfuss, I. 1987. *The Moral Society: Its Structure and Effects*. Department of Philosophy, Research School of Social Sciences, Australian National University.

Horgan, T. and M. Timmons. 2007. 'Moorean Moral Phenomenology'. In *Themes from G. E. Moore: New Essays in Epistemology and Ethics*, edited by S. Nuccetelli and G. Seay. Oxford: Oxford University Press: 203–26.

Huemer, M. 2005. *Ethical Intuitionism*. Basingstoke: Palgrave Macmillan.

Hume, D. 1975 [1748, 1751]. *Enquiries concerning Human Understanding and concerning the Principles of Morals*, 3rd edn, edited by L. A. Selby-Bigge & P. H. Nidditch. Oxford: Clarendon Press.

Hume, D. 1978 [1739–40]. *A Treatise of Human Nature*, 2nd edn, edited by L. A. Selby-Bigge & P. H. Nidditch. Oxford: Clarendon Press.

Hume, D. 1985 [1777]. *Essays, Moral, Political, and Literary*, edited by E. F. Miller. Indianapolis: Liberty Fund.

Hume, D. 1998 [1751]. *An Enquiry concerning the Principles of Morals*, edited by T. L. Beauchamp. Oxford: Oxford University Press.

Hume, D. 2000 [1739–40]. *A Treatise of Human Nature*, edited by D. F. Norton & M. J. Norton. Oxford: Clarendon Press.

Hussain, N. 2007. 'Honest Illusions: Valuing for Nietzsche's Free Spirits'. In *Nietzsche and Morality*, edited by B. Leiter & N. Sinhababu. Oxford: Oxford University Press.

Jackson, F. 1998. *From Metaphysics to Ethics: A Defence of Conceptual Analysis*. Oxford: Clarendon Press.

Joyce, R. 2001. *The Myth of Morality*. Cambridge: Cambridge University Press.

Joyce, R. 2005. 'Moral Fictionalism'. In *Fictionalism in Metaphysics*, edited by M. E. Kalderon. Oxford: Oxford University Press, 287–313.

Joyce, R. 2006. *The Evolution of Morality*. Cambridge, MA: MIT Press.

Joyce, R. 2007. 'Morality, Schmorality'. In *Morality and Self-Interest*, edited by P. Bloomfield. Oxford: Oxford University Press, 51–75.

Joyce, R. 2009. 'Is Moral Projectivism Empirically Tractable?' *Ethical Theory and Moral Practice* 12: 53–75.

Joyce, R. 2010. 'Expressivism, Motivation Internalism, and Hume'. In *Humeon Motivation and Virtue*, edited by C. Pigden. Basingstoke: Palgrave Macmillan, 30–56.

Joyce, R. 2011a. 'The Error in "The Error in the Error Theory"', *Australasian Journal of Philosophy* 89: 519–34.

Joyce, R. 2011b. 'The Accidental Error Theorist'. In *Oxford Studies in Metaethics* vol 6, edited by R. Shafer-Landau. Oxford: Oxford University Press, 153–80.

Joyce, R. and S. Kirchin, eds. 2010. *A World Without Values*. Dordrecht: Springer.

Kail, P. J. E. 2007. *Projection and Realism in Hume's Philosophy*. Oxford: Oxford University Press.

Kalderon, M. E. 2005. *Moral Fictionalism*. Oxford: Oxford University Press.

Karlander, K. 2008. *The Normativity of Thought and Meaning*. Doct. diss. Stockholm University.

Kelly, T. 2006. 'Evidence'. In *The Stanford Encyclopedia of Philosophy*, edited by E. N. Zalta. At http://plato.stanford.edu/entries/evidence/

Kelly, T. 2007. 'Evidence and Normativity: Reply to Leite', *Philosophy and Phenomenological Research* 75: 465–74.

Kirchin, S. 2010. 'A Tension in the Moral Error Theory'. In *A World Without Values*, edited by R. Joyce and S. Kirchin. Dordrecht: Springer, 167–82.

Kitcher, P. 2011. *The Ethical Project*. Cambridge, MA: Harvard University Press.

Kolodny, N. 2005. 'Why be Rational?' *Mind* 114: 509–63.

Kramer, M. 2009. *Moral Realism as a Moral Doctrine*. Oxford: Wiley-Blackwell.

Kymlicka, W. 2002. *Contemporary Political Philosophy: An Introduction*, second edition. Oxford: Oxford University Press.

Leite, A. 2007. 'Epistemic Instrumentalism and Reasons for Belief: Reply to Tom Kelly's "Epistemic Rationality as Instrumental Rationality: A Critique"', *Philosophy and Phenomenological Research* 75: 456–64.

Leiter, B. 2011. 'Nietzsche's Moral and Political Philosophy'. In *The Stanford Encyclopedia of Philosophy*, edited by E. N. Zalta. At http://plato.stanford.edu/entries/nietzsche-moral-political/

Lenman, J. 2008. 'Against Moral Fictionalism', *Philosophical Books* 49: 23–32.

Lewis, D. 1983. 'Truth in Fiction'. In his *Philosophical Papers* vol. 1. Oxford: Oxford University Press.

Lewis, D. 1989. 'Dispositional Theories of Value', *Proceedings of the Aristotelian Society* 63: 113–37.

Lycan, W. G. 2000. *Philosophy of Language: A Contemporary Introduction*. London: Routledge.

Mackie, J. L. 1946. 'A Refutation of Morals', *Australasian Journal of Philosophy* 24: 77–90.

Mackie, J. L. 1976. *Problems from Locke*. Oxford: Clarendon Press.

Mackie, J. L. 1977. *Ethics: Inventing Right and Wrong*. Harmondsworth: Penguin Books.

Mackie, J. L. 1980. *Hume's Moral Theory*. London: Routledge.

Mackie, J. L. 1982. *The Miracle of Theism: Arguments for and against the Existence of God*. Oxford: Oxford University Press.

Mackie, J. L. 1985a. 'Morality and the Retributive Emotions'. In Mackie 1985c, 206–19. Reprinted from *Edward Westermarck: Essays on His Life and Works*, edited by T. Stroup. Helsinki 1982.

Mackie, J. L. 1985b. 'Cooperation, Competition, and Moral Philosophy'. In Mackie 1985c, 152–69. Reprinted from *Cooperation and Competition in Humans and Animals*, edited by A. M. Colman. Wokingham, 1982.

Mackie, J. L. 1985c. *Persons and Values: Selected Papers* vol. 2, edited by J. Mackie & P. Mackie. Oxford: Clarendon Press.

Majors, B. 2005. 'Moral Discourse and Descriptive Properties', *Philosophical Quarterly* 55: 475–94.

Makinson, D. C. 1965. 'Paradox of the Preface', *Analysis* 25: 205–7.

McPherson, T. 2009. 'Moorean Arguments and Moral Revisionism'. *Journal of Ethics and Social Philosophy*, www.jesp.org, vol.3, no. 2.

McPherson, T. 2012. 'Ethical Non-naturalism and the Metaphysics of Supervenience'. In *Oxford Studies in Metaethics* 7, edited by R. Shafer-Landau. Oxford: Oxford University Press, 205–34.

Mill, J. S. 1998 [1861]. *Utilitarianism*, edited by R. Crisp. Oxford: Oxford University Press.

Miller, A. 2003. *An Introduction to Contemporary Metaethics*. Cambridge: Polity Press.

Mindus, P. 2009. *A Real Mind: The Life and Work of Axel Hägerström*. Dordrecht: Springer.

Moore, G. E. 1993 [1903]. *Principia Ethica*, revised edition, edited by T. Baldwin. Cambridge: Cambridge University Press.

Moore, G. E. 1993 [1922]. 'The Conception of Intrinsic Value'. In his *Principia Ethica*, 280–98. Reprinted from his *Philosophical Studies*, London: Kegan Paul, Trench, Trubner & co, 1922.

Moore, G. E. 1942. 'A Reply to My Critics'. In *The Philosophy of G. E. Moore*, edited by P. A. Schilpp. Evanston, IL: Northwestern University Press: 533–677.

Moore, G. E. 1959. *Philosophical Papers*. London: George, Allen and Unwin.

Nagel, T. 1986. *The View from Nowhere*. Oxford: Oxford University Press.

Nagel, T. 1996. *The Last Word*. New York: Oxford University Press.

Nichols, S. 2004. *Sentimental Rules*. New York: Oxford University Press.

Nolan, D., G. Restall, and C. West. 2005. 'Moral Fictionalism versus the Rest', *Australasian Journal of Philosophy* 83: 307–30.

Norton, D. F. 1982. *David Hume: Commonsense Moralist, Skeptical Metaphysician*. Princeton, NJ: Princeton University Press.

Oddie, G. 2005. *Value, Reality, and Desire*. Oxford: Oxford University Press.

Olson, J. 2009. 'Reasons and the New Naturalism'. In *Spheres of Reasons*, edited by S. Robertson. Oxford: Oxford University Press, 164–82.

Olson, J. 2010. 'The Freshman Objection to Expressivism and What to Make of It', *Ratio* 23: 87–101.

Olson, J. 2011a. 'Error Theory and Reasons for Belief'. In *Reasons for Belief*, edited by A. Reisner and A. Steglich-Petersen. Cambridge: Cambridge University Press, 75–93.

Olson, J. 2011b. 'Getting Real about Moral Fictionalism'. In *Oxford Studies in Metaethics* vol. 6, edited by R. Shafer-Landau. Oxford: Oxford University Press, 181–204.

Olson, J. and M. Timmons. 2011. 'A. C. Ewing's First and Second Thoughts on Metaethics'. In *Underivative Duty: British Moral Philosophers from Sidgwick to Ewing*, edited by T. Hurka. Oxford: Oxford University Press, 183–211.

Ott, W. 2006. 'Hume on Meaning', *Hume Studies* 32: 233–52.

Parfit, D. 2001. 'Rationality and Reasons'. In *Exploring Practical Philosophy*, edited by D. Egonsson, et al. Aldershot: Ashgate, 17–41.

Parfit, D. 2006. 'Normativity'. In *Oxford Studies in Metaethics* 1, edited by R. Shafer-Landau. Oxford: Oxford University Press, 325–80.

Parfit, D. 2011. *On What Matters*, vol. 2. Oxford: Oxford University Press.

Pascal, B. *Pensées*, edited and translated by W. F. Trotter. Grand Rapids, MI: Christian Classics Ethereal Library.

Pereboom, D. 2005. 'Living Without Free Will: The Case for Hard Incompatibilism'. In *The Oxford Handbook of Free Will*, edited by R. Kane. New York: Oxford University Press, 477–88.

Persson, I. 2005. *The Retreat of Reason: A Dilemma in the Philosophy of Life*. New York: Oxford University Press.

Petersson, B. 1973. *Axel Hägerströms värdeteori*. Doct. diss, Uppsala University.

Petersson, B. 2011. 'Axel Hägerström and his Early Version of Error Theory', *Theoria* 77: 55–70.

Pigden, C. 1999. *Russell on Ethics*. London: Routledge.

Pigden, C. 2007. 'Nihilism, Nietzsche, and the Doppelganger Problem', *Ethical Theory and Moral Practice* 10: 441–56.

Pitson, A. E. 1989. 'Projectionism, Realism, and Hume's Moral Theory', *Hume Studies* 15: 61–92.

Plato. 1956. *Protagoras and Meno*, translated by W. K. C. Guthrie. London: Penguin Books.

Platts, M. 1980. 'Moral Reality and the End of Desire'. In *Reference, Truth, and Reality: Essays on the Philosophy of Language*, edited by M. Platts. London: Routledge and Kegan Paul, 69–82.

Price, R. 1991 [1787]. 'A Review of the Principal Questions in Morals'. In *British Moralists 1650–1800: II. Hume–Bentham*, edited by D. D. Raphael. Indianapolis: Hackett, 129–98. Originally published by Oxford University Press, 1969.

Reid, T. 1991 [1788]. 'Essays on the Active Powers of Man'. In *British Moralists 1650–1800: II. Hume–Bentham*, edited by D. D. Raphael. Indianapolis: Hackett, 263–310. Originally published by Oxford University Press, 1969.

Raphael, D. D., ed. 1991a. *British Moralists 1650–1800: I. Hobbes–Gay*. Indianapolis: Hackett. Originally published by Oxford University Press 1969.

Raphael, D. D., ed. 1991b. *British Moralists 1650–1800: II. Hume–Bentham*. Indianapolis: Hackett. Originally published by Oxford University Press 1969.

Rawls, J. 1999 [1971]. *A Theory of Justice*, revised edn. Cambridge, MA: Harvard University Press.

Robertson, S. J. 2008. 'How to be an Error Theorist about Morality', *Polish Journal of Philosophy* 2: 107–25.

Robinson, R. 1948. 'The Emotive Theory of Ethics', *Proceedings of the Aristotelian Society* supp. vol. 22: 79–106.

Ross, W. D. 2002 [1930]. *The Right and the Good*, edited by P. Stratton-Lake. Oxford: Clarendon Press.

Ross, W. D. 1939. *Foundations of Ethics*. Oxford: Oxford University Press.

Rowland, R. 2013. 'Moral Error Theory and the Argument from Epistemic Reasons', *Journal of Ethics and Social Philosophy*, www.jesp.org, vol. 7, no.1.
Russell, B. 1905. 'On Denoting', *Mind* 14: 479–93.
Russell, B. 1946. 'Reply to My Critics'. In *The Philosophy of Bertrand Russell*, edited by P. A. Schilpp. Evanston, IL: The Library of Living Philosophers.
Russell, B. 1999. 'Is there an Absolute Good?' In *Russell on Ethics*, edited by, C. Pigden. London: Routledge, 119–24. Lecture written and delivered in 1922.
Sainsbury, M. 1998. 'Projections and Relations', *The Monist* 81: 133–61.
Satris, S. 1987. *Ethical Emotivism*. Dordrecht: Martinus Nijhoff Publishers.
Sayre-McCord, G. 1988. 'Moral Theory and Explanatory Impotence'. In *Essays on Moral Realism*, edited by G. Sayre-McCord. Ithaca: Cornell University Press, 256–81.
Scanlon, T. M. 1998. *What We Owe to Each Other*. Cambridge, MA: Harvard UP.
Schiffer, S. 1990. 'Meaning and Value', *Journal of Philosophy* 87: 602–14.
Schroeder, M. 2007. *Slaves of the Passions*. Oxford: Oxford University Press.
Schroeder, M. 2008. *Being For: Evaluating the Semantic Program of Expressivism*. Oxford: Oxford University Press.
Schroeder, M. 2010. *Non-Cognitivism in Ethics*. London: Routledge.
Searle, J. R. 2010. *Making the Social World*. Oxford: Oxford University Press.
Shah, N. and D. Velleman. 2005. 'Doxastic Deliberation', *Philosophical Review* 114: 497–534.
Shafer-Landau, R. 2003. *Moral Realism: A Defence*. Oxford: Oxford University Press.
Shafer-Landau, R. 2009. 'A Defence of Categorical Reasons', *Proceedings of the Aristotelian Society* 109: 189–206.
Shafer-Landau, R. ms. 'On the Positive Case for Robust Metaethical Realism'. Unpublished manuscript.
Shepski, L. 2008. 'The Vanishing Argument from Queerness', *Australasian Journal of Philosophy* 86: 371–87.
Sidgwick, H. 1981 [1907]. *The Methods of Ethics*, 7th edn, edited by J. Rawls. Indianapolis: Hackett.
Sinnott-Armstrong, W. 2006. *Moral Skepticisms*. New York: Oxford University Press.
Sinnott-Armstrong, W. 2010. 'Mackie's Internalisms'. In *A World Without Values*, edited by R. Joyce and S. Kirchin. Dordrecht: Springer, 55–70.
Smilansky, S. 2000. *Free Will and Illusion*. Oxford: Oxford University Press.
Smith, A. 1982 [1791]. *The Theory of Moral Sentiments*, edited by D. D. Raphael & A. L. Macfie. Indianapolis: Liberty Fund.
Smith, M. 1994. *The Moral Problem*. Oxford: Blackwell.
Smith, M. 2000. 'Does the Evaluative Supervene on the Natural?' In *Well-Being and Morality: Essays in Honour of James Griffin*, edited by R. Crisp & B. Hooker. Oxford: Clarendon Press.

Sobel, J. H. 2009: *Walls and Vaults: A Natural Science of Morals (Virtue Ethics According to David Hume)*. Hoboken, NJ: Wiley.

Sobel, J. H. ms. *Good and Gold: A Judgmental History of Metaethics from Moore through Mackie*. Unpublished manuscript.

Sober, E. 1982. 'Why Logically Equivalent Predicates May Pick Out Different Properties', *American Philosophical Quarterly* 19: 183–90.

Steglich-Petersen, A. 2008. 'Against Essential Normativity of the Mental', *Philosophical Studies* 140: 263–83.

Stevenson, C. L. 1937. 'The Emotive Meaning of Ethical Terms', *Mind* 46: 14–31.

Stevenson, C. L. 1944. *Ethics and Language*. New Haven, CT: Yale University Press.

Stratton-Lake, P. 2002a. 'Introduction'. In *Ethical Intuitionism: Re-evaluations*, edited by P. Stratton-Lake. Oxford: Clarendon Press, 1–28.

Stratton-Lake, P. 2002b. 'Introduction'. In W. D. Ross, *The Right and the Good*, edited by P. Stratton-Lake. Oxford: Clarendon Press, ix–l.

Strawson, G. 1994. 'The Impossibility of Moral Responsibility', *Philosophical Studies* 75: 5–24.

Streumer, B. 2008. 'Are There Irreducibly Normative Properties?' *Australasian Journal of Philosophy* 86: 537–61.

Streumer, B. 2013a. 'Are There Really No Irreducibly Normative Properties?' In *Thinking about Reasons: Essays in Honour of Jonathan Dancy*, edited by D. Bakhurst. Oxford: Oxford University Press, 310–36.

Streumer, B. 2013b. 'Can We Believe the Error Theory?' *Journal of Philosophy* 110: 194–212.

Streumer, B. 2014. 'Do Normative Judgements Aim to Represent the World?' In *Irrealism in Ethics*, edited by B. Streumer. Oxford: Wiley-Blackwell, 101–20.

Stroud, B. 1968. 'Transcendental Arguments', *Journal of Philosophy* 65: 241–56.

Stroud, B. 1977. *Hume*. London: Routledge.

Sturgeon, N. L. 2001. 'Moral Skepticism and Moral Naturalism in Hume's *Treatise*', *Hume Studies* 27: 3–83.

Sturgeon, N. L. 2006a. 'Ethical Naturalism'. In *The Oxford Handbook of Ethical Theory*, edited by D. Copp. New York: Oxford University Press, 91–121.

Sturgeon, N. L. 2006b. 'Moral Explanations Defended'. In *Contemporary Debates in Moral Theory*, edited by J. Dreier. Oxford: Blackwell, 241–62.

Sturgeon, N. L. 2009. 'Doubts about the Supervenience of the Evaluative'. In *Oxford Studies in Metaethics* 4, edited by R. Shafer-Landau. Oxford: Oxford University Press, 53–90.

Suikkanen, J. 2010. 'Non-Naturalism: The Jackson Challenge'. In *Oxford Studies in Metaethics* 5, edited by R. Shafer-Landau. Oxford: Oxford University Press, 87–110.

Tännsjö, T. 2010. *From Reasons to Norms: On the Basic Question in Ethics.* Dordrecht: Springer.

Taylor, S. E. and J. D. Brown. 1988. 'Illusion and Well-being: A Social Psychological Perspective on Mental Health', *Psychological Bulletin* 103: 193–210.

Tegen, E. 1944. 'The Basic Problem in the Theory of Value', *Theoria* 10: 28–52.

Tersman, F. 2006. *Moral Disagreement.* Cambridge: Cambridge University Press.

Thomson, J. J. 1985. 'The Trolley Problem', *Yale Law Journal* 94: 1395–415.

Tresan, J. 2006. '*De Dicto* Internalist Cognitivism', *Nous* 40: 143–65.

Warnock, G. 1971. *The Object of Morality.* London: Routledge and Kegan Paul.

Wedgwood, R. 2007. *The Nature of Normativity.* Oxford: Oxford University Press.

West, C. 2010. 'Business as Usual? The Error Theory, Internalism, and the Function of Morality'. In *A World Without Values*, edited by R. Joyce and S. Kirchin. Dordrecht: Springer, 183–98.

Westermarck, E. 1932. *Ethical Relativity.* London: Kegan Paul, Trench, Trubner & Co., Ltd.

Wielenberg, E. 2011. 'The Failure of Brown's New Supervenience Argument', *Journal of Ethics and Social Philosophy*, www.jesp.org, (Discussion Note, October 2011).

Wielenberg, E. 'Three Ways the Moral Can Supervene'. Unpublished manuscript.

Williams, B. 1981. 'Internal and External Reasons'. In his *Moral Luck.* Cambridge: Cambridge University Press, 101–14.

Williams, B. 2006 [1985]. *Ethics and the Limits of Philosophy*, edited by A. W. Moore. London: Routledge.

Wilson, J. 2010. 'Hume's Dictum—What it is and why believe it', *Philosophy and Phenomenological Research* 80: 595–637.

Wittgenstein, L. 1965. 'A Lecture on Ethics', *Philosophical Review* 74: 3–12.

Wittgenstein, L. 1999 [1922]. *Tractatus Logico-Philosophicus*, translated by C. K. Ogden. Mineola, NY: Dover.

Wood, P. B. 1986. 'David Hume on Thomas Reid's *An Inquiry into the Human Mind: On the Principles of Commonsense*: A New Letter to Hugh Blair from July 1762', *Mind* 95: 411–16.

Zangwill, N.1995. 'Moral Supervenience', *Midwest Studies in Philosophy* 20: 240–62.

Index

The manufacturer's authorised representative in the EU for product safety is Oxford University Press España S.A. of El Parque Empresarial San Fernando de Henares, Avenida de Castilla, 2 - 28830 Madrid (www.oup.es/en or product.safety@oup.com). OUP España S.A. also acts as importer into Spain of products made by the manufacturer.
Printed and bound by CPI Group (UK) Ltd, Croydon, CR0 4YY
14/04/2025
01844708-0001